TEXTS IN GERMAN PHILOSOPHY

UNTIMELY MEDITATIONS

TEXTS IN GERMAN PHILOSOPHY

General Editor: CHARLES TAYLOR

Advisory Board: RÜDIGER BUBNER, RAYMOND GEUSS, PETER HEATH, GARBIS KORTIAN, WILHELM VOSSENKUHL, MARX WARTOFSKY

The purpose of this series is to make available, in English, central works of German philosophy from Kant to the present. Although there is rapidly growing interest in the English-speaking world in different aspects of the German philosophical tradition as an extremely fertile source of study and inspiration, many of its crucial texts are not available in English or exist only in inadequate or dated translations. The series is intended to remedy that situation, and the translations where appropriate will be accompanied by historical and philosophical introductions and notes. Single works, selections from a single author and anthologies will all be represented.

Friedrich Nietzsche *Daybreak*

J. G. Fichte *The Science of Knowledge*

Lawrence S. Stepelevich (ed.) *The Young Hegelians: an anthology*

FRIEDRICH NIETZSCHE

UNTIMELY
MEDITATIONS

TRANSLATED BY
R. J. HOLLINGDALE

WITH AN INTRODUCTION BY
J. P. STERN

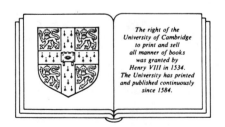

The right of the
University of Cambridge
to print and sell
all manner of books
was granted by
Henry VIII in 1534.
The University has printed
and published continuously
since 1584.

CAMBRIDGE UNIVERSITY PRESS

CAMBRIDGE
NEW YORK   NEW ROCHELLE
MELBOURNE   SYDNEY

Published by the Press Syndicate of the University of Cambridge
The Pitt Building, Trumpington Street, Cambridge CB2 1RP
32 East 57th Street, New York, NY 10022, USA
10 Stamford Road, Oakleigh, Melbourne 3166, Australia

First published 1983
Reprinted 1985, 1986, 1987, 1988

Printed in the United States of America

Library of Congress catalog card number: 83-6609

British Library Cataloguing in Publication Data
Nietzsche, Friedrich
Untimely Meditations. – (Texts in German Philosophy)
1. Philosophy, German
I. Title   II. Hollingdale, R.J.
III. Unzeitgemässe Betrachtungen. *English*
IV. Series
193   B3317
ISBN 0 521 24740 3 hard covers
ISBN 0 521 28927 0 paperback

CONTENTS

INTRODUCTION

by J. P. Stern

When in February 1869 – a few months after his twenty-fourth birthday – Friedrich Nietzsche was appointed professor of Greek philology at the University of Basel, his future career and the direction of his intellectual development alike seemed assured. Classics at the University, which included linguistic, literary and philosophical studies, as well as teaching in the top form of the local grammar school (which was part of his duties) seemed to give full scope to his outstanding talents. His ambitions as a brilliant classical scholar and his aims as a pedagogue did not appear to be seriously at odds with the ethos of the profession he had chosen, nor were his musical and philosophical interests – his ardent concern with Wagner and Schopenhauer – incompatible with it. By the time, seven years later, the last of these four 'untimely meditations' appeared, his perspective on the world had changed, and with it his conception not simply of his future career, but of 'the life-task' he felt his daimon was imposing on him. Yet there were underlying continuities. Strenuous thinking about life and its tasks had formed the basis of his friendships as a pupil at Schulpforta, and the teacher's passion was to be with him to the end; as late as *Ecce Homo* of 1888 he wrote proudly that even the laziest boys he had taught at the Basel *Paedagogium* had worked hard at their Greek.

The change had begun with the publication, on 2 January 1872, of his first book, *The Birth of Tragedy*. Its scholarly respectability impugned, its pedagogic and national purpose unrecognized and its philosophical purport ignored, the book was greeted with a barrage of severe professional criticism, occasionally outright derision, which led, in the following winter, to the collapse of Nietzsche's classical seminar at the University. What praise the book received came from outside the profession: from the Wagners (in whose presence much of it had been planned and discussed), from artists and men and women of letters, and (Nietzsche noted with ambivalent but increasingly positive feelings) from Jewish intellectuals. Although in the following years his academic reputation recovered, the reception of his book gave him a first glimpse of the essential incompatibility of his 'task' with any institutional framework, even that of a small, liberal yet municipally cosseted university like that of Basel.

Several visits to Bayreuth (spring and October 1873, the latter to take part in the founding of the Festival Society with an 'Exhortation to the Germans' which fell on deaf ears) left Nietzsche increasingly ill at ease in the presence of Wagner, who was turning out to be the supremo among musical managers. On a final, by now reluctant, visit (July–August 1876, by which time the fourth and final Meditation was already in Wagner's hands), Nietzsche attended the solemn opening of the first festival with its première of *The Ring*. Finding the music overlaid with irrelevances of production and publicity, Nietzsche left before the end of the festival with feelings of disillusion, revulsion and physical distress.

Nietzsche's illnesses – acute myopia, colics and other stomach upsets, nervous disorders of various kinds, period of almost unendurable headaches – go back to his schooldays. But from the summer of 1874 on these obviously psychosomatic states intensified to the point of determining his working capacity and the pattern of his life, until in the summer of 1876 he was obliged to apply for, and was granted, a year's leave of absence from his teaching duties.

The *Meditations*, then, mark the first of several changes in the direction of Nietzsche's philosophizing – changes which are invariably accompanied by periods of great agitation and euphoria alternating with psychosomatic disorders. Nietzsche certainly lives his philosophical experiences to the full. Yet, to one side of the extensive publicity these states have received, it must be emphasized that all these changes (except the last, the terrible breakdown in Turin of Christmas 1888 and January 1889, from which he never recovered) were the outcome of perceptions and evaluations of perceptions which, whatever else one's view of them, must be assessed as rational. As with all products of the mind, the value of Nietzsche's insights must be assessed not by their genesis but by the illumination they afford us; not, ultimately, by their truthfulness but by their truth.

Thirteen essays were planned. The four he completed bring together a group of themes which, in the context of *The Birth of Tragedy*, could only be considered from afar or by way of contrast. All these themes hinge on a concern with the state of contemporary

German culture, a concern which in itself was anything but 'untimely'. The brilliant opening of the first Meditation, which promises a vigour in argumentation that is not maintained, indicates Nietzsche's attitude throughout. He does not deplore the Franco-Prussian War (in which he briefly served as a volunteer stretcher-bearer) or Germany's victory, and his critical attitude toward the newly founded Reich is not – at least not directly – political; all is subordinated to his hopes and fears for the future of Germany's intellectual and artistic life, that is, of her culture. What he deplores and warns against is the 'ease-and-contentment theory' dominant in contemporary society, according to which the victory of German arms is being ascribed to, or said to be the harbinger of, the superiority of German culture. 'Bildungsphilister' – 'cultural philistines': the butt of Nietzsche's polemic throughout – are those who don't know or refuse to know that the way toward a national culture is difficult and supremely strenuous; that some of the truths which must be faced by those who would lead the nation are unpleasant and in some ways even destructive, while there are other truths which, having a harmful effect on the growth of a healthy national culture, had better be ignored; and that the real enemies of such a culture are those who believe that the values to be striven for in the modern world are 'progress' – meaning improvements in material conditions – and the 'democratic' rule of mediocrity through the placatory politics of socialism. As with all major concepts of Nietzsche's thinking throughout his work, 'culture' as a value-free concept is not available to him.

Thus the tone of these essays is predominantly critical, polemical, occasionally satirical and abusive, and Nietzsche, uneasily aware of this, tries again and again to switch to positive statement and affirmation. The reader, on the other hand, is made equally uneasy by references to the concepts – or at least the notions – of 'Life' and of a '*healthy* culture', which are set up as norms and indications of value: these vaguely Darwinian notions determine what is to be affirmed as positive. True, the last two meditations are paeans in praise of Schopenhauer and Wagner, the twin deities which encompass most of the argument. The contradiction this entails in respect of 'Life' is not faced, but in the end it doesn't *have* to be faced. These last two essays remind one of the well-known meniscus analogy: another drop of praise will bring the argument to overflowing, praise will turn into disillusionment and, eventually, bitter rejection.

No critic (except the Marxist polemicists) has ever doubted

Nietzsche's literary gifts. These gifts are to be seen at their best in the aphorism and in the reflection, in the extended metaphor and sometimes in the parable, but not, in spite of his admiration for Montaigne, in the essay. Nietzsche's great philosophical and literary discovery – that his 'philosophy' might take the form of 'notes toward . . .' – is still to come. The freedom the essay gives him (which is different in kind from the freedom of the aphorist and the writer of 'notes toward . . .') is not always helpful to his present undertaking: 'the thought', to quote from his favourite aphorist, G. C. Lichtenberg, 'has still too much room in the expression', for sometimes there isn't enough thought to fill the expression. The brilliant insights are not always organically connected with the essay form.

The *Meditations* appeared separately: the first two in Leipzig, I in August 1873, II in February 1874; the other two in Schlosschemnitz, III in October 1874, and IV, after delays and with misgivings on Nietzsche's part, in July 1876. Although Nietzsche writes a vigorous defence of them in his autobiographical survey in *Ecce Homo*, they were not included among the books he himself re-published; and it was not until 1893, that is four years after his mental breakdown, that they were collected in the book form in which they are familiar to us, by his friend Heinrich Köselitz (pseud. 'Peter Gast'), and published in two volumes as 'Second Edition' by C. G. Naumann of Leipzig. As always with Nietzsche, numerous thematically related notes precede and accompany the completion of the manuscripts; the sections of the *Nachlass* in which they now appear (Friedrich Nietzsche: *Sämtliche Werke, Kritische Studienausgabe*, eds. Giorgio Colli and Mazzino Montinari, München–Berlin–New York 1980ff., vols. 1, 7 and 8) are as extensive as the essays themselves.

I The use of polemics

Born in 1808, David Friedrich Strauss was at the end of his career as a writer when Nietzsche launched his polemic against him. Strauss's publication of *Das Leben Jesu, kritisch bearbeitet* in 1835 (translated by George Eliot as *The Life of Jesus Critically Examined*, 1846) had led to his dismissal from a junior post at Tübingen University; and in 1839 he was forced to refuse the professorship of theology offered to him at Zurich, even before he was able to take up the post. His attitude to the opposition he had to face, including threats of violence from the Swiss peasantry (who came down from their Alpine pastures, bearing sticks) was admirable throughout, and was known to have been admirable. After the Zurich episode Strauss gave up all idea of an academic position and lived the life of a freelance man of letters. *Der alte und neue Glaube* (1872; translated as *The Old Faith and the New*, 1873), which Nietzsche attacks in the First Meditation, is the complacent and somewhat prolix work of an old man.

In *The Life of Jesus* Strauss undertook to challenge the historical evidence of the supernatural in Jesus's life by scrutinizing the inconsistencies of the synoptic Gospels, and to demonstrate that the claims made on behalf of Jesus's 'mythical' status reflected the needs of the Jewish community of his time, a community informed by special mythopoeic gifts. However, Strauss's criticism is far from radical. He argues that the figure of Jesus is a compound of what he calls 'pure myth' (arising from the messianic visions of the Old Testament) and 'historical myth' (the mythologized episodes from the life of the contemporary Jewish community). Yet even though this de-mythologizing reduces the role of the Church to that of a mere propagator and organiser of such myths, the Christian religion (Strauss claims) will survive unharmed because it is a moral faith, based not on facts, but ideas: not the historical Jesus, but 'the ideal Christ' is 'mankind's moral exemplar'. This is not how the book was generally understood. The young Nietzsche's reading of it as a student of theology at Bonn (1864–5) completed a process begun during his last year at Schulpforta; it led to his rejection of the Christian faith and his refusal, at Easter 1865, to take Communion.

The Old Faith and the New goes further than *The Life of Jesus*. Strauss now rejects the idea of a personal God of any kind as well as the Christian faith in all its forms, and puts in its place a scientific materialism based on a Darwinian cosmology. These cosmological speculations, of which 'the New Faith' is composed, are followed by a series of good-natured if rather home-spun animadversions on the role of the arts and music, literature and philosophy, science and politics in the life of a society founded on Darwinian premises. The result is a rather English 'book of practical wisdom', a potboiler of the kind Bertrand Russell, Dean Inge or G. B. Shaw would be writing half a century later, though it has none of Shaw's wit or distinction of style.

Seeing that Nietzsche was at all times a highly selective and economical reader, one is bound to ask why he should have bothered to give this book so much attention and write an elaborate refutation of it. There are three reasons.

The first, obvious, one is that Wagner, who in 1865 had been publicly criticized by Strauss (for having persuaded Ludwig II to dismiss a rival composer), read the book, found it to be 'terribly shallow', and asked Nietzsche point-blank to pay off the old debt for him.

The second reason, emphasized by Nietzsche himself throughout the essay, is his critical concern with the state of German culture. Strauss's book was certainly a great popular success. Its facile style (Nietzsche argues), to which this success is due, makes it representative of all that is facile, cheap and expedient – 'materialistic' – in contemporary Germany. Thus (to adopt the term used in *Ecce Homo*) 'Strauss' now figures as the 'semiotic code' ('die Semiotik') for all that hinders the revival of a tragic culture – the culture Nietzsche had envisaged, in the last sections of *The Birth of Tragedy*, as a worthy and attainable goal for Germany, identifying that culture with the literary, philosophical and musical totality of the art of Richard Wagner.

A good part of Nietzsche's attack, especially in the second half of the essay, is directed against Strauss's metaphors and diction, and against the unstrenuous logic of his arguments. The extensive (not to say excessive) quotations Nietzsche assembles are used not only to refute the book, but to discredit its author. In impugning the courage and integrity of the man, as he does at length, Nietzsche seems at best to be ignorant of the actual circumstances of Strauss's public existence. The procedure he follows is basic to all quotational satire: he identifies certain locutions as clichés and *idées reçues*, dissects them, and uses the result as evidence of the author's 'infamous vulgarity of mind', bad taste and lack of intellectual rigour. This procedure was used in an essay of Wagner's ('Herr Devrient and his Style', 1869), which Nietzsche is sure to have known, but its originator is Schopenhauer. Schopenhauer is probably the first writer in German to extend Buffon's 'Le stile est l'homme même' to the point where certain characteristic verbal turns (it might be something as innocuous as the use of certain prepositions or tenses) are made to betray the character of a writer and to indicate the 'real' values by which he lives. It is a questionable device at the best of times, and Nietzsche will never again use it as extensively and uncritically as he does here. The view of language it implies (language seen as a reliable revealer of Strauss's turpitudes) is incompatible with the linguistic views expressed elsewhere in Nietzsche's early writings. More important, what this satirical procedure amounts to is a condemnation of certain moral conceptions and attitudes by means of an *aesthetic* evaluation of them. And this aesthetic re-valuation Nietzsche will frequently resort to in his later work, for he regards it as the least boring and least contaminating way of dealing with false moralities.

Finally, there is a rather more personal reason for Nietzsche's concern with the book. Shorn of their clichés and occasional solecisms, some of Strauss's views must have found instant and spontaneous response in Nietzsche's mind. Among them are the subverting of all ideas of the supernatural and of a compensatory transcendence, the attacks on the Church and the hierarchy of organized religion, and above all the idea of a myth born of the living need of a people, a poetic 'reality' that comes into being as a socially sanctioned lie. These arguments, taken over from *The Life of Jesus* into the opening sections of *The Old Faith and the New*, come very close to ideas Nietzsche himself developed in his later writings; but they also lead back to the inquiry into the function of myth conducted in *The Birth of Tragedy*. And the functionalizing of static concepts is one of Nietzsche's characteristic philosophical moves.

There is thus a close and not in the least 'untimely' affinity between some central aspects of Strauss's two books and a major strand of Nietzsche's thinking throughout his life as a philosopher. Of course, the form these thoughts will eventually assume in Nietzsche is incomparably more searching and memorable – more interesting – than anything dreamt of in Strauss's philosophy. Thus the idea that 'God is dead' because men no longer need him (formulated in Book III, § 125 of *The Gay Science*, 1882, and again in the Preface to *Thus Spoke Zarathustra*, written in January 1883) belongs to the same kind of thinking as does Strauss's idea that the Jews created the myth of a God only when there was a communal need for such a myth, but it is just as certain that Nietzsche, not Strauss, has the imagination to draw such a *dramatic* implication from the idea. Of course, the whole style of Nietzsche's philosophizing is different, and he is aware of this difference. The very fact that he is able to separate the style and form of Strauss's book from its matter and ideas is to him evidence of its 'modern barbarism'. Yet the initial impetus to his own philosophical insights will always come while doing battle with his adversaries, his 'flashes of lightning' be ignited by striking inert ideas and beliefs. And if that is so, then the polemical task Richard Wagner set him was more appropriate than he – Wagner – may have thought. Nietzsche's harping on Strauss's cliché-ridden mind must then be seen as an early example of that long-standing campaign he waged against potential allies and fellow spirits, not all of them more significant than Strauss. This is part of Nietzsche's half-acknowledged *agon* with his anticipators. And seeing that what separates his work beyond any doubt from other contemporary 'philosophies' is their literary, aesthetic inferiority, it is hardly surprising that that quality above all should be given paramount importance.

These remarks are intended as a criticism of Nietzsche's procedure, not of his diagnosis. Here (as almost everywhere else) his indictment is illuminating of the world around him and of things to come. Public life in Germany *did* indeed coarsen greatly as a consequence of the War of 1870, the process *was* accelerated by the victory in that war, though this happened not only in the press, the arts and the world of learning, but above all in such areas as trade, finance and party politics, in which Nietzsche was hardly interested. It is plausible to connect Strauss indirectly with this process of decline, yet it is odd to give him pride of place in it. But then, this is what critics of culture are prone to do at all times: to seek out and magnify the intellectual and literary agents of the decline they castigate, if only because, being of a feather, the *literati* are the easier target.

Postscript. Nietzsche to his friend Gersdorff, 11 February 1874 (i.e. six months after the publication of his essay): 'Yesterday at Ludwigsburg they buried David Strauss. I very much hope that I did not sadden his last months, and that he died without knowing anything about me. It's rather on my mind.'

However, Strauss to his friend Rapp, 19 December 1873: 'First they draw and quarter you, then they hang you. The only thing I find interesting about the fellow is the psychological point – how one can get into such a rage with a person whose path one has never crossed, in brief, the real motive of this passionate hatred.'

II A surfeit of history

This essay is not an inquiry into the nature of history, but into history's foreign affairs. Nietzsche does not ask such traditional epistemic questions as, What kind of knowledge does the study of history yield? or, How reliable is our knowledge of the past? These problems interest him only to the extent that they contribute to reflecting on 'the uses and disadvantages', that is, on the *function and value* of the coherent recollection of the past in the outlook of a given community, its rulers and its intellectuals. Nietzsche writes in the full and explicit conviction that this is not an abstract technical problem, but a very concrete existential-philosophical one; a problem that is not to be considered academically ('scientifically'), if only because to consider it adequately means to render the academic outlook itself problematic. Thus the inquiry is once again predominantly critical: its purpose is to subvert the *'wissenschaftlich'* ethos with its *a priori* assumptions that knowledge is to be pursued for its own sake, that all knowledge is valuable and one kind of knowledge is as good as another, and that the study of history is, or should be, a self-regulating and self-justifying pursuit. To put it another way: the attack is directed against the only absolute we recognize.

The force of the argument, but also its direction, is determined by Nietzsche's choice of his central metaphor of affirmation. What makes for the originality of the essay, and for the occasional strangeness of its wordings, is his exhortation, sustained throughout, that the past is not to be seen and studied as an immutable object of knowledge, but to be fully experienced as a living thing: as a living plant or being that can overgrow and stunt or destroy the present, that can be cultivated and fructified, trained and pruned, so as to be of use to 'life'.

There is no need to emphasize what must be obvious to any reader of Nietzsche: he does not proceed from a stable definition of the concepts he uses. Indeed, he regards any such defining as an impossibility, and the demand for it as part of the ethos he is setting out to challenge. Instead, he describes three kinds of history – he calls them the monumental, the antiquarian and the critical – distinguished by the different ways in which they contribute to or detract from 'life', which is here to be seen quite simply as the enemy of academicism, abstraction, dry-as-dust scholarship and the like. D. H. Lawrence's invocations of 'life' in his novels and letters provide apt and specific embodiment of Nietzsche's general meaning.

Illustrations from our recent past may help to make clear these three approaches. The 'monumental' history is clearly to be seen as the Churchillian notion of a sympathetic study of a nation's heroes, conducted in order to invoke them in all their greatness as exemplars that should provide the present with encouragement and enthusiasm. The 'antiquarian' approach of Nietzsche's scheme is not simply that of the heedless collector of past facts and figures; it is

T. S. Eliot's attitude toward the history of England in *Four Quartets*: history as consolation and reassurance, as the positive continuity that provides a people with its identity. (And both Nietzsche and Eliot in *After Strange Gods* have a good deal to say about the intellectuals who, with their 'rootless cosmopolitanism', undermine that continuity.) Finally there is the 'critical' approach to the past, but here I think *our* 'experienced knowledge of the past' suggests implications which Nietzsche fails to see.

Only in its mildest form is this 'critical' history critical in any respectable sense of the word: when Nietzsche says that a people may be endangering its present by living too much in the past, and that there are times and circumstances when we must free ourselves from the hold the past has on us in order to live fully, confidently, courageously in the present, we are likely to agree as readily as when he praises the healing power of oblivion. Yet who decides what should be forgotten? The most perceptive moves in West Germany's foreign policy since 1948 have been born of the fear of her politicians lest they should forget what was done in her name before 1945. This is not a situation provided for by Nietzsche's scheme, even though he argues – and here is his thinking at its best – that the manner in which each of the three kinds of history is to be pursued must be *relative* to the needs of a particular time and place. History as a deterrent is not considered. Accordingly, we are left with the uncomfortable impression that the full adverse consequences of the 'critical' approach he advocates escape him. For when we are told that 'life' may require of us a 'temporary destruction of the past', or 'an as it were *a posteriori* construction' of the past, we are invited to condone the sort of corruption that was practised in our times by the Fascist ideologists. But not only by them. When the critic Walter Benjamin wrote that the destruction practised by the tyrants of his day was so total that it included their victims' past and the very memory of their lives, their deeds, their books, all for the sake of a healthy new 'life', he was in effect describing the consequences of Nietzsche's 'critical' history; though when Benjamin added that Marxism–Leninism would put an end to all that, he, an official visitor to Moscow in the months of the purges, was practising precisely what he so bitterly attacked.

Katyn, Auschwitz, the Japanese massacres of Hong Kong are the stigmata of *our* experience of 'critical history'. Listing them, are we not moving into an area of the politics of violence beyond Nietzsche's ken? We cannot be sure. For here we come face to face with an ambivalence that is entirely characteristic of his thinking at such danger points. Endowed with a powerful imagination that functions in unpredictable ways, he does undoubtedly envisage some of the consequences inherent in the planned obliteration of the past. Every present, he tells us (though without giving an example), is founded in past crimes. The suppression of such knowledge must be faced for the sake of a healthy national culture and life. In any event, he adds – and again this is a wholly characteristic turn – the suppression and destruction is always atoned for: by the exceptional *individual*, the ruler or thinker who takes upon himself the odium of the liar, the simplifier, the conscious or instinctive suppressor of the inconvenient past. (The individual's atonement is kin to the morality of Dostoyevsky's Grand Inquisitor.) The idea is not followed up in the present essay. In the perspective of Nietzsche's later writings, however, we recognize it as an early example of his constant pre-occupation with the morality of strenuousness. Accordingly, an individual's sacrifice of his sense of justice, of his righteousness and good conscience, is to be seen not only as justifying his destructive act (which in the essay before us is done for the sake of a collective good), but as a criterion of his personal value: the greater the sacrifice and the cost of it to him, the greater his value as a human being.

The few hints we are given here of this strange morality of strenuousness, among them the suggestion that there is no justice the exercise of which is not repugnant, do not allow us to discuss it at length. Instead, we must ask what this advocacy of the individual's atonement for the planned and purposeful subversion of the past has to do with *the study* we call history. What has removed the argument from the domain of historical research is not the central question Nietzsche is attempting to answer – the question of what criteria we ought to follow in choosing one subject of research rather than another – but the metaphor which determines his answer. History, on fully becoming a 'living' thing, ceases to be itself, ceases to be a study, and becomes an adjunct of the politics of violence. Put more generally: history pursued for an end outside itself ceases to be history.

Again we must ask whether the full consequences of this switch from an attack on abstract book learning to a suppression of the memory of past crimes are really part of Nietzsche's 'lived', '*erlebt*', knowledge of the past. And if we conclude that they are not, then this hiatus of his imagination turns out to be of a piece with what he is attacking; then he himself has inadvertently joined the ranks of those to whom the content of their study is mere 'words, words, words', the *savants* with the imagination of bookworms and philological hamsters.

But there is a further paradox. Seen in its social context, the notion of history in the service of 'life' amounts to placing it, as well as all concerted knowledge and culture generally, within the domain of the state. He certainly does not see it in that way. On the contrary, in the last sections of the essay (and in countless later reflections) he will attack the Hegelians precisely because they worship 'the State' and by doing so encourage spinelessness and the indiscriminate worship of success. Yet by denying historical research any independent goals (because to pursue such goals is to work to the detriment of the 'life' of 'the community' or 'the people'), he is – again inadvertently – placing it in the service of the state, for the simple reason that, in the Germany (and Europe) in which and for which he writes, there is no other effective 'community' or 'people' than that sanctioned and protected by the powerful modern state.

Nietzsche does not see this. His anti-Hegelianism makes him think of 'the State' as an avoidable option. His most serious concern is with the single solitary man; 'the community' and 'the people' (exalted at the expense of 'the masses') are hardly more than concessions to human sociability.

The argument of the concluding sections is good knock-about invective, directed against the 'ruthless optimism' of the Hegelian Left as well as the state worship of the Right. What Nietzsche attacks is the belief (common to both groups) that history is an ameliorative process which reaches its apogee in the age of Hegel, and that this development toward a goal is guaranteed by history's own immutable laws; in brief, the villain of the piece is history as progress. There is no 'total world process of history', Nietzsche insists, and belief in immutable historical laws that lead to progress, or subservience to 'the tyranny of facts', are merely bad for one's character (Nietzsche seems to think that facts and laws have much the same status). Against those who excuse their complacency or passivity by deterministic arguments, he invokes the non-historical or suprahistorical beings whose existence cannot be foreseen – it certainly does not depend on any cyclical theory or organic metaphor (so much for Spengler's claim that his view of history is derived from Nietzsche).

No age is unique and none is privileged; however, in each epoch the human potential at its highest may be present. With this insight,

the essence of Nietzsche's overall undertaking is
first time. His philosophizing from now on may
journeys in search of the values inherent in the
search of what is the best in man; and the conc
recurrence of the same' in *Zarathustra* springs f
endless repeatability of the opposite of 'the
majority of mankind.

The supreme human being is 'possible at
gives an era its unity of style, and thus its
Wagner's role.) In no sense is he a 'product of history'. Individual in
all he does, such a man 'stands above history' in the sense of being
the creator of the values inherent in religion, philosophy and art.
(Women are not considered.) And if 'history' has any purpose, it is to
be the framework of such suprahistorical figures, who live in the
moment and create for eternity. This emphasis on the artistic com-
ponent of genius reflects Jacob Burckhardt's lectures, which
Nietzsche attended throughout the autumn of 1870. Of one of these,
'On Human Greatness', he writes to a friend (7 November) that it is
conceived 'entirely from within *our* sphere of thought and feeling',
adding that 'in the course of our friendly walks [Burckhardt] calls
Schopenhauer "our philosopher" '. Indeed, the triad – religion,
philosophy, art – of human achievement at its highest, as well as the
omission of politics from the list of *valuable* human activities, is
pure Schopenhauer.

Though they cannot create such exceptional individuals, education and the acquisition of legitimate knowledge can at least bring
about circumstances propitious to their coming. And so Nietzsche
turns once more to the central question of the essay, which may now
be restated: What kind of living knowledge is appropriate to those
great life-enhancing and creative figures, as well as to all those others
whose existence they are sent to enhance? What use our specialisms?
How are they to be delimited? Nietzsche offers no stable, general
answer. All he can do is to stress the need for such an answer, the
need for '*a doctrine of the hygiene of life*'. History and every other body of
knowledge – every science – is to be pursued in such a way and to
such lengths that it should sustain and further 'life', it is to be abandoned when it ceases to contribute to this end. It is a splendid
thought, but one is left to wonder how Nietzsche would have reacted
to national-socialist ('Aryan') mathematics or Lysenkovian biology,
both of which were conceived with this sort of imperative in
mind.

This is indeed a vital problem – even more vital to our civilization

...n it was to Nietzsche's – and the great and lasting merit of the essay is that it draws our attention to it. But having done that the argument runs aground, once again held captive by a metaphor. The kind of knowledge required in order to formulate the rules of hygiene is, in theory at least, finite; hence we speak of a body of knowledge which, once attained, will provide the required remedies, rules or hygienic standards. But a body of knowledge of this delimited kind does not yield an appropriate analogy to all the other kinds of 'Wissenschaften' Nietzsche has in mind. They are not finite in this sense. The results of an anthropological inquiry may or may not be predictable, its effects are certainly not. The medical spin-offs of modern physics were unforeseeable by the scientists of Los Alamos. What is the evidence for Nietzsche's claim that the rational study of religion is incompatible with a strong religious faith? Or again: at what point does the world-picture of Einsteinian physics offend against 'the hygiene of life'? Answers to such questions are chimeras.

We have certainly learned to distrust the absolute imperative of research (which is, to pursue any given inquiry regardless of its consequences, according to the motto, as Nietzsche puts it, '*Fiat veritas, pereat vita!*'). Yet the ethical limits which our scientists are at last beginning to impose on their investigations are bound to be determined by arguments of a more concrete and technical kind than Nietzsche envisages; their decisions of where to stop and where to go on are bound to be based on scientific and legal considerations – all of which Nietzsche is not even theoretically interested in – rather than on a large metaphysical notion of 'life'. And, as we have seen, the position in the humanities is similar. The way Nietzsche's peremptory thinking about 'critical' history leads to dire conclusions (conclusions he himself would have repudiated) is evidence that in the humanities too the pursuit of knowledge cannot be switched on and off according to some premeditated notion of the needs of 'life', for all knowledge pursued with any intensity – all *interesting* knowledge – leads into the unforeseeable, while at the same time the connections between different subject-matters are closer, less arbitrary than Nietzsche assumes.

Certainly, Nietzsche gives us some help as we steer our way between the Scylla of an absolute pursuit of knowledge and the Charybdis of Soviet or Maoist ideology (research in the service of whatever happens to be the current party line). But the help we receive is limited to his insistence *that* a major problem awaits sol-

ution; *how* it is to be solved he does not say. There is no *a priori* that
would enable us to decide whether a prospect opening up in the
advancement of science is illusory or real, destructive or life-
enhancing. The glory and foolishness of scholarship are in-
separable.

Postscript. Burkhardt to Nietzsche, 25 February 1874: 'In thanking
you very warmly, and having merely rushed through this immensely
significant essay, I can say only a word or two in reply. As yet I have
really no right to do this, for the work demands that it be given
mature consideration and perused step by step, but the matter is so
close to the heart of the likes of us that one is tempted to say something straightaway. Above all my wretched head has never been
capable of reflecting even from afar on the last reasons, goals and
needs of the science of history, the way you can. But as a teacher and
lecturer I may say that I have never taught history for the sake of what
is called, with much pathos, World History, but I have taught it
essentially as a propaedeutic subject. I have done all I could to guide
[my students] toward their own grasp of the past, hoping at least not
to make them dislike it . . .'

III 'A philosophy to live by'?

The experience of reading Nietzsche's tribute to Schopenhauer is at
once exhilarating – by virtue of the generous enthusiasm it conveys –
and disconcerting – in respect of the expectations it does not fulfil.
The essay is neither biography nor an introduction to or a critical
appraisal of Schopenhauer's philosophy. Rather is it a series of
invocations of the mind Nietzsche senses at work behind thè
philosophy – 'that ideal man who holds sway in and around
Schopenhauer, as his Platonic idea, so to speak' – and a timely
meditation on the effects this philosophy has, or rather should have,
on its readers. A book Nietzsche planned but never completed,
'Philosophy in the Tragic Age of the Greeks' (1873), contains a suc-
cinct aphoristic account of his present undertaking. In writing of the
pre-Socratic philosophers from Thales onwards, Nietzsche blends
'story' and 'history' in the same way as he does in his portrait of
Schopenhauer:

I tell the story of these philosophers in simplified form: I merely wish to
bring out in each system that point which represents a piece of the person-

ality, and which history must preserve as a part of what is irrefutable and indisputable. It's a start, intended to recapture and recreate those natures by means of comparisons . . . My task is to throw a light on that which we must always love and revere, of which no subsequent knowledge can rob us: man in his greatness . . .'

Not the philosophical – only the human is irrefutable. When Nietzsche writes 'der grosse Mensch' he does not mean simply the great, heroic personality. The heroism exalted in this essay is of a special, intricate kind.

The essay contains no exposition of doctrine. Schopenhauer's demonstration of the universal, all-encompassing 'Will' and its creation of a harsh world of conflicting interests, brief pleasures, unabating fears and false hopes; his distinction between the faculty of the 'understanding' which acts in the service of that will and the faculty of 'reason' which is capable of transcending the will and its products; his doctrine of the ethical value of pity and charity; even Schopenhauer's basic dichotomy between the 'acquired' and 'intelligible' aspects of character – all these are taken for granted. Thus Schopenhauer's grand conclusion – the non-violent renunciation of all life and the world itself, and his commendation of artist, philosopher and saint as the exemplary practitioners and teachers of that renunciation – is put before us without supporting argument or criticism of any kind. Nietzsche's style is at its most volatile. Again and again it makes him skirt the philosophy, leads him past the 'educational' influence exerted through it, to a lively but not greatly varied account of contemporary social attitudes toward philosophy as such; and the few biographical anecdotes (about Schopenhauer's parents, his views on the 1848 Revolution etc.) are brought in whenever the argument looks like floating away from its ostensible subject altogether.

Three ingrained turns of style and thought characterize the essay (as indeed they characterize most of Nietzsche's writings).

(1) Once again metaphors are allowed to shape long stretches of the argument, though now they relate to 'nature' rather than 'life'. 'Nature' is brought into a positive but unsteady relationship to 'culture'. At times 'culture' is seen as the fulfilment of 'nature', at other times as a perfecting and improvement of it – in either case its end-purpose must be the production of genius, or rather of the conditions that make the birth of 'man in his greatness' possible. As before, there is a Darwinian undertone to this argument. 'Nature' is said to be immensely wasteful in producing genius, just as the works

of genius are lavishly in excess of their effects on the rest – the inane bulk – of humankind. Nietzsche's attitude to this avowedly 'natural' process is ambivalent: he condemns the wastage caused by all the dullness, smugness and insensitivity of the age as the pyrrhic victory of mediocrity over greatness, yet at the same time he rejoices in it too. Seen as a necessary aspect of man's existence in the world, the excess of individual creative effort over collective pedagogic results turns out to be simply another confirmation of the tragic view of life. (The Romantics' note of 'the joy of suffering' in all this is unmistakable.) He deplores the lack of understanding Schopenhauer's philosophy has encountered; insists that the age is deeply in need of its message yet wholly incapable of grasping it; and is prepared to push the argument to the point (familiar to us from Franz Kafka's novels) where the claim that a message has been understood is read as proof positive that it has been misunderstood. The very fact that philosophy is *taught* at the universities, that people are *paid* to *lecture* on it, whether or not they have anything to *say* (the butt of Wittgenstein's wrath), proves conclusively either that the philosophy in question is bad (Hegel's) or that it is good but trivialized and misinterpreted (Schopenhauer's).

(2) Nietzsche does not distinguish between 'generation' and 'subsistence': when he identifies and evaluates a given intellectual or literary pursuit not by what it is but by the way it came into being, this is not an inadvertent confusion, but part of his philosophical programme. When he insists that what matters is 'the man behind the philosophy', this is not primarily because he wishes to produce a psychological portrait of the man, but because he believes that an incalculable loss occurs in the transition from generating causes to achieved product or form, and that the conflating of causes with achievement reduces the loss. The finished work – e.g. the philosophical system – cannot (Nietzsche believes) by its very nature contain the richness, the undiminished truthfulness of the man who created it; the reason for this necessary defect in the product lies in the very nature of its medium – language – and its deficiencies vis-à-vis (supposedly non-linguistic) experience – 'life'. It is one of Nietzsche's fundamental convictions – in the Wagner essay he will call it 'Urerfahrung' – that 'man in the fulness of his being' is always more, is always greater than, any of his works; is always diminished and betrayed by the means he has to use to make himself manifest: to utter (this, the reader may think, comes well from Nietzsche . . .) is always to dissipate.

(3) At every stage the Meditation is steeped in value judgments. Disinterestedness, description implying neutrality or indifference are not available to Nietzsche: every argument is a taking of sides, a black or a white. Dispassionate investigation is foreclosed by polemic or paean of praise. The subtleties – e.g. in the description of the dangers surrounding Schopenhauer the man in his time – presuppose a distribution of authorial sympathies and thus of values that is never challenged, never defended. We are told a good many positive things about philosophy and a good many negative things about the age in which it is said to languish. But the question of the limits of philosophy – the limits of the influence of thought on social action – is never raised. The sovereignty of philosophy over other forms of discourse is absolute; and art – at least in this essay – is uneasily assimilated to it.

Philosophy, for Nietzsche, is not the inquiry into first principles or ultimate truths, nor is it simply love of the wisdom by which to live – it is all these in the service of the heroism that Schopenhauer 'the Educator' is said to embody in an exemplary way. Nietzsche sees this heroism in Schopenhauer's determination to go through with his chosen task of true enlightenment, facing and conveying the worst about the world cheerfully, free from bitterness and resentment. Paraphrasing Schopenhauer's dichotomy of 'the World as Will and Idea', Nietzsche writes (in a note of 1873): 'It is splendid to contemplate things, it is terrible to be them.' Without despairing at this 'terrible truth', without taking refuge in illusory hopes, but also without allowing his insights to harden into cynicism, Schopenhauer 'educates' us to face *and* renounce the world and its grim 'reality', to assist in the generation of all those who see beyond the world and its trivia, who know better than *it* knows, and are in the world without being of it.

At this point Schopenhauer's philosophy, in spite of his protests to the contrary, comes close to the Stoic-Christian ideal, and eventually Nietzsche will denounce it for that very reason. Here he merely modifies the Stoic view by advocating not the avoidance of suffering, but the 'heroism' that seeks it out, embodies and fully realizes it: to 'live by a philosophy' – any true philosophy, but Schopenhauer's above all others – is to live in constant awareness of the worst that is to be said against world and life, and to transmute that awareness into – what?

Here Nietzsche parts company with his preceptor. Schopenhauer's clear answer to that question is, ultimately, 'Nirvana'; and Nietzsche quotes, approvingly, more than one passage from his writings in which this 'mortifying' conclusion is drawn. Yet at the same time Nietzsche wishes to advocate this Schopenhauerian 'heroism' with its deep contempt of all that the world cherishes as a basis for a *national* culture – a thing not merely in the world, but of the world too. And when he begins to do this, the Meditation's ostensible cultural strain turns out to be incompatible with its philosophical, Schopenhauerian strain, and the long quotation from Emerson with which the essay closes does nothing to reconcile the two. Whatever the 'new degree of culture' may be, of which Emerson claims that it 'would instantly revolutionize the entire system of human pursuits', it cannot possibly be derived (as Nietzsche proposes to derive it) from a philosophical scheme as contemptuous of the world and all it cares for as is Schopenhauer's. If Schopenhauer 'educates' us for anything, it is, as Thomas Buddenbrook sensed, for death. Is Nietzsche aware of the incompatibility of 'the philosophical truth' with his cultural hopes? In the last of these Meditations he will try to resolve the paradox by experimenting with the notion of a culture that is formed by a people united by suffering and something very much like the love of death. Before long both Schopenhauer 'the educator' *and* Nietzsche's hopes for a cultural renewal will have to be sacrificed: that grand 'revaluation of all values' in which he will come to see his 'all-encompassing life task' lies beyond Schopenhauer, and beyond culture too.

IV Homage to Wagner?

The fourth and last Meditation is devoted to a portrait of Richard Wagner, the man and artist, in 1876, the year in which the Bayreuth opera house was opened; it is a portrait painted with much the same palette and in the same technique as was Schopenhauer's some two years earlier. With the tetralogy, *Der Ring des Nibelungen*, completed, Wagner's entire musical *oeuvre* except *Parsifal* (first performed in 1882, a year before Wagner's death) lay before Nietzsche and was deeply familiar to him, and so were most of Wagner's theoretical and polemical writings as well as most of his autobiography. The essay, which incorporates a considerable number of unacknowledged quotations from Wagner's own writings, is clearly designed as an act of homage; yet it does not read easily.

It is not only Nietzsche's eventual repudiation of Wagner which makes one ask how sincere this act of homage is. Nietzsche's own notebooks of 1874 (and to a lesser extent those of the following year) contain observations, either omitted from the essay or considerably modified, which strike a highly critical note. Here are some of them:

No doubt he accounted immoderateness and lack of restraint as natural.

Whatever strongly affected Wagner, that he wished to do. He understood his models only insofar as he could imitate them. Actor's nature.

His music is not worth much, nor is the poetry, nor is the plot, the dramaturgy is often mere rhetoric – but, broadly viewed, all is *one* and on one level. [*A later version has*: His early music etc.]

Wagner's first problem: 'Why doesn't the effect come off, seeing that *I* experience it?' It is this that drives him on, to criticize the public, the state, society. As between artist and public, he posits the relationship of subject to object – quite naively.

Wagner's serenity is the secure feeling of one who has returned from supreme perils and dissipations to a world that is limited and homely; all the people with whom he has dealings are such limited *segments of his life* (at least, that's all there is to them as far as he is concerned) – which is why he can be serene and feel superior, for here he can *play* with all afflictions and scruples.

His other quality is a great histrionic gift, which, being misplaced, fails to find its outlet in the most direct ways: to find *that*, he lacks stature, voice and the necessary modesty.

If Goethe is a misplaced painter, Schiller a misplaced orator, then Wagner is a misplaced actor. Music especially is what he adds.

A born actor but, like Goethe, as it were a painter without the painter's hands.

None of our great composers was such a poor musician at the age of 28 as Wagner [who by this time had completed *Rienzi* and *Der fliegende Holländer*].

He measures the state, society, virtue, the people, everything by the standard of his art; and whenever he feels dissatisfied, he wishes the world would go under.

He has not kept himself free from giving thought to policial aspirations – this is his misfortune in his contact with the King of Bavaria; to start with, the King did not put his work on the stage, then he half abandoned it by producing it in a provisional way, and finally he made Wagner exceedingly unpopular because people generally ascribed the Prince's excesses to his influence. His involvement with the Revolution was equally unfortunate: he lost wealthy protectors, frightened people, yet in the eyes of the socialists was bound to appear as a defector – all this without any profit to his art and without any real need, and moreover as a sign of imprudence, for he entirely failed to understand the situation of 1849.

Furthermore he offended the Jews, who in Germany nowadays own most of the money and the press. To start with, it was done without cause or reason, later by way of revenge.

Whether he is right to put such great hopes in Bismarck, the not-too-distant future will show.

Wagner's youth was the youth of a manysided dilettante who is unlikely to turn out to be good at anything.

As an actor he wished merely to imitate man at his most effective and at his most real – that is, man at his most passionate, because, thanks to his own extreme nature, he saw in all other conditions merely weakness and untruth. For the artist there is an extraordinary danger in depicting excessive emotion. Intoxication, ecstasy, the sudden, the state of being moved at all costs –terrible tendencies!

A man who feels himself capable of these immense raptures and transports will hardly retain any modesty, for only the knower feels called to content himself – the unknowing enthusiast is heedless. Add to this the cult of genius, nourished by Schopenhauer.

N.B.: Wagner's art speaks a *theatrical* language, a language that doesn't belong indoors, inside a room. It is a popular language, and as such it is bound to coarsen even the noblest [sentiments]. It is intended to act at a distance and to glue together the national chaos. E.g. his *Kaisermarsch.*

His attitude to music is that of an actor – that is why he can as it were speak from the souls of different musicians and place before us quite different worlds (*Tristan, Die Meistersinger*).

The organic unity [of Wagner's work] lies in the drama, and that is why it (often) fails to penetrate to the music, or indeed to the text. The text gives the impression of something improvised, a quality which is only valuable in artists who have achieved perfection, not in those who are on the way toward it; but the improvised deceives, and gives *an impression* of abundance.

There is something comic in Wagner's inability to persuade the Germans to take the theatre seriously. They remain cold and unmoved – he gets worked up as though their salvation depended on it. Nowadays especially, the Germans believe that they are engaged in more important matters, and that someone should concern himself so solemnly with art strikes them as a funny *Schwärmerei.*

Above all: the significance which Wagner ascribes to art does not fit our national circumstances. Hence [his public's] instinctive aversion to what is unsuitable.

For a German, Wagner lacks modesty; think of Luther, of our military commanders.

How did Wagner get his followers? Singers who became interesting as dramatic actors and found a brand-new chance to achieve effects, perhaps with an inferior voice. Musicians who were able to learn from the Master of performance: the performance must be so brilliant that the work itself [?] fails to reach the consciousness. Orchestral musicians who previously were bored. Musicians who intoxicated or bewitched the public in a direct manner and now learned the colour-effects of the Wagnerian orchestra. All sorts of discontented people who hoped for personal gain from every coup. People who go into raptures over every kind of so-called 'progress'. Those who were bored with all existing music and now found their nerves more powerfully stirred. Very soon he had the virtuoso performers on his side, then a section of the composers – neither of them can do without him. Literary men with all sorts of reformist ambitions. Artists who admire his way of living independently.

The tyrant who suppresses all individuality other than his own and his followers'. This is Wagner's great danger: to refuse to accept Brahms, etc.; or the Jews.

Wagner is a modern man, incapable of deriving encouragement or strength from a belief in God. He does not believe that he is in the safekeeping of a benevolent being, but he believes in himself. Nobody who believes only in himself can be entirely honest. Wagner gets rid of his weaknesses by loading them on to his time and his enemies.

And this, precisely, is what Nietzsche does in parts of this Meditation. His difficulties in completing it (only sections 1–6 were written in one go), his doubts whether it was publishable (doubts eventually overcome by Peter Gast, his new musician friend), his inability to give it a discernible structure and to avoid passages of heavy bathos (as in the opening scene, tolerable only as a surrealist joke, of Wagner with a carriageful of disciples in the Bayreuth rain) – all these suggest a deeply divided mind. Yet there is an important affinity between the mind at work on the essay and the mind whose portrait is sketched in the fragmentary notes. Both proceed not by way of organic development, but by single flashes of insight, and it is the momentum generated by the rhetoric which links one *aperçu* to the next.

A Hegelian diagnosis of the age, contained in a note written in 1875, forms the major premise of Nietzsche's argument: 'This is the character of our new culture: *knowledge* is its foundation, *use* its soul . . . Use makes bestial, knowledge mummifies.' In the essay itself this is reformulated in the claim that modern man encounters 'the real' with greater awareness of himself and his world, with a more disillusioning knowingness, than did his ancestors. This is the reason (Nietzsche now abandons the Hegelian view) why modern man has a greater need of art than they did, but it must be an art that will encompass the new knowledge. Combining criticism and naivety, art assumes a new importance: 'Lest the bow should snap, there is art.'

Wagner's *oeuvre*, then (Nietzsche proceeds), is built on a radical denial of the present and a return to the distant past. (In *Beyond Good and Evil* of 1886, Nietzsche will describe the Germans as 'a people of the day before yesterday and the day after tomorrow – they haven't yet a today'.) Wagner's achievement is to have founded a tradition by creating a complex art form – or rather, a form which appears complex but is elemental – that will imbue men with the tragic, metaphysical sense of life, and thus will help them to face their new, 'graver' reality. At the same time he is also the prisoner of his age – an age characterized by false feeling and false thinking; an age which speaks a language that is overextended and debased; has a literature that is derivative and merely 'interesting', and a grand opera (a dig, this, at Meyerbeer, Wagner's friend and ally in Paris) which strains after mere 'effects' and offers mere entertainment. In such an age and faced with such a public, Wagner's achievement must go unrecognized or be misrepresented. The best that can be said of the present is that the War of 1870–1 has brought out those 'qualities of simple courage and thoughtfulness' which had been overlaid by the contemporary pseudo-culture: on these 'essentially *German*' virtues Wagner may hope to draw in order to accomplish his task. (The contradiction with the opening of the First Meditation is patent.) Even so, his supreme creativeness – a synthesis of music, drama and *mise-en-scène* issuing in 'tönendes Dasein', 'existence transformed into sound' – belongs to and must be directed toward the future. (There is no doubt that Nietzsche's hostile view of the German public was strongly influenced by his discussions with Wagner in the early 1870s; yet a few years later Wagner could speak of the new Germany as 'the nation of high-minded dreamers and deep thinkers'.)

In this somewhat generalized tirade a sudden striking perception looms up: 'Everything nowadays has an expectantly apologetic character.' Wagner's art, however, is anything but apologetic and claims absolute, final validity; and so, asserting itself against the halfheartedness of contemporary culture, it must appear negative and destructive. The psychological pattern Nietzsche had hit on in the Schopenhauer essay is repeated: in his supreme struggle to achieve his vision Wagner too is beset by dangers and temptations. Almost all the failings Nietzsche had ascribed to him in the preliminary notes now figure as temptations resolutely overcome, trials strenuously undergone and since won. Wagner's histrionics (that 'comedy-actor's talent' which the later Nietzsche will reduce to 'the art of a mountebank') are ascribed to Wagner's early life and work;

his political trimming is presented as so many sacrifices on the altar of his artistic and cultural mission; the immense sophistication of his greatest operas – their wholly conscious and calculated adaptation of primitive legend and myth – is accounted a mere phase in Wagner's development; and that development is now seen, miraculously, as leading from the complex and derivative, histrionic and conventional to the chthonic and populist, the authentic and simple. In other words: Nietzsche is attempting to unravel what he had come to regard as the central enigma of Wagner's art – the enigma of a mythopoeic imagination of unique power at work in a prosy age. That such an imagination might create a 'tragic' culture after the pattern of Aeschylus was Nietzsche's hope in the last sections of *The Birth of Tragedy* of 1872. Here the existence of that imagination is confirmed, its *official* genealogy is sketched out, the hopes for a cultural revival are renewed, and the enigma is resolved – by invoking Wagner's populism and his 'German' qualities. It is not a solution that Nietzsche could believe in for long. By the time the tribute lay in his master's hands, his disappointment with Bayreuth, the institution designed to give reality to those populist hopes, was complete. In these circumstances, was it not just as well that in the Meditation itself he had kept as close as possible to Wagner's own broad hints and theories?

In August 1876, on the first day of the first Bayreuth festival, Wagner wrote a 'Last Request to my Dear Comrades', which begins with the single word, '*Deutlichkeit*!' It is a *cri de coeur* for 'clarity' in the presentation, not of a mood or dramatic plot, not of mimesis or 'interesting' entertainment, but of '*Pathos*', defined here as the circumstances of human existence concentrated in a single, distinct, individuated passion. In this 'clarity' Nietzsche now sees the summit of Wagner's art, in its service all its diverse elements are united. It is an illuminating definition – at least, any reader who seeks illumination in definitions and in this kind of generalized, non-technical language is sure to find it so.

The inference seems irresistible that the divided mind has carried the essay to conclusions which are at odds with the notes of 1874–5. Yet this is not the whole story; Nietzsche's attitude is more complex. Beneath the rhetorical momentum and its superlatives a dark undertone is present throughout, which bears true witness to his deepest sympathy and concern with Wagner the man and his art. This *basso continuo* is heard wherever the words 'Not' ('need') and 'Notwendigkeit' ('necessity') are sounded – words of venerable lineage in

German, with metaphysical overtones, enshrined in some of the greatest moments of Wagner's own art. Even more strongly than Schopenhauer, Wagner is characterized as a *modern* hero, one whose finest achievements are the fruits of dire need and inward compulsion, of strenuous labour, self-denial and self-sacrifice, he and his *oeuvre* are said to be informed by a veritable ideology of suffering and deprivation. The moments of serenity and joyfulness, too, of his '*German* serenity', we are told, are most dearly purchased. Even where the dominant value of Wagner's life and work is designated as 'Treue', the loyalty and trust evoked are seen to spring not from an abundance of love, but from a love embattled against falsehood, betrayal and sacrilege. All these – quasi-Christian – tributaries of 'Not' are praised as signs of Wagner's greatness, a greatness which, ignoring the cliquish intellectuals, will make its direct appeal to 'the People'. And when Nietzsche goes on to ask what sort of public reception Wagner's work is to have – what, in other words, is to be the purpose of Bayreuth and 'the art-work of the future' – the answer is the opposite of any meliorist utopia. It is to become the lodestar of a people united by common suffering and want, a people that ennobles the word 'common' by its suffering and want.

That 'reality' – 'das Wirkliche' – as the object of experience is fundamentally hostile to human kind and its art, that art is a shield against 'reality' and that '*life is what one suffers from*' are all assertions put before us without supporting argument other than that their opposite is philistine and untragic. Coming after a hundred years during which this ideology has held sway, we may be forgiven for thinking it questionable, and for seeking Wagner's achievement elsewhere. But there is no doubt that, assenting to it, Nietzsche gives expression to his innermost beliefs. There is no consensus on Wagner's operas: disagreement over their evaluation and meanings remains as irreconcilable as it was in Nietzsche's day. All the same, a critic who regards the *oeuvre* as a paradigm of superabundant vitality and believes that it refreshes and invigorates its public, must establish his view against Nietzsche's innermost experience of it as a negative transcending of life; nor is it Nietzsche the hostile polemicist of the 1880s who challenges that view, but Nietzsche the writer of this act of homage.

*   *   *

There is nothing particularly 'untimely' about these four Meditations, either in their several subject-matters and leading arguments, or in the dominant attitudes they express. They are at their weakest not where the criticism is at its most detailed and timely, but where the subject-matter fails to provide an adequate foil. They are at their best where we are shown a searching philosophical mind engaged in vigorous critical controversy with its contemporary culture, and criticism is surely the most timely of intellectual pursuits.

Nietzsche's own view of the book seems somewhat different. Looking back on it in *Ecce Homo* of 1888, the reading he proposes is likely to confirm his critics' worst suspicions:

On an overall view I took hold of two famous and as yet unclassified types, the way one takes hold of an opportunity, in order to give voice to something – in order to have available a few more formulae, signs, linguistic means . . . In this manner Plato made use of Socrates, as a semiotic code [als einer Semiotik] for Plato. Looking back on these writings from some distance I do not wish to deny that fundamentally they speak only of me. 'Wagner in Bayreuth' is a vision of my future; in 'Schopenhauer as Educator', on the other hand, my innermost story, my own *becoming* is inscribed. Above all my *vow*!

Can we take this reading seriously? Is it not of the kind to discredit everything he says? Yet the reading is not as bizarre or as solipsistic as it may seem – given, that is, Nietzsche's view of himself as representative, and given, too, that the truly representative is never the average but the exceptional.

We note that the passage from *Ecce Homo* says nothing about what I have called the cultural concern of the book. This does not mean that this concern is marginal, but that we must see it as a means to an end: and that end is neither national nor political, nor directly social, but above all individual. Uninterested in the actual arrangements of contemporary German society, Nietzsche levels his irony, invective, and radical criticism against its intellectual pretensions. It is through these, he argues, that society fails to sustain the exceptionally gifted individual in his striving for the full expansion of his potentialities. (That expansion he will later call 'the will to power'.) It impedes him in the fulfilment of his destiny, especially where that destiny is tragic. If that individual is 'Nietzsche', then this is not the concrete person of that name, any more than it was Socrates in the passage just quoted. And for this 'Nietzsche', German society – indeed any modern society – is never anything more than the prisonhouse or hunting ground of the gifted individual.

1
David Strauss,
the confessor and the writer

1

Public opinion in Germany seems almost to forbid discussion of the evil and perilous consequences of a war, and especially of one that has ended victoriously: there is thus all the more ready an ear for those writers who know no weightier authority than this public opinion and who therefore vie with one another in lauding a war and in seeking out the mighty influence it has exerted on morality, culture and art. This notwithstanding, it has to be said that a great victory is a great danger. Human nature finds it harder to endure a victory than a defeat; indeed, it seems to be easier to achieve a victory than to endure it in such a way that it does not in fact turn into a defeat. Of all the evil consequences, however, which have followed the recent war with France* perhaps the worst is a widespread, indeed universal, error: the error, committed by public opinion and by all who express their opinions publicly, that German culture too was victorious in that struggle and must therefore now be loaded with garlands appropriate to such an extraordinary achievement. This delusion is in the highest degree destructive: not because it is a delusion – for there exist very salutary and productive errors – but because it is capable of turning our victory into a defeat: *into the defeat, if not the extirpation, of the German spirit for the benefit of the 'German Reich'.*

Even supposing that a war of this kind were in fact a war between two cultures, the value of the victor would still be a very relative one and could certainly not justify choruses of victory or acts of self-glorification. For one would have to know what the defeated culture had been worth: perhaps it was worth very little: in which case the victory of the victorious culture, even if attended by the most magnificent success in arms, would constitute no invitation to ecstatic triumphs. On the other hand, in the present case there can be no question of a victory of German culture, for the simple reason that French culture continues to exist as heretofore, and we are dependent upon it as heretofore. Our culture played no part even in our success in arms. Stern discipline, natural bravery and endurance, superior generalship, unity and obedience in the ranks, in

*The 'recent war with France' is the Franco-Prussian War of 1870–1. (This and all subsequent notes are by the translator.)

3

short, elements that have nothing to do with culture, procured for us the victory over opponents in whom the most important of these elements were lacking: the wonder is that that which at present calls itself 'culture' in Germany proved so small an obstacle to the military demands which had to be met for the achievement of a great success – perhaps it was only because that which calls itself culture foresaw a greater advantage in subordinating itself this time. But if it is now allowed to grow and luxuriate, if it is pampered with the flattering delusion that the victory belonged to *it*, then it will, as I have said, have the power to extirpate the German spirit – and who knows whether the German body remaining will be of any use whatever!

If it were possible to take that calm and tenacious bravery which the German demonstrated against the emotional and shortlived impetuosity of the French and turn it against the enemy within, against that highly ambiguous and in any case alien 'cultivatedness' which is nowadays dangerously misunderstood to constitute culture, then all hope for the creation of a genuine German culture, the antithesis of this cultivatedness, would not be lost: for the Germans have never lacked clear-sighted and courageous leaders and generals – though these have frequently lacked Germans. But whether it is in fact possible to redirect German bravery in this way seems to me more and more doubtful and, after the late war, daily more improbable; for I see how everyone is convinced that struggle and bravery are no longer required, but that, on the contrary, most things are regulated in the finest possible way and that in any case everything that needed doing has long since been done – in short, that the finest seeds of culture have everywhere been sown and are in places bursting into leaf and even into luxuriant blossom. In this realm it is not mere complacency, but joy and jubilation which reign. I sense this joy and jubilation in the incomparable self-assurance of our German journalists and manufacturers of novels, tragedies, songs and histories: for these types patently belong together in a single guild which seems to have entered into a conspiracy to take charge of the leisure and ruminative hours of modern man – that is to say, his 'cultural moments' – and in these to stun him with printed paper. Since the war, all is happiness, dignity and self-awareness in this guild: after such 'successes of German culture' it feels itself not merely confirmed and sanctioned, but almost sacrosanct; and it therefore speaks more solemnly, takes pleasure in addressing itself to the German people, publishes collected editions in the manner of the classics, and goes so far as to employ those international journals which stand at its service to proclaim certain individuals from its midst as the new German classics and model writers. One might perhaps have expected that the more thoughtful and learned among cultivated Germans would have recognized the dangers inherent in such a *misuse of success*, or at least have felt this spectacle as painful: for what could be more painful than the sight of a deformed man pluming himself before the mirror like a cockerel and exchanging admiring glances with his reflection? But the learned classes are happy to let happen what is happening, and have in any case quite enough to do in maintaining themselves without the additional burden of looking after the welfare of the German spirit. Its members are, moreover, supremely convinced that their own culture is the ripest and fairest fruit of the age, indeed of all the ages, and cannot comprehend why anyone should need to look after the welfare of German culture in general, since they themselves and countless numbers like them have already gone far, far beyond all such considerations. The more cautious observer, however, especially if he is a foreigner, cannot help noticing that what the German scholar now calls his culture and that jubilant culture of the new German classics differ from one another only in the extent of their knowledge: wherever the question is one not of knowledge and information, but of art and ability – wherever, that is to say, life bears witness to the culture – there is now only *one* German culture: and is it this that is supposed to have triumphed over France?

Such an assertion seems completely incomprehensible: all impartial judges, and finally the French themselves, have seen Germany's decisive advantage to have lain in the more extensive knowledge possessed by its officers, in the superior training of its troops, and in the greater science of its conduct of the war. In what sense, then, can German culture be said to have triumphed, if one thinks to deduct from it German erudition? In no sense: for the moral qualities of stricter discipline and readier obedience have nothing to do with culture – though they distinguished the Macedonian soldiery from the Greek, for example, the latter were incomparably more cultured. It can only be the result of confusion if one speaks of the victory of German culture, a confusion originating in the fact that in Germany there no longer exists any clear conception of what culture is.

Culture is, above all, unity of style in all the expressions of the life of a people. Much knowledge and learning is neither an essential means to culture nor a sign of it, and if needs be can get along very well with the opposite of culture, barbarism, which is lack of style or a chaotic jumble of all styles.

It is in such a chaotic jumble of styles that the German of our day dwells: and one seriously wonders how, with all his erudition, he can possibly fail to notice it, but, on the contrary, rejoices from the very heart at the 'culture' he at present possesses. For everything ought to instruct him: every glance he casts at his clothes, his room, his home, every walk he takes through the streets of his town, every visit he pays to a fashionable shop; in his social life he ought to be aware of the origin of his manners and deportment, in the world of our artistic institutions, of our concerts, theatres and museums, he ought to notice the grotesque juxtaposition and confusion of different styles. The German amasses around him the forms and colours, productions and curiosities of every age and every clime, and produces that modern fairground motley which his learned colleagues are then obliged to observe and classify as the 'modern as such', while he himself remains seated calmly in the midst of the tumult. But with this kind of 'culture', which is in fact only a phlegmatic lack of all feeling for culture, one cannot overcome enemies, least of all those who, like the French, actually possess a real and productive culture, regardless of what its value may be, and from whom we have hitherto copied everything, though usually with little skill.

If we had in fact ceased to copy it we would not thereby have triumphed over it, but only have liberated ourselves from it: only if we had imposed upon the French an original German culture could there be any question of a victory of German culture. In the meantime, we should not forget that we are still dependent on Paris in all matters of form, just as before – and that we have to go on being dependent, for up to now there has been no original German culture.

We all ought to have been aware of this from our own knowledge: in addition to which, one of the few who had a right to speak to the Germans of it in a tone of reproach has publicly revealed it. 'We Germans are of yesterday', Goethe once said to Eckermann; 'it is true that we have been soundly cultivating ourselves for a century, but another couple of centuries may have to pass before sufficient spirit and higher culture has penetrated our countrymen and become general for it to be possible to say of them: it is a long time *since they were barbarians.*'*

*Goethe to Eckermann, on 3 May 1827.

2

If, however, our public and private life so manifestly does not
the stamp of a productive and stylistically secure culture, if our great
artists, moreover, have admitted and continue to admit this dreadful
and, for a gifted people, profoundly humiliating fact, how is it possible that the greatest self-satisfaction nonetheless continues to reign
among educated Germans: a self-satisfaction which since the recent
war has shown itself ready to burst out in cries of jubilation and
triumph? In any event, there exists a steadfast belief that we are in
possession of a genuine culture: the enormous incongruity between
this complacent, indeed exultant belief and an in fact notorious
cultural deficiency seems to be apparent only to the select few. For
all those whose views coincide with public opinion have covered
their eyes and stopped their ears – the incongruity must not be
admitted to exist. How is this possible? What force is so powerful as
to dictate such a 'must not'? What species of man must have come to
dominate in Germany that such strong and simple feelings can be
prohibited and expression of them obstructed? I shall call this
power, this species of man, by its name – it is the *cultural
philistine*.

The word 'philistine', as is well known, belongs to the student
vocabulary, and signifies, in its wider, popular sense, the antithesis
of a son of the muses, of the artist, of the man of genuine culture. The
cultural philistine, however – the study of whom, and the hearing of
whose confessions when he makes them, has now become a disagreeable duty – distinguishes himself from the general idea of the
species 'philistine' through a superstition: he fancies that he is himself a son of the muses and man of culture; an incomprehensible
delusion which reveals that he does not even know what a philistine,
and the antithesis of a philistine, is: so we shall not be surprised to
find that usually he solemnly denies he is a philistine. With this lack
of all self-knowledge, he feels firmly convinced that his 'culture' is
the complete expression of true German culture: and since he
everywhere discovers cultivated people of his own kind, and finds all
public institutions, schools and cultural and artistic bodies organized
in accordance with his kind of cultivation and in the service of his
requirements, he also bears with him everywhere the triumphant
feeling of being the worthy representative of contemporary German
culture and frames his demands and pretensions accordingly. If,
however, true culture must in any event presuppose unity of style,

7

and even an inferior and degenerate culture cannot be thought of as failing to exhibit a stylistic unity within which the manifold phenomena which characterize it are harmonized, this confusion reigning in the deluded mind of the cultural philistine may well orginate in the fact that, discovering everywhere identical reproductions of himself, he infers from this identity of all 'cultivated' people the existence of a unity of style and thus the existence of a German culture. He perceives around him nothing but needs identical with and views similar to his own; wherever he goes he is at once embraced by a bond of tacit conventions in regard to many things, especially in the realms of religion and art: this impressive homogeneity, this *tutti unisono** which no one commands but which is always ready to break forth, seduces him to the belief that a culture here holds sway. But systematic and oppressive philistinism does not constitute a culture, even an inferior culture, merely because it possesses system: it must always be the antithesis of a culture, namely a permanently established barbarity. For that uniformity which is so striking in the cultivated people of Germany today is a unity only through the conscious or unconscious exclusion and negation of every artistically productive form and the demand of a true style. An unhappy contortion must have taken place in the brain of the cultural philistine: he regards as culture precisely that which negates culture, and since he is accustomed to proceed with consistency he finally acquires a coherent collection of such negations, a system of un-culture, to which one might even concede a certain 'unity of style' if it made any sense to speak of a barbarism with style. If he is allowed to choose between a stylistically agreeable action and one of the opposite kind, he invariably elects the latter, and because he always does so all his actions bear the same negative stamp. It is precisely this negative stamp which enables him to recognize the nature of the 'German culture' he has patented: whatever does not correspond to it he adjudges hostile and inimical to him. In this case the cultural philistine does no more than defend himself: he denies, secretes, stops his ears, averts his eyes, he is a negative being even in his hatred and hostility. The person he hates most of all, however, is him who treats him as a philistine and tells him what he is: a hindrance to the strong and creative, a labyrinth for all who doubt and go astray, a swamp to the feet of the weary, a fetter to all who would pursue lofty goals, a poisonous mist to new buds, a parching desert

---

*tutti unisono: everybody, together

to the German spirit seeking and thirsting for new life. For it *seeks*, this German spirit! and you hate it because it seeks and refuses to believe you when you say you have already found what it is seeking. How is it possible that a type such as the cultural philistine could have come into existence and, once extant, could acquire the authority of supreme arbiter over all the problems of German culture; how is this possible, after there has filed past us a whole line of great heroic figures whose every movement, every feature, whose questioning voice, whose burning eye, betrayed but one thing: *that they were seekers*, and that what they were seeking with such perseverence was precisely that which the cultural philistine fancied he already possessed: a genuine, original German culture. Is there a ground, they seemed to ask, so pure, so untouched, of such virginal holiness, that the German spirit may raise its house upon this ground and upon no other? Questioning thus, they made their way through the wilderness and thorns of wretched and meagre ages, and as seekers they passed from our sight: so that one of them, speaking for all, could say in his old age; 'I have toiled for half a century and allowed myself no rest, but have continually striven and sought and worked as well and as hard as I could.'*

But what view does our philistine culture take of these seekers? It assumes them to be finders, not seekers, and seems to forget that it was as seekers that they regarded themselves. 'We have our culture, do we not?' they say, 'for we have our classics, do we not? Not only have the foundations been laid, but the building itself stands already upon them – we ourselves are this building.' And the philistine raises his hand to his own brow.

Thus to misjudge our classics, however, and in thinking to honour them thus to damn them, it is necessary not to know them: and this is indeed the universal fact. For otherwise it would be known that there is only one way of honouring them, and that is to go on seeking in their spirit and with their courage, and not to grow weary of doing so. On the other hand, to affix to them the suspect word 'classic' and from time to time to 'edify' oneself with their works is to resign oneself to those feeble and egoistic sensations promised by our concert halls and theatres to anyone who can pay for them; the same applies to the erection of statues of them and the naming of festivals and societies after them – all these things are merely cash payments by means of which the cultural philistine settles accounts with them so

*Goethe to Eckermann, 14 March 1830.

as not to have to follow after them and to go on seeking. For 'All seeking is at an end' is the motto of the philistines.

There was a time when this motto was to some extent sensible: the time when, during the first decade of the present century, so much confused seeking, experimenting, wrecking, promising, surmising, hoping was going on in Germany that the spiritual middle class was right to fear for its own safety. At that time it was right to reject with a shrug of the shoulders the brew of fantastic and language-twisting philosophies and tendentious historiographies, a carnival of all the gods and myths, which the Romantics had mixed together, and to reject too the current poetic fashions and follies dreamed up in a state of intoxication – right, that is, because the philistine does not have the right even to a debauch. With the craftiness pertaining to baser natures, however, he took the opportunity thus afforded to cast suspicion on seeking as such and to promote a comfortable consciousness of having already found. His eyes were opened to the joys of philistinism: he saved himself from all the wild experimentation going on by a flight into the idyllic, and to the restlessly creative drive of the artist he opposed a certain easy complacency, a self-contentment in one's own limitations, one's own placidity, even in one's own narrow-mindedness. His attenuated finger pointed, without any false modesty, to the hidden and secret corners of his life, to the many moving and naive pleasures which sprang up like blushing flowers in the most wretched depths of the uncultivated existence and as it were mire of the philistine world.

There were a number of representational talents who, with a gentle brush, depicted the happiness, the cosiness, the prosaicness, the bucolic health, the ease and contentment to be found in the nursery, the scholar's study and the farmhouse. With such picture-books of reality in their hands, these self-satisfied people then sought to come to terms once and for all with the classics they found so unsettling and with the demand for further seeking which proceeded from them; they devised the concept of the epigone-age with the object of obtaining peace and quiet and so as to meet every uncomfortable innovation with the condemnatory verdict 'epigone-work'. It was these same self-contented people who, with the same end in view of guaranteeing their own peace, took charge of history and sought to transform every science which might be expected to disturb their complacency into an historical discipline, especially so in the case of philosophy and classical philology. Through historical awareness they saved themselves from enthusiasm – for history was

10

no longer supposed to engender enthusiasm, even though Goethe might think it did: stupefaction is now the goal of these unphilosophical admirers of *nil admirari** when they seek to understand everything historically. While professing to hate fanaticism and intolerance in any form, what they really hated was the dominating genius and the tyranny of the real demands of culture; and that is why they employed all their powers in paralyzing, stupefying or disrupting all those quarters where fresh and powerful movements might be expected to appear. A philosophy which chastely concealed behind arabesque flourishes the philistine confession of its author invented in addition a formula for the apotheosis of the commonplace: it spoke of the rationality of the real, and thus ingratiated itself with the cultural philistine, who also loves arabesque flourishes but above all conceives himself alone to be real and treats his reality as the standard of reason in the world. He now permitted everyone, himself included, to reflect, to research, to aestheticize, above all to compose poetry and music, to paint pictures, even to create entire philosophies: the sole proviso was that everything must remain as it was before, that nothing should at any price undermine the 'rational' and the 'real', that is to say, the philistine. The latter, to be sure, is very partial to abandoning himself from time to time to the pleasant and daring extravagances of art and sceptical historiography and knows how to appreciate the charm of such forms of entertainment and distraction; but he sternly segregates the 'serious things of life' – that is to say profession, business, wife and child – from its pleasures: and to the latter belongs more or less everything that has anything to do with culture. Therefore woe to an art that starts to take itself seriously and makes demands that touch upon his livelihood, his business and his habits, in short, his philistine 'serious things of life' – he averts his eyes from such an art as though from something indecent, and with the air of a duenna he warns every defenceless virtue not to look.

Being so fond of dissuading, he is grateful to the artist who pays heed to him and lets himself be dissuaded; he gives him to understand that henceforth no sublime masterpieces are to be demanded of him, but only two much easier things: either imitation of actuality to the point of mimicry in idylls or gently humorous satires, or free copies of the most familiar and famous of the classics, though incorporating timid concessions to the taste of the time. For when he

*nil admirari: to wonder at nothing

11

values only the imitations of an epigone or the icon-like portraiture of the present, he knows that the latter will glorify him and augment general contentment with 'actuality', while the former, as well as being quite harmless, will even enhance his reputation as a judge of classical taste – for he has, as aforesaid, come to terms once and for all with the classics themselves. Finally, he invents for his habits, modes of thinking, likes and dislikes, the general formula 'healthiness', and dismisses every uncomfortable disturber of the peace as being sick and neurotic. Thus David Strauss, a true *satisfait* with the state of our culture and a typical philistine, once spoke characteristically of 'Arthur Schopenhauer's ingenious but in many ways unhealthy and unprofitable philosophizing'. For it is a cruel fact that 'the spirit' is accustomed most often to descend upon the 'unhealthy and unprofitable', and on those occasions when he is *honest* with himself even the philistine is aware that the philosophies his kind produce and bring to market are in many ways spiritless, though they are of course extremely healthy and profitable.

For now and then the philistines, when they are alone by themselves, take wine together and recall, in honest, naive and loquacious fashion, the great deeds of the war; on these occasions many things come to light that are otherwise anxiously concealed, and sometimes one of them even lets out the fundamental secrets of the entire brotherhood. Such a thing occurred very recently in the case of a celebrated aesthetician of the Hegelian school of reasoning. The provocation was, to be sure, sufficiently unusual: a circle of philistines was celebrating the memory of a true and genuine non-philistine, and one moreover who in the strictest sense of the word perished by the philistines: the memory of the glorious Hölderlin; and the well-known aesthetician thus had a right on this occasion to speak of tragic souls which perish through contact with 'reality' – the word reality here understood in the sense, already alluded to, of philistine rationality. But 'reality' is now something different from what it was in Hölderlin's day, and it may well be asked whether he would have been able to find his way in the present great age. 'I do not know', said Friedrich Vischer, 'whether his gentle soul could have endured all the harshness involved in any war or all the rottenness we have seen advancing since the war in every sphere of life. Perhaps he would again have sunk back into despair. He was one of the unarmed souls, he was the Werther of Greece, a lover without hope; his was a life full of gentleness and desire, but there was also strength and substance in his will, and greatness, richness and life in his style, which now and then reminds us of Aeschylus. Only his spirit had too little of hardness in it; he lacked the weapon of humour; *he could not admit that one can be a philistine without being a barbarian.*' It is this last confession, and not the sugary condolences of the after-dinner speaker, that concerns us. Yes, one admits to being a philistine – but a barbarian! Not at any price. Poor Hölderlin was, alas, incapable of drawing such fine distinctions. If, to be sure, one understands by the word barbarian the opposite of civilization, or even equates it with such things as piracy and cannibalism, then the distinction is justified; but what the aesthetician is plainly trying to say is that one can be a philistine and at the same time a man of culture – this is the joke that poor Hölderlin had not the humour to see and the lack of which destroyed him.

On this occasion a second admission escaped the speaker: 'It is not always strength of will, *but weakness*, which enables *us* to transcend that longing for the beautiful experienced so profoundly 'by tragic souls' – that, or something like it, was the confession, deposed in the name of the assembled 'we', that is to say the 'transcenders', the 'transcenders through weakness'! Let us be content with these admissions! For we now know two things, and from the mouth of an initiate: first, that this 'we' has really got free of the desire for beauty, has indeed actually transcended it; and, secondly, that this was accomplished through weakness! In less indiscrete moments this weakness had been called by a fairer name: it was the celebrated 'healthiness' of the cultural philistines. After this latest information, however, it might be advisable henceforth to refer to them, not as the 'healthy', but as the weaklings or, more strongly, as the *weak*. If only these weak were not in possession of the power! What can it matter to them what they are called! For they are the masters, and he is no genuine master who cannot endure a mocking nickname. Indeed, provided one possesses the power, one is even free to mock at oneself. It does not really matter then whether one exposes oneself to attack: for what does the purple, the mantle of triumph, not protect! The strength of the cultural philistine comes to light when he admits his weakness: and the more often and more cynically he admits it, the more clearly he betrays his feelings of self-importance and superiority. This is the age of cynical philistine confessions. As Friedrich Vischer made aural confession, so David Strauss has confessed with a book: that aural confession was cynical, and so is this book of confessions.

3

David Strauss makes a twofold confession regarding philistine culture: confession by word and confession by deed – *the word of the confessor and the deed of the writer*. His book entitled *The Old Faith and the New* is, with regard to its content and with regard to its quality as a book and the production of a writer, an uninterrupted confession; and that he should permit himself to make public confession as to his beliefs at all already constitutes a confession.* – It may be that everyone over forty has the right to compile an autobiography, for even the humblest of us may have experienced and seen from closer quarters things which the thinker may find worth noticing. But to depose a confession of one's beliefs must be considered incomparably more presumptuous, since it presupposes that the writer accords value, not merely to what he has experienced or discovered or seen during his life, but even to what he has believed. Now, the last thing the real thinker will wish to know is what kind of beliefs are agreeable to such natures as Strauss or what it is they 'have half dreamily cobbled together' (p. 10) in regard to things of which only he who knows them at first hand has a right to speak. Who could need the confessions of belief of a Ranke or a Mommsen, even though they are scholars and historians of an order quite different from David Strauss? As soon as they sought to interest us in their beliefs rather than in their knowledge they would be overstepping their bounds in a very annoying fashion. But this is what Strauss does when he tells us of his beliefs. No one wishes to know anything about them, except perhaps certain narrow-minded opponents of the Straussian dogmas who feel that there must lie behind them a system of truly diabolical principles and would no doubt want Strauss to compromise his learned utterances by betraying this diabolical background. Perhaps these uncouth fellows have even benefited from Strauss's latest book; the rest of us, however, who have had no reason to suspect the existence of such a diabolical background, have done no such thing – we would, indeed, have been grateful if we *had* found a little diabolism in these pages. For the voice of Strauss speaking of his new faith is certainly not the voice of an evil spirit: it is not the voice of a spirit at all, let alone that of an actual genius. It is the voice of those people whom Strauss introduces to us as his 'we' – they are, he says, 'scholars and artists,

* Strauss's *Der alte und neue Glaube* was published in 1872. Nietzsche's page references are to the original edition. An English translation by Mathilde Blind appeared in 1873.

office workers and soldiers, tradesman and landed proprietors, in their thousands and by no means the worst in the land' – and who, when they tell us of their beliefs, bore us even more than when they tell us of their dreams. When they choose to break their silence and noise their confessions, the volume of their *unisono* must not be allowed to deceive us as to the poverty and vulgarity of the tune they sing. How can the knowledge that a belief is shared by many make us more favourably disposed towards it when we also know that if any one of the many ventured to tell us of it we should not let him finish but interrupt him with a yawn? If you have such a belief, we should have to tell him, for God's sake keep quiet about it. It may be that in earlier years a few simple people sought a thinker in David Strauss: now they have discovered him to be a believer and are disappointed. If he had stayed silent* he would have remained a philosopher, at least so far as these people are concerned: now he is a philosopher to no one. But he no longer desires the honour of being a thinker; he wants only to be a new believer, and is proud of his 'new faith'. Confessing it in writing, he thinks he is inscribing the catechism 'of modern ideas' and constructing the broad 'universal highway of the future'. In fact, our philistine no longer hesitates to say anything, but has grown self-assured to the point of cynicism. There was a time – a very distant time, to be sure – when the philistine was tolerated as something that said nothing and of which nothing was said: there was another time when one flattered his oddities, found him amusing and talked about him. This attention gradually turned him into a coxcomb and he began to take an inordinate pride in his oddities and ingenuous queer-headedness: now he himself talks, often in the manner of Riehl's music for the home. 'But what is this I see! Is it phantom or reality? How long and broad my poodle grows!'† For now he is already trundling like a hippopotamus along the 'universal highway of the future' and his growling and barking has changed into the proud accents of the founder of a religion. Are you perhaps thinking, Master, of founding the religion of the future? 'It seems to me that the time has not yet come. It does not even occur to me to want to destroy any existing church' (p. 8). – But why not, Master? All that matters is that one is able to. Besides, to speak frankly, you yourself believe you are able to: you have only to look at the last page of your book. There you say that your new highway 'is the sole uni-

---

*'if he had stayed silent': Nietzsche's German version of the Latin 'si tacuisses, philosophus mansisses'
†From Goethe's *Faust*, Part I Scene 3.

versal highway of the future, which needs only to be gradually completed and above all more travelled along for it to become pleasant and comfortable'. Therefore deny it no longer: the founder of a religion has been unmasked, the new, pleasant and comfortable road to the Straussian paradise has been constructed. All you are not yet content with, you modest man, is the carriage in which you wish to drive us; you tell us in your closing words: 'that the carriage to which my valued readers have had to entrust themselves with me meets every requirement I would not venture to assert' (p. 367): 'we have been much buffeted about'. Ah ha! you are fishing for compliments, you coquettish religion-founder! We, however, would prefer to tell you the truth. If your reader prescribes himself the 368 pages of your religious catechism at the rate of one page every day of the year – if, that is to say, he takes it in the smallest possible doses – we believe that at the end of it he will feel unwell: out of vexation that it has failed to produce any effect. Gulped down in mouthfuls, however, as much as possible at once according to the prescription for all timely books, the draught can do no harm: far from feeling vexed and unwell, the drinker will be in a merry and happy mood, just as though nothing has happened, no religion had been destroyed, no universal highway constructed, no confession made – and that is what I call an effect! Physician and medicaments and sickness all forgotten! And the joyful laughter! The continual incitement to laughter! You are to be envied, dear sir, for you have founded the most agreeable religion in the world: a religion whose founder is continually honoured by being laughed at.

4

The philistine as the founder of the religion of the future – that is the new faith in its most impressive shape; the philistine become a visionary – that is the unheard-of phenomenon that distinguishes Germany today. Let us, however, preserve for the moment a degree of caution in regard to this visionary enthusiasm: has David Strauss himself not urged such caution upon us, in the following passage (p. 80), in which, to be sure, we are supposed to recognize in the first instance not Strauss but the founder of Christianity: 'We know there have been noble, gifted visionaries, a visionary can arouse and exalt us, and can produce a very lasting effect historically; but let us not choose him as our life-guide. He will lead us astray if we do not subject his influence to the control of reason.' We know even more, indeed: there have also been ungifted visionaries, visionaries who do not arouse and fire us and yet intend to produce a very lasting effect historically as life-guides and to dominate the future: how much more is it incumbent upon us to subject their visionary enthusiasm to the control of reason. Lichtenberg even says: 'There are enthusiastic visionaries devoid of ability, and these are truly dangerous people.' For the present, and in aid of this control by reason, we would like an honest answer to three questions. First: how does the new believer imagine his Heaven? Secondly: how far does the courage bestowed on him by the new faith extend? And thirdly: how does he write his books? Strauss the confessor shall answer the first and second questions for us, Strauss the writer the third.

The Heaven of the new believer will naturally have to be a Heaven on earth: for the Christian 'prospect of an immortal Heavenly life' has, together with the other consolations of Christianity, 'irrevocably fallen away' for him who has 'even one foot' in the Straussian camp (p. 364). There is some significance in how a religion elects to depict its Heaven: and if it be true that Christianity knows no other Heavenly occupation than music-making and singing, then the Straussian philistine cannot very well be expected to look forward to it. The confessional book does, however, contain one paradisial page, page 294: unroll this parchment first of all, most fortunate philistine! All Heaven will there climb down to you. 'We shall give only an indication', Strauss says, 'of what we do, of what we have done these many years. Besides our profession – for we belong to the most varied professions, we are by no means only scholars or artists but also office workers and soldiers, tradesmen and landed proprietors, and, to say it again, there are not a few of us but many thousands and not the worst in any country – besides our profession, I say, we try to keep our minds as open as possible to all the higher interests of mankind: during recent years we have participated in the liveliest way in the great national war and the construction of the German state, and we feel ourselves profoundly uplifted by this turn, as glorious as it was unexpected, in the history of our much-tried nation. We assist our understanding of these things through historical studies, which have now been made easy even for the unlearned by a series of attractive and popularly written historical works; at the same time, we seek to broaden our knowledge of nature, for which there is likewise no lack of aids accessible to the common understanding; and lastly, we find in the writings of our great poets, in performances of the works of our great composers, a

17

stimulus for the spirit and the heart, for the imagination and the sense of humour, that leaves nothing to be desired. Thus we live and go our way rejoicing.'

This is our man, cries the philistine who reads this: for that is how we live, how we live every day!* And what a nice turn of phrase he has to describe things! When, for example, he refers to historical studies by means of which we assist our understanding of the political situation, what can he be referring to but newspaper-reading, and when he speaks of our lively participation in the construction of the German state, what can he mean but our daily visits to the public house? and is a stroll through the zoo not what is meant by 'aids accessible to the common understanding' through which we broaden our knowledge of nature? And finally – the theatres and concerts from which we take home 'stimuli for the imagination and sense of humour' which 'leave nothing to be desired' – how wittily he dignifies these dubious activities! This is our man: for his Heaven is our Heaven!

Thus the philistine cries and rejoices: and if we are not as contented as he is, the reason is that we wanted to know more. Scaliger asked: 'What is it to us whether Montaigne drank red wine or white!' But in this more important case how much we should treasure such detailed information! If only we could know how many pipes the philistine must smoke each day according to the dictates of the new faith, and whether he prefers the Spener or the National-Zeitung when he is drinking his coffee. Our thirst for knowledge is not satisfied! On only one point do we receive something of what we desire, but this, happily, concerns the philistine's Heaven of Heavens: the private little aesthetic closets consecrated to the great poets and composers in which the philistine not merely 'edifies' himself but in which, according to his confession, 'all his blemishes are effaced and washed away' (p. 363); so that we appear to have to envisage these closets as kinds of little bathrooms. 'But that is only for fleeting moments, it happens only in the realm of the imagination and is valid only therein; as soon as we return to rude reality and the daily round, the old cares descend upon us again from all sides' – thus sighs our teacher, Strauss. Yet if we employ the fleeting moments for which we are allowed to linger in those little closets, there will be just enough time to view from all sides a picture of the ideal philistine, that is to say *the philistine from whom all blemishes have been washed away* and who is now the philistine type in all its purity. What here pre-

*This phrase is from a German students' song.

sents itself is, in all seriousness, instructive: let no one who has fallen victim to the confessional book let it go without having read the excursus 'on our great poets' or that 'on our great composers'. Here there extends the rainbow of the new guild, and he who cannot take joy in it 'is beyond all help', is, as Strauss says on another occasion but could also say here, 'not yet ripe for our viewpoint'. For we are, remember, in the Heaven of Heavens. The enthusiastic peripatetic sets about leading us around, and apologizes if, carried away by the pleasure he takes in all these wonderful things, he talks a little too much. 'If I perchance grow more loquacious than is thought appropriate to the occasion', he tells us, 'I ask the reader's indulgence: out of the fullness of the heart the mouth speaketh. Let him be assured, however, that what he is now going to read is not drawn from earlier writings and inserted here, but written for the present purpose and the present place' (p. 296). This confession momentarily staggers us. Of what interest can it be to us whether or not these charming little chapters are newly written! If only it were a matter of writing! Between ourselves, I wish they had been written 25 years ago: for then I would know why the ideas in them seem to me so pallid and why the odour of mouldering antiques adheres to them. But that something written in 1872 should smell mouldy in 1872 arouses my suspicions. Suppose someone fell asleep while reading these chapters and imbibing their odour – what would he be likely to dream about? A friend of mine gave me the answer, for it happened to him. He dreamed of a waxworks show: the classic authors stood there, delicately imitated in wax and gems. They moved their arms and eyes and a screw inside them squeaked as they did so. He then saw something uncanny, a formless figure draped in ribbons and gilt paper with a label hanging from its mouth and 'Lessing' written on it; my friend said he stepped closer and learned the worst: it was the Homeric chimera, Strauss in front, Gervinus behind, in the middle chimera – *in summa*, Lessing. This discovery wrung from him a scream of fear, he awoke and read no further. Why, Master, did you ever write such mouldy little chapters!

We do, to be sure, learn a few novelties from them: for example, that Gervinus has taught us how and why Goethe possessed no talent for the drama, that in the second part of *Faust* he has produced only a schematic allegory; that Wallenstein is a Macbeth who is at the same time Hamlet;* that the Straussian reader plucks out the stories from the *Wanderjahre* in the way illbred children pluck the almonds and

---

*In Schiller's three-part drama *Wallenstein*.

19

raisins out of a tough cake;* that without thrills and extreme situations nothing on the stage can make any real effect; and that Schiller emerged from Kant as from a hydropathic establishment. All this is certainly new and striking, even if it does not strike us very pleasantly; and, as surely as it is new, just as surely it will never grow old, for it was never young: it came into the world already old. What ideas the new-style blessed come across in their aesthetic Heaven! And why have they not forgotten at any rate some of them, especially when they are as unaesthetic and earthly-ephemeral and bear the stamp of stupidity as visibly as, for example, some of the opinions of Gervinus! But it almost seems as though the modest greatness of a Strauss and the immodest minimality of a Gervinus can get on together only too well: and so hail to all these blessed ones, and hail to us unblessed ones as well, if this undoubted judge of art goes on teaching his acquired enthusiasm and his coach-horse gallop, of which honest Grillparzer has spoken with all due clarity, and all Heaven resounds with the hoofbeats of this galloping enthusiasm! Things would at least be a bit livelier than they are at present, when the creeping carpet-slippered enthusiasm of our heavenly leader and the lukewarm eloquence of his mouth in the long run only weary and disgust us. I would like to know how a Hallelujah would sound in the mouth of Strauss: I imagine one would have to listen very closely or it would sound like a polite apology or a whispered compliment. I can relate an instructive and appalling example of this. Strauss took grave exception to references by one of his opponents to his bowing and scraping before Lessing – the unfortunate man had misunderstood him –; Strauss, to be sure, asserted that the man must be a numbskull not to recognize that the simple words he had used of Lessing in section 90† had come straight from the warmth of his heart. Now, I have no doubt at all as to the existence of this warmth; on the contrary, I have always felt that this warmth of approval of Lessing on the part of Strauss had something suspect about it; I find the same suspect approval of Lessing raised to steam-heat in Gervinus; indeed, none of the great German writers is in general so popular with the little German writers as Lessing is; and yet they deserve no thanks for it: for what is it in Lessing that really wins their approval? First, his universality: he is a critic and a poet, an archaeologist and a philosopher, a theorist of drama and a

---

*Goethe's novel *Wilhelm Meisters Wanderjahre* (1821–9), which contains inset stories.
†'section 90' refers to *The Old Faith and the New.*

theologian. Then, 'this unity of the writer and the man, of the head and the heart'. The latter quality distinguishes every great writer, and sometimes even the little writer, for a narrow mind gets on fabulously well with a narrow heart. And the former quality, universality, is in itself no distinction at all, especially as in Lessing's case it was a mere necessity. What is, rather, to be marvelled at in these Lessing enthusiasts is precisely that they fail to notice this consuming necessity which pursued Lessing throughout his life and forced upon him his 'universality'; that they fail to realize that such a man is consumed too quickly, like a flame, and are not indignant that this tender, ardent being was darkened, tormented and suffocated by the vulgar narrowness and poverty of his whole environment, and especially that of his learned contemporaries; that they fail to understand, indeed, that this admired universality is something that ought to evoke, not admiration, but a profound feeling of pity. 'Commiserate with the extraordinary man', Goethe cries to us, 'that he lived in so miserable an age he had constantly to exert himself polemically.'* How, my dear philistines, can you think of Lessing without a feeling of shame: he who perished of your stupidity, in conflict with your ludicrous totems and idols, through the wretched state of your theatres, your scholars, your theologians, without even once being able to venture that eternal flight for which he had come into the world. And what do you feel when you remember Winckelmann, who, to free his sight of your grotesque absurdities, went begging for help to the Jesuits and whose shameful conversion dishonours not him but you? Do you even dare to speak the name of Schiller and not blush? Look at this picture! The flashing eyes that gaze contemptuously out over your heads, the deathly flushed cheeks – do these say nothing to you? Here was a glorious, divine toy which you broke. And if this curtailed and mortally harassed life had been deprived of Goethe's friendship it would have been your part to extinguish it even sooner! None of your great geniuses has ever received any assistance from you, and do you now want to make it a dogma that none ever shall receive any? To each of them you were that 'resistance of the obtuse world' which Goethe names in his epilogue to Schiller's *Glocke*; to each of them you showed annoyance and lack of understanding, or envious narrow-mindedness, or malice and egoism: it was in spite of you they created their works, against you they directed their attacks, and it was thanks to you they

*Goethe to Eckermann, 7 February 1827.

sank down too soon, their work unfinished, broken or deadened by the struggle. And are you now to be permitted, *tamquam re bene gesta,** to praise such men! and to do so in words which reveal unmistakably whom it is you have in mind when you utter such praise, which then 'gushes so warmly from the heart' that one would have to be blind not to see towards whom your obeisances are really directed. Even in his day, Goethe felt impelled to exclaim: 'Truly, we are in need of a Lessing!' and woe to all vain teachers and to the whole aesthetic heavenly kingdom if the young tiger, his restless energy visible in swelling muscles and the glance of his eye, should ever set out in search of prey!

5

How wise my friend was that, enlightened by this chimerical figure as to the nature of the Straussian Lessing and of Strauss himself, he forbore to read further. We read further, however, and went on to beg entry into the *musical* sanctum of the new faith. The Master opened the door, attended at our side, explained, named names – at last we stopped mistrustfully and looked at him: were we not experiencing the same thing as happened to our poor friend in his dream? So long as he was speaking of them, the composers of whom Strauss spoke seemed to us to be wrongly named, and we felt he must be referring to someone else, if not to mere teasing phantoms. When, for example, he takes, with the same warmth as had made us suspicious when he praised Lessing, the name of Haydn into his mouth and gives himself out for an epopt and priest of a Haydnesque mystery cult, while at the same time (p. 362) comparing Haydn with 'honest soup' and Beethoven with 'confectionary' (in reference to the quartets, of all things), we are certain of only one thing: *his* confectionary-Beethoven is not *our* Beethoven, and his soup-Haydn is not *our* Haydn. The Master finds, moreover, that our orchestras are too good to perform his Haydn and believes that this music is suited only to the most modestly competent dilettanti – again a proof that he is referring to a different artist and to different works of art (perhaps to Riehl's music for the home).

But who could this Straussian confectionary-Beethoven be? He is supposed to have written nine symphonies, of which the 'Pastoral' is 'the least inspired'; we discover that at every third of them he is

tamquam re bene gesta: as if the thing were done well

impelled 'to kick over the traces and go off on an adventure', which almost suggests to us a cross-bred creature, half horse, half knight errant. In regard to a certain 'Eroica' it is seriously stated of this centaur that he has failed to make it clear 'whether what is going on is a conflict on the battlefield or in the depths of the human heart'. In the 'Pastoral' there is an 'excellent storm' which is, however, far too good to interrupt a mere peasants' dance; and it is through this 'capricious continual association' of the music with its 'trivial underlying occasion', as Strauss so neatly and correctly calls it, that this symphony is 'the least inspired' – an even harsher word seems to have hovered in the mind of our classical Master but, as he tells us, he preferred to express himself here 'with befitting modesty'. But no, here he is for once in the wrong, here he really is too modest. For who else is to instruct us about the confectionary-Beethoven if not Strauss himself, the only one who seems to know him? There immediately follows, moreover, the enunciation of a firm and befittingly *immodest* judgment, this time on the Ninth Symphony: this work, it seems, may be loved only by those to whom 'the baroque counts as a mark of genius and the formless as the sublime' (p. 359). It is true that so stern a critic as Gervinus gave it a welcome, namely as a confirmation of one of his own dogmas: he, Strauss, is however very far from seeking the merits of *his* Beethoven in such 'problematic productions'. 'It is a pity', sighs our Master sadly, 'that our enjoyment of Beethoven and the admiration we gladly accord him must be diminished by reservations of this kind.' For our Master is a favourite of the muses, and they have told him that they went only a stretch of the way with Beethoven and that he thereafter again lost sight of them. 'This is a defect', he cries, 'but can one believe that it also appears as a merit?' 'He who trundles along the musical idea with toil and out of breath will appear to be the stronger and to move what is heavier' (pp. 355–6). This is a confession, and in regard not only to Beethoven but to the 'classic prose-writer' himself: the muses never let go of *him*, the celebrated author: from the lightest play of wit – Straussian wit, that is – to the heights of seriousness – Straussian seriousness, that is – they stay imperturbably at his side. He, the classic artist in writing, carries his burden with playful ease, while Beethoven trundles his along out of breath. He seems to dally with his load: there is a merit; but can one believe that it might appear as a defect? – But at the most only to those to whom the baroque counts as a mark of genius and the formless as the sublime – is that not so, you dallying favourite of the muses?

23

We begrudge no one the edification he acquires for himself in the silence of his room or in the new heavenly kingdom arranged for the purpose; but of all possible forms of edification the Straussian is one of the strangest; for he edifies himself at a little sacrificial fire into which he casually casts the sublimest works of the German nation in order to perfume his idols with the smoke they produce. Let us imagine for a moment that the 'Eroica', the 'Pastoral' and the Ninth had chanced to get into the hands of our priest of the muses and that it had then depended upon him to keep Beethoven's image spotless through the removal of such 'problematical productions' – who can doubt that he would have burned them? And that is how the Strausses of our day in fact proceed: they want to know of an artist only that by which he is suited for their domestic service, and can see no alternative but using him as perfume or burning him. This, of course, they should be at liberty to do: the only strange thing about it is that public opinion in aesthetic matters is so insipid, uncertain and easily misled that it beholds such an exhibition of the sorriest philistinism without protest, that it lacks, indeed, any feeling for the comicality of a scene in which an unaesthetic magistrate sits in judgment on Beethoven. And as for Mozart, there ought truly to apply to him what Aristotle said of Plato: 'the *bad man* is not permitted even to praise him'. Here, however, all shame has been lost, on the part of the public as much as on that of the Master; not only is he permitted to cross himself before the greatest and purest products of the German genius as though he had beheld something godless and indecent, but his candid confessions of sins are received with delight, especially as he confesses not sins he himself has committed, but those supposedly committed by our great spirits. 'Ah, if only our Master really was always right!' his admiring readers sometimes think in an access of doubt; he himself, however, stands there, smiling and certain, perorating, damning and blessing, doffing his hat to himself, and capable at any moment of saying what the duchess Delaforte said to Madame de Staël: 'I have to admit, my dear friend, that I know of nobody who is always right except me.'

6

To the worm a corpse is a pleasant thought, and to everything living a worm is a dreadful one. The worm's idea of Heaven is a fat carcass, the philosophy professor's is grubbing about in the entrails of Schopenhauer, and as long as there are rats there will also be a rat

Heaven. This provides the answer to our first question: how does the new believer imagine his Heaven? The Straussian philistine lodges in the works of our great poets and composers like a worm which lives by destroying, admires by consuming, reveres by digesting.

Now we come to our second question: how far does the courage bestowed on him by the new faith extend? This too would already have been answered if courage were identical with immodesty: for in that case Strauss would possess the courage of a Mameluke – for that befitting modesty of which he speaks in the passage on Beethoven just alluded to is only a stylistic device, not a moral position. Strauss has sufficient of that impudence to which every victorious hero feels himself entitled; every flower that blooms belongs to him, the victor, alone, and he lauds the sun for illuminating *his* window. Even the ancient, venerable universe does not remain untouched by his commendations, as though they alone could consecrate it and it must henceforth revolve only about the central monad, Strauss. The universe, he informs us, is a machine with iron wheels and cogs and heavy pistons and rams, 'but merciless cogs are not all that move within it, there also flows a soothing oil' (p. 365). The universe will not be precisely grateful to our image-mad Master that he can find no better metaphor with which to commend it, if indeed it takes any pleasure at all in being commended by Strauss. What is this oil called which trickles down on to the pistons and rams? And of what consolation could it be to the worker within this machine to know that this oil is being poured on to him while the machine continues to hold him in its grip? Let us say simply that the metaphor is an unfortunate one and turn our attention to another procedure through which Strauss seeks to convey how he really feels towards the universe and in the course of which there hovers upon his lips the question Gretchen kept asking: 'He loves me – he loves me not – he loves me?'* If while he is doing this Strauss does not pluck the petals from a flower or count the buttons on a coat, what he does do is no less harmless, though it perhaps requires a little more courage. Strauss wants to see whether or not his feeling for the 'cosmos' has become paralysed and dead, and he jabs himself: for he knows that one can jab one's arm with a needle quite painlessly so long as the arm is paralysed and dead. In reality, to be sure, he does not jab himself, he chooses an even more violent procedure, which he describes thus: 'We open Schopenhauer, who loses no opportunity of striking

---

*In Goethe's *Faust*, Part I Scene 12.

our idea in the face' (p. 143). But since it is not an idea, even the fairest Straussian idea of the universe, that has a face, but he who has the idea, the procedure here described consists of the following individual acts: Strauss opens Schopenhauer, whereupon Schopenhauer takes the opportunity to strike Strauss in the face. Strauss now 'reacts', and does so 'religiously', that is to say he strikes back at Schopenhauer, berates him, speaks of absurdities, blasphemies, infamies, even asserts that Schopenhauer was out of his mind. The outcome of this cudgelling: 'we demand for our universe the same piety as the devout of the old stamp do for their God' – more briefly: 'he loves me!' He makes things hard for himself, our favourite of the muses, but he is as brave as a Mameluke and fears neither the Devil nor Schopenhauer. How much 'soothing oil' would he not use up if he indulged in such procedures very often!

On the other hand, we realize the debt Strauss actually owes to the titillating, jabbing and cudgelling Schopenhauer; and the following express act of kindness towards him therefore fails to occasion in us any further surprise. 'It is necessary only to leaf through Arthur Schopenhauer's writings, though one would also do well, not merely to leaf through them, but to study them' etc. (p. 141). To whom is the chieftain of the philistines really addressing these words? – he of whom it can be proved that he has never studied Schopenhauer, he of whom Schopenhauer himself would have to have said: 'this is an author who does not deserve to be leafed through, let alone studied'. It is obvious that he swallowed Schopenhauer the wrong way: by coughing and spluttering he is trying to get rid of him. But so that the measure of naive commendation shall be full, Strauss permits himself to recommend old Kant: he calls Kant's *Allgemeine Geschichte und Theorie des Himmels* of 1755 'a work which has always seemed to me no less significant than his later critique of reason. If in the latter what one must admire is profundity of insight, in the former it is extensiveness of outlook; if in the latter we see the aged philosopher engaged in securing a domain of knowledge, even if a limited one, in the former we encounter a man filled with all the courage of the spiritual discoverer and conqueror.' This judgment of Kant on the part of Strauss has always seemed to me no more modest than his judgment of Schopenhauer: if in the latter we see the chieftain engaged above all in securing the expression of a judgment, albeit a very limited one, in the former we encounter the celebrated prose-writer who, with all the courage of ignorance, empties his vial of commendation even upon Kant. The quite incredible fact that Strauss has no notion how to derive from Kant's critique of reason support for his testament of modern ideas, and that everywhere he flatters nothing but the crudest kind of realism, is among the most striking characteristics of this new gospel, which presents itself moreover only as the arduously attained outcome of continuous historical and scientific research and therewith denies any involvement with philosophy at all. For the philistine chieftain and his 'we' there is no such thing as the Kantian philosophy. He has no notion of the fundamental antinomies of idealism or of the extreme relativity of all science and reason. Or: it is precisely reason that ought to tell him how little of the in-itself of things can be determined by reason. But it is true that people of a certain age find it impossible to understand Kant, especially if in their youth they have, like Strauss, understood, or thought they understood, the 'gigantic spirit' Hegel, and have also had to occupy themselves with Schleiermacher, 'who', as Strauss says, 'possessed almost too much acuteness'. It will sound strange to Strauss when I tell him that even now he is in a state of 'absolute dependence' on Hegel and Schleiermacher, and that his doctrine of the universe, his way of regarding things *sub specie bienni*,* his grovelling before the realities of present-day Germany, above all his shameless philistine optimism, are to be elucidated by reference to certain early youthful impressions, habits and pathological phenomena. He who has once contracted Hegelism and Schleiermacherism is never quite cured of them.

There is one passage in the confessional book in which this incurable optimism goes strolling along with a downright holiday air of complacency (pp. 142–3). 'If the world is a thing that it were better did not exist', says Strauss, 'well then, the thought of the philosopher, which constitutes a piece of this world, is a thought that it were better was not thought. The pessimistic philosopher does not see that he declares his own thought bad when his thought declares the world bad; but if a thought which declares the world bad is itself bad thinking, then the world is, on the contrary, good. Optimism may as a rule make things too easy for itself, and here Schopenhauer's insistence on the role which pain and evil play in the world is quite in order; but every true philosophy is necessarily optimistic, since otherwise it denies its own right to exist.' If this refutation of Schopenhauer is not

---

*sub specie bienni: literally, 'under the aspect of two years' – Nietzsche's ironic adaptation of the well-known phrase 'sub specie aeternitatis'.

the same as that which in another place Strauss calls a 'refutation to the loud rejoicing of the higher spheres', then I do not understand this theatrical expression, which he once employed against an opponent. Optimism has here for once deliberately made things too easy for itself. But the trick of the thing was precisely to make it look as though refuting Schopenhauer was no bother at all and to cast one's burden off with such playful ease that the three muses would take continual delight in the dallying optimist. This is to be achieved by showing that there is no need whatever to take a pessimist seriously: the vainest sophistries will do for dealing with so 'unhealthy and unprofitable' a philosophy as Schopenhauer's, upon which one needs to expend, not reasons, but at the most jokes and phrases. In the light of such passages as this, one comprehends Schopenhauer's solemn assertion that, where it is not the thoughtless chatter of those beneath whose flat cranium there are no thoughts but only words, optimism seems to him not merely an absurd but also a *truly infamous mode of thinking*, a bitter mockery of the nameless sufferings of mankind. When the philistine reduces it to a system, as Strauss does, he also reduces it to an infamous mode of thinking, that is to say to an inordinately stupid ease-and-contentment doctrine for the benefit of the 'ego', or of his 'we', and he arouses indignation.

Who, for example, could read the following psychological elucidation without feeling indignation, since it can quite clearly have sprung only from the stem of this infamous ease-and-contentment theory: 'Beethoven said he would never have been able to compose such a text as *Figaro* or *Don Giovanni*. *Life had not smiled upon him to the extent that he could have adopted so cheerful a view of it as to take the weaknesses of mankind so lightly*' (p. 361). But the worst example of this infamous vulgarity of mind is supplied in the fact that Strauss knows no other way of explaining to himself the whole dreadfully serious drive to self-abnegation and to salvation in asceticism evidenced in the first centuries of Christianity than by supposing it to have originated in a preceding surfeit of sexual indulgence of all kinds and the disgust and nausea that resulted:

> 'The Persians call it *bidamag buden*,
> The Germans say *Katzenjammer*.'*

Strauss himself quotes these lines and is not ashamed. We, however, turn aside for a moment to overcome our disgust.

*Katzenjammer: a hangover; remorse for the previous night's debauch. The couplet is from Goethe's *West-Östliche Divan*.

7

Our philistine chieftain is indeed brave with words to the point of rashness whenever he believes he will give delight to his noble 'we' through such bravery. Thus, the asceticism and self-abnegation of the saints and hermits of old may count as a form of *Katzenjammer*, Jesus may be described as a visionary who would in our day hardly escape the madhouse, the story of the resurrection may be called a 'piece of world-historical humbug' – let us for once let all this pass, so that we may study the singular courage of which Strauss, our 'classic philistine', is capable.

Let us first hear his confession: 'To tell the world what it least wants to hear is, to be sure, a displeasing and thankless office. It likes to live unstintingly, like a great lord, it receives and pays out for as long as it has anything to pay with: but when someone comes along to reckon up the items and hands it the bill, it regards him as a mischief-maker. And precisely that is what my head and heart have always impelled me to do.' Such a head and heart may well be called courageous, yet it remains doubtful whether this courage is natural and original, or whether it is not rather acquired and artificial; perhaps Strauss accustomed himself to being a mischief-maker by profession only gradually, until he had acquired from this pro-fession the courage for it. That would accord very well with natural cowardice, such as is proper to the philistine: it reveals itself especially in the inconsequentiality of those assertions which it takes courage to make; there is the sound of thunder, but there follows no clearing of the air. He cannot manage an aggressive act, only aggressive words, but he chooses the most offensive words he can find and exhausts all his force and energy in uncouth and blustering expressions: when his words have died away he is more cowardly than he who has never spoken. Even the phantom form of actions, ethics, reveals that he is a hero only of words, and that he avoids every occasion on which it is necessary to proceed from words to grim earnest. He announces with admirable frankness that he is no longer a Christian, but he does not wish to disturb anyone's peace of mind; it seems to him contradictory to found an association in order to overthrow an association – which is in fact not so very contradic-tory. With a certain rude contentment he covers himself in the hairy cloak of our ape-genealogists and praises Darwin as one of the greatest benefactors of mankind – but it confuses us to see that his ethics are constructed entirely independently of the question: 'What is our conception of the world?' Here was an opportunity to exhibit native courage: for here he ought to have turned his back on his 'we' and boldly derived a moral code for life out of the *bellum omnium contra omnes** and the privileges of the strong – though such a code would, to be sure, have to originate in an intrepid mind such as that of Hobbes, and in a grand love of truth quite different from that which explodes only in angry outbursts against priests, miracles and the 'world-historical humbug' of the resurrection. For with a genuine Darwinian ethic, seriously and consistently carried through, he would have had against him the philistine whom with such outbursts he attracts to his side.

'All moral behaviour' says Strauss, 'is a self-determination of the individual according to the idea of the species.' Translated into comprehensible language, all this means is: Live as a man and not as an ape or a seal! Unfortunately this imperative is altogether without force and useless, because the concept of man yokes together the most diverse and manifold things, for example the Patagonian and Master Strauss, and because no one will venture to demand: 'Live as a Patagonian!' and at the same time 'Live as Master Strauss!' If, however, anyone should go so far as to demand of himself: 'Live as a genius', that is to say as the ideal expression of the species man, but happened to be either a Patagonian or Master Strauss, how we would then have to suffer from the importunities of natural fools thirsting for genius – Lichtenberg in his day already had to complain of their mushroom-like growth in Germany – and demanding of us with wild cries that we listen to their latest confessions of faith. Strauss has not yet even learned that no idea can ever make men better or more moral, and that preaching morals is as easy as finding grounds for them is difficult; his task was much rather to take the phenomena of human goodness, compassion, love and self-abnegation, which do in fact exist, and derive and explain them from his Darwinist presuppositions: while he preferred by a leap into the imperative to flee from the task of *explanation*. In making this leap he is even able to elude, with an easy and frivolous hop, Darwin's fundamental proposition. 'Do not ever forget', says Struass, 'that you are a man and not a mere creature of nature: do not ever forget that all others are likewise men, that is to say, with all their individual differences the same as you, with the same needs and demands as you – that is the epitome of all morality.' But whence sounds this imperative? How can man possess it in himself, since, according to Darwin, he is pre-

bellum omnium contra omnes: war of all against all

30

cisely a creature of nature and nothing else, and has evolved to the height of being man by quite other laws: precisely, in fact, by always forgetting that other creatures similar to him possessed equivalent rights, precisely by feeling himself the stronger and gradually eliminating the other, weaker examples of his species? While Strauss is obliged to assume that no two creatures have been exactly similar, and that the entire evolution of man from the level of the animals up to the heights of the cultural philistine depends upon the law of differences between individuals, he finds no difficulty in enunciating the opposite: 'behave as though there were no differences between individuals!' Where has the moral teaching of Strauss–Darwin now gone, where has any courage whatever gone!

We are at once given a fresh demonstration of the point at which courage is transposed into its opposite. For Strauss continues: 'Do not ever forget that you and all that you are aware of within and around you is no disconnected fragment, no wild chaos of atoms and accidents, but that everything proceeds according to eternal laws out of the one primeval source of all life, all reason and all goodness – that is the epitome of religion.' Out of this 'one primeval source' however, there at the same time flows all destruction, all unreason, all evil, and Strauss calls this source the universe. But how, given it possesses so contradictory and self-annulling a character, should this be worthy of religious veneration and be addressed by the name 'God', as Strauss himself addresses it (p. 365): 'our God does not take us into his arms from outside' – here one expects as an antithesis a certainly very strange 'taking us into his arms from within'! – 'he opens to us sources of consolation within us. He shows us that, while chance would be an irrational master of the world, necessity, i.e. the chain of causes in the world, is reason itself' (a piece of surreptitiousness which only the 'we' can fail to recognize as such because they were raised in this Hegelian worship of the real as the rational, that is to say in the *deification of success*). 'He teaches us to see that to desire an exception to the fulfilment of a single law of nature would be to desire the destruction of the cosmos.' On the contrary, Master: an honest natural scientist believes that the world conforms unconditionally to laws, without however asserting anything as to the ethical or intellectual value of these laws: he would regard any such assertions as the extreme anthropomorphism of a reason that has overstepped the bounds of the permitted. But it is at precisely the point at which the honest natural scientist resigns that Strauss 'reacts' – to employ his own choice expression – 'religiously', and goes on to pursue a consciously dishonest kind of natural science; he assumes without question that all events possess the *highest* intellectual value and are thus absolutely rational and purposeful, and then that they contain a revelation of eternal goodness itself. He is thus in need of a complete cosmodicy and at a disadvantage compared with those who are concerned only with a theodicy, who conceive the entire existence of man as, for example, a punishment or a process of purification. At this point, and thus embarrassed, Strauss goes so far as to venture for once a metaphysical hypothesis – the driest and most palsied there has ever been and at bottom no more than an unconscious parody of a saying of Lessing's. 'That other saying of Lessing's', he says on page 219, 'that, if God held all truth in his right hand and in his left the never-sleeping quest for truth with the condition of continually erring in this quest, and then offered him a choice between them, he would humbly fall upon God's left hand and beg for the contents of it – this saying has always been regarded as among the finest he left to us. There has been found in it an expression of his restless desire for action and investigation. This saying has always made so powerful an impression upon me because behind its subjective significance I have heard resounding an objective one of immense range. For does it not contain the best reply to Schopenhauer's crude conception of an ill-advised God who knows of nothing better to do than to enter into so wretched a world as this is? May it not be that the Creator himself shares Lessing's opinion and prefers continual striving to peaceful possession?' A God, that is to say, who reserves to himself *continual error* and at the same time a striving for truth, and who perhaps humbly falls upon Strauss's left hand and says to him: all truth is for you. If ever a God or a man were ill-advised it is this Straussian God, with his partiality for error and failure, and the Straussian man, who has to pay for this partiality – here indeed one can 'hear resounding a significance of immense range', here there flows Strauss's universal soothing oil, here one senses something of the rationality of all evolution and natural law! Does one really? Or would our world not be, rather, as Lichtenberg once called it, the work of a subordinate being who as yet lacked a full understanding of his task, and thus an experiment? a novice's test-piece which was still being worked on? So that Strauss himself would have to concede that our world is an arena, *not* of rationality, but of error, and that its laws and purposefulness are no source of consolation, since they proceed from a God who is not merely in error but takes pleasure in being in error. It is a truly delicious spectacle to behold Strauss as a metaphysical architect building up into the clouds. But for whom is this spectacle mounted? For the noble and contented 'we', so as to preserve their contentment: perhaps they were overcome by fear in the midst of those merciless wheels of the universal machine and tremblingly begged their leader for help. Whereupon Strauss started the 'soothing oil' flowing, led on a God who errs out of a passion for error, and assumed for once the wholly uncongenial role of a metaphysical architect. He does all this because his 'we' are afraid and he himself is afraid – and here we discover the limits of his courage, even with respect to his 'we'. For he does not dare to tell them honestly: I have liberated you from a merciful God, the universe is only a rigid machine, take care you are not mangled in its wheels! This he dares not do: so he has to call in the sorceress, that is to say metaphysics. To the philistine, however, even a Straussian metaphysic is preferable to the Christian, and the idea of an erring God more attractive than that of a miracle-working one. For he himself, the philistine, commits errors, but has never yet performed a miracle.

It is for this very reason that the philistine hates the genius: for the genius has the justified reputation of performing miracles; and that is why it is in the highest degree instructive to see why, in one solitary passage, Strauss for once presents himself as the daring defender of the genius and of the aristocratic natures of the spirit. Why does he do it? From fear, this time fear of the social democrats. He refers them to Bismarck, Moltke, 'whose greatness can be the less denied as they advance into the realm of palpable action. Now even the most stiff-necked and surly of these fellows must be constrained to look upwards a little, so as to get a sight of these exalted figures, even if only to the knee.' Do you perhaps desire, Master, to give the social democrats instruction in how to get kicked? The will to deliver such kicks is to be found everywhere, after all, and that those who are to get kicked can see only 'to the knee' of these exalted figures seems to ensure that the kicks will be successfully delivered. 'In the domain of art and science too', Strauss goes on, 'there will never be a lack of kings who build and who give work to a host of carters.' Good – but suppose the carters themselves start to build? It does happen, metaphysical Master, you know that – then the kings will have to grin and bear it.

This union of audacity and weakness, of rash words and cowardly acquiescence, this subtle assessment of how and with what expressions one can now impress the philistine, now flatter him, this lack of character and strength masquerading as strength and character, this defectiveness in wisdom with the affectation of superiority and mature experience – all this, in fact, is what I hate in this book. If I thought that young men could endure such a book, even treasure it, I would sadly renounce all hope for their future. This confession of a pitiful, hopeless and truly contemptible philistinism presents itself as an expression of the views of those many thousands of 'we's of whom Strauss speaks, and these 'we's are in turn the fathers of the coming generation! These are gruesome presuppositions for anyone who wants to assist the coming generation to that which the present does not possess – to a truly German culture. To such a one the ground seems strewn with ashes and all the stars appear obscured; every dead tree, every desolate field cries to him: Unfruitful! Lost! Here there will be no more spring! He has to feel as the youthful Goethe felt when he looked into the sad atheistical twilight of the *Système de la nature*: the book seemed to him so grey, so stagnant, so dead, that it cost him an effort to endure its proximity, and he shuddered in its presence as in the presence of a ghost.*

8

We are now sufficiently instructed as to the new believer's Heaven and his courage to be able to pose our final question: how does he write his books? and what is the nature of the scriptures of his religion?

To him who can answer this question rigorously and without prejudice, the fact that Strauss's portable oracle for the German philistine has been in demand to the extent of six editions will present a problem of the most thought-provoking kind, especially when he hears that it has also received a warm welcome in scholarly circles and even in German universities. Students are said to have greeted it as a syllabus for the training of strong minds and professors are said not to have objected: here and there the book has been received as a *sacred scripture for scholars*. Strauss himself gives us to understand that the confessional book is not intended to offer instruction *only* to scholars and the cultivated, but we adhere to the view that it is directed at these in the first instance, and particularly at the scholars,

---

*Système de la nature: Baron d'Holbach's once celebrated defence of atheistic materialism and determinism, published in 1770. Goethe refers to it in *Dichtung und Wahrheit III*.

and that it holds up to them the reflection of a life such as they themselves live. For this is the trick of the thing: the Master affects to be outlining the ideal of a new philosophy of life, and now he hears himself praised on every side, since everyone is in a position to think that this is precisely how *he* thinks and that Strauss would see already fulfilled in him that which he has demanded only of the future. This is part of the explanation of the extraordinary success of this book: 'as is here written so do we live and go our way rejoicing!' the scholar cries to him, and is glad when he finds that others feel the same. Whether he happens to differ from the Master on individual points – over Darwin, for example, or capital punishment – is to him of little moment, since he is on the whole so certain of breathing his own air and hearing the echo of *his* voice and *his* needs. The painfulness of this unanimity for any true friend of German culture must not deter him from acknowledging it to himself or from making the fact public.

We all know how our age is typified by its pursuit of science; we know it because it is part of our life: and that precisely is the reason almost no one asks himself what the consequences of such an involvement with the sciences could be for culture, even supposing that the will and the capacity to promote culture were everywhere to hand. For the nature of scientific man (quite apart from the form he assumes at present) contains a real paradox: he behaves like the proudest idler of fortune, as though existence were not a dreadful and questionable thing but a firm possession guaranteed to last for ever. He seems to be permitted to squander his life on questions whose answer could at bottom be of consequence only to someone assured of an eternity. The heir of but a few hours, he is ringed around with frightful abysses, and every step he takes ought to make him ask: Whither? Whence? To what end? But his soul is warmed with the task of counting the stamens of a flower or breaking up the stones of the pathway, and all the interest, joy, strength and desire he possesses is absorbed in this work. Now, this paradox, the scientific man, has in recent years got into a frantic hurry in Germany, as though science were a factory and every minute's slacking incurred punishment. Nowadays he works as hard as the fourth estate, the slaves; his study is no longer an occupation but a necessity, he looks neither to right nor left and goes through all the business of life, and its more questionable aspects, with the half-consciousness or the repellent need for entertainment characteristic of the exhausted worker.

Now this is his attitude towards culture too. He behaves as though life were to him only *otium* but *sine dignitate*:* and even in his dreams he does not throw off his yoke, like a slave who even when freed still dreams of servitude and beatings. Our scholars are hardly to be distinguished – and then not to their advantage – from farmers who want to increase the tiny property they have inherited and are assiduously employed all day and far into the night in tilling the field, leading the plough and encouraging the oxen. Now, Pascal believes quite generally that men pursue their business and their sciences so eagerly only so as to elude the most important questions which would press upon them in a state of solitude or if they were truly idle, that is to say precisely those questions as to Whither, Whence and Why. Amazingly, the most obvious question fails to occur to our scholars: what is their work, their hurry, their painful frenzy supposed to be for? To earn bread or acquire positions of honour, perhaps? Not at all. Yet you exert yourselves like those in need of food, indeed you tear it from the table of science as greedily and as utterly unselectively as though you were on the point of starvation. But if you, as men of science, treat science in the way a worker treats the tasks that are to furnish his means of life, what will become of a culture condemned to await the hour of its birth and redemption in the midst of such excitement and breathless confusion? No one has time for it – and yet what is science for *at all* if it has no time for culture? At least reply to this question: what is the Whence, Whither, To what end of science if it is not to lead to culture? To lead to barbarism, perhaps? That our learned class has already gone frighteningly far in this direction is evident when we think that such superficial books as Strauss's are sufficient to meet the demands of their present cultural level. For it is precisely in such books that we find that repellent need for entertainment and that casual, only-half-listening accommodation with philosophy and culture and with the serious things of life in general. One is reminded of the social world of the learned classes, where too, when the shop talk is exhausted, there is evidence only of weariness, of a desire for diversion at any price, of a tattered memory and incoherent personal experience. When we hear Strauss speak of the problems of life – whether it be the problem of marriage or of war or of capital punishment – we are appalled at his lack of real experience, of any native insight into the nature of man: all his judgments are so uniformly bookish, indeed at

otium sine dignitate: idleness without dignity

36

bottom merely of the sort found in the newspapers; literary reminiscences take the place of genuine ideas and insights, an affected moderation and knowingness is supposed to compensate us for the lack of real wisdom and maturity of thought. How exactly this corresponds to the spirit which informs the noisily advertised high seats of learning in the cities of Germany! How congenial this spirit must find the spirit of Strauss: for it is in precisely those places that culture is most completely lacking, it is precisely there that the germination of a new culture is totally thwarted; noisy preparation for the sciences there pursued goes with a herdlike stampede for the disciplines most in favour at the cost of deserting those of most consequence. With what kind of lantern would one have to search here for men capable of inward contemplation and an undivided devotion to the genius and possessing the strength and courage to conjure up demons which have deserted our age! Viewed externally, these places display all the pomp of culture, with their imposing apparatus they resemble an arsenal choked with cannon and other weapons of war: we behold such preparations and industrious activity as though Heaven itself were to be stormed and truth fetched up out of the deepest well, and yet in warfare it is often the biggest pieces of apparatus that are worst deployed. Genuine culture likewise avoids these places as it conducts its campaigns, feeling instinctively that it has nothing to hope for and much to fear in them. For the only form of culture with which the inflamed eye and the blunted brain of the learned working class want to occupy themselves is precisely that *philistine culture* whose gospel has been proclaimed by Strauss.

If we consider for a moment the principal grounds of that congeniality which links the learned working class and philistine culture we shall also discover the path that leads us to our final main theme: consideration of Strauss as a *writer* recognized as a classic.

In the first place, this culture wears an expression of complacency and will have nothing essential changed in the present condition of German education; it is above all seriously convinced of the superiority of all German educational institutions, especially the grammar schools and universities, never ceases to recommend them to foreigners as models, and does not doubt for a moment that they have made the German people into the most educated and judicious nation in the world. Philistine culture believes in itself and therefore in the means and methods available to it. In the second place, however, it lays the final arbitration as to all questions of taste and culture in the hands of the scholar and regards itself as an ever-growing compendium of learned opinions on art, literature and philosophy; it is concerned to constrain the scholar to express his opinions and then to administer them to the German people, admixed, diluted or systematized, as a medicinal draught. Whatever may develop outside this circle is listened to with doubt and inattentively, or not listened to at all, until at length a single voice, no matter whose it may be so long as it bears the firm stamp of the scholarly species, is heard from within those sacred halls where the traditional infallibility in matters of taste is supposed to dwell: and from then on public opinion possesses one opinion more and repeats this single voice with a hundredfold echo. In reality, however, this supposed aesthetic infallibility is very questionable, so questionable indeed that one may assume that a scholar in fact lacks taste, ideas and aesthetic judgment until he has demonstrated the opposite. And only a few will be able to do so. For, after the panting and harassment of the daily race which the world of the sciences is today, how many of them will be able to maintain that courageous and steady glance that characterizes the champion of culture even if they ever possessed it – that glance which condemns this daily race itself as a source of barbarism? That is why these few must, moreover, live in a state of opposition: what can they achieve against the uniform belief of countless thousands who have one and all made of public opinion their patron saint and who sustain and support one another in this belief? Of what good is it for an individual to declare himself against Strauss when the many have decided in his favour and the masses they lead have learned to thirst for repeated draughts of the Master's philistine sleeping-potion?

If we have herewith assumed without further ado that the Straussian confessional book has scored a victory with public opinion and has been welcomed as a victor, its author may perhaps draw our attention to the fact that the diverse judgments on his book in the public prints are by no means unanimous and certainly not uniformly favourable, and that he himself has had to protest in a postscript against the sometimes extremely hostile tone and impudent and challenging manner of some of these newspaper warriors. How can there be one public opinion about my book, he will expostulate, when every journalist regards me as fair game, an outlaw to be mishandled at will! This contradiction is easily resolved as soon as we distinguish between two aspects of the Straussian book, the theological and the literary: it is only in the latter aspect that the book impinges on German culture. Through its theological colouring it stands outside our German culture and awakens the antipathy of the various theological parties, indeed of every individual German insofar as he is a theological sectarian by nature and invents his own strange private theology so as to be able to dissent from every other. But just hear all these theological sectarians as soon as Strauss is spoken of as a *writer*; at once the theological dissonances die away and we hear in the purest unison as though from the mouth of *one* community: nonetheless he is a *classic writer*! Now everyone, even the most sullenly orthodox, flatters Strauss to his face as a writer, though it may be no more than a word in commendation of his almost Lessing-like dialectics or the freedom, beauty and validity of his aesthetic views. As a book, it seems, the Straussian production corresponds exactly to the ideal of a book. His theological opponents, though they spoke loudest, are in this case only a small fragment of the great public: and even in relation to them Strauss is right when he says: 'Compared with my thousands of readers, my couple of dozen detractors are a vanishing minority, and it will be hard for them to prove that they are faithful interpreters of the former. If, in such a matter as this is, those who disagree have spoken up, while those who agree have contented themselves with silent approval, that lies in the nature of the case.' Apart from the scandal which Strauss may here and there have provoked among the theological confessions, as to Strauss the *writer* there thus reigns unanimity even among his fanatical opponents to whom his voice is like the voice of the beast from the abyss. And the treatment Strauss has received at the hands of the literary day-labourers of the theological parties therefore proves nothing against our proposition that in this book philistine culture has celebrated a triumph.

It must be admitted that the educated philistine is on average a degree less candid than Strauss, or at least is more reserved when he speaks publicly: but candour in another is therefore all the more edifying for him; at home and among his own kind he loudly applauds it, and it is only in writing that he declines to confess how much all that Strauss says is after his own heart. For, as we already know, our culture philistine is somewhat cowardly, even when he is strongly moved: and it is precisely the fact that Strauss is a degree less cowardly that makes him a leader, while on the other hand there are very definite limits to *his* courage. If he were to overstep *these* limits, as Schopenhauer for instance does with almost every sentence, he would no longer lead on the philistines as their chieftain but would be deserted as precipitately as he is now followed. If anyone thought to call this moderation and *mediocritas* in courage, which if not wise is at any rate prudent, an Aristotelean virtue he would be in error: for this species of courage is the mean, not between two faults, but between a fault and a virtue – and it is within this mean between virtue and fault that *all* the qualities of the philistine lie.

9

'But nonetheless he is a classic writer!' We shall now see.

It might perhaps be in order to go on to speak of Strauss the stylist and artist in language, but let us first of all consider whether as a writer he is capable of constructing his house, whether he really understands the architecture of a book. This will determine whether he is a genuine, thoughtful and practised maker of books; and if we have to answer in the negative, his fame can always take refuge in his claim to be a 'classic writer of prose'. The latter capacity without the former would, to be sure, not suffice to raise him to the rank of a classic author, but at best to that of the classic improvisers or virtuosi of style who, with all their skill in expression, reveal in the actual erection of the building the clumsy hand and ignorant eye of the bungler. We shall therefore ask whether Strauss possesses the artistic power to construct a whole, *totum ponere.**

As a rule the first written draft suffices to show whether the author has envisaged his work as a whole and found the general tempo and correct proportions appropriate to what he has envisaged. If this most vital of tasks has been achieved and the building itself erected with proper scale and balance, there nonetheless remains a great deal still to do: how many minor errors must be corrected, how many holes stopped, here and there a provisional partition or a false floor must be replaced, dust and rubble lie everywhere, and wherever you look you can see signs of the labour that has been going on; the house as a whole is still uninhabitable and uncomfortable: all the walls are bare and the wind whistles through the open windows. Whether Strauss has done the great and wearisome work now needed will not concern us very long when we ask if he has produced the building itself in fair proportions and visualized it as a whole. The opposite of this, to put a book together out of bits and pieces, is well known to be the way of scholars. They trust that these bits and pieces will cohere of themselves and thereby confuse logical

---

*totum ponere: to construct a whole (repeating previous phrase)

cohesion with artistic. In any event, the relation between the four main questions which designate the divisions of Strauss's book is not logical: 'Are we still Christians? Do we still possess religion? How do we conceive the world? How do we order our life?', and their relation is not logical because the third question has nothing to do with the second, the fourth nothing to do with the third, and all three have nothing to do with the first. The natural scientist, for example, who poses the third question, demonstrates the immaculateness of his sense for truth precisely in that he passes by the second in silence; and that the themes of the fourth section – marriage, society, capital punishment – would only be confused and darkened by the introduction of Darwinist theories from the third section seems to be grasped by Strauss himself, for he in fact pays no further regard to these theories. But the question 'are we still Christians?' at once prejudices freedom of philosophical reflection and gives it an unpleasant theological colouring; in addition to which he has quite forgotten that even today the greater part of mankind is still Buddhist and not Christian. Why should we without more ado think at the words 'old faith' of Christianity alone! If Strauss herewith reveals that he has never ceased to be a Christian theologian and has thus never learned to become a philosopher, he further surprises us by his inability to distinguish between faith and knowledge and by continually naming his so-called 'new faith' and the contemporary sciences in the same breath. Or should we regard the new faith as only an ironical accommodation to linguistic usage? It almost seems so when we see that here and there he innocently lets new faith and contemporary science deputize for one another, for example on page 11, where he asks on which side, that of the old faith or that of contemporary science, 'there are to be found more of the obscurities and inadequacies unavoidable in human affairs'. According to his introduction, moreover, he intends to present the evidence upon which the modern philosophy of life depends: all this evidence he borrows from science and here too he adopts wholly the posture of a man of knowledge, not that of a believer.

At bottom, then, the new religion is not a new faith but precisely on a par with modern science and thus not religion at all. If Strauss nevertheless asserts that he does have a religion, the reasons for it lie outside the domain of contemporary science. Only a minute portion of Strauss's book, amounting to no more than a few scattered pages, treats of that which Strauss could have a right to call a faith: namely that feeling for the cosmos for which he demands the same piety as

41

the believer of the old stamp feels towards his God. In these pages at least the scientific spirit is certainly not in evidence: but we could wish for a little more strength and naturalness of faith! For what is so extremely striking is the artificiality of the procedures our author has to adopt in order to convince himself he still possesses a faith and a religion at all: as we have seen, he has to resort to jabbing and cudgelling. It creeps weakly along, this stimulated faith: we freeze at the sight of it.

Strauss promises in his introduction to test whether this new faith is capable of doing for the new believer what the old faith does for the believer of the old stamp, but in the end he himself comes to think he has promised too much. For when he deals with the subject he does so in a quite offhand, indeed almost embarrassed manner, in a couple of pages (pp. 366f.), even resorting to the desperate ploy: 'whoever cannot help himself here is beyond help and is not yet ripe for our point of view' (p. 366). Consider with what weight of conviction the Stoic of antiquity believed in the cosmos and in the rationality of the cosmos, and contrast with it even the claim to originality which Strauss makes for his faith! But, as we have said, whether it is new or old, original or imitated, would be a matter of indifference if only it exhibited naturalness, health and strength. Strauss himself leaves this distilled emergency faith in the lurch whenever the claims of knowledge constrain him to do so and in order to present his newly acquired scientific perceptions to his 'we' with a quieter conscience. The timidity with which he speaks of his faith is matched by his loud orotundity whenever he cites the greatest benefactor of most recent mankind, Darwin: here he demands faith, not merely in the new Messiah, but in himself, the new apostle, too; for example when, dealing with the most intricate theme of natural science, he pronounces with a truly antique pride: 'I shall be told I am speaking of things I do not understand. Good; but others will come who understand them and who have also understood me.' From this it seems almost as though the celebrated 'we' are to be obligated to a faith, not only in the cosmos, but in Strauss the natural scientist too; in that case all we would ask is that the latter faith should not require for its realization such cruel and painful procedures as the former did. Or can it be that in this instance the 'religious reaction' which is the mark of the 'new faith' will be produced in the believer by the jabbing and cudgelling, not of the believer himself, but of the object of the belief? If so, how we should profit from the religiosity of these 'we'!

For otherwise it is almost to be feared that modern men will be able to get along without bothering overmuch with the ingredients of Strauss's religious faith, just as they have in fact hitherto got along without the principle of the rationality of the cosmos. Modern natural science and study of history have nothing whatever to do with the Straussian faith in the cosmos, and that the modern philistine does not need it either is shown by the description of his life which Strauss himself gives in the section 'How do we order our life?' He is therefore right to doubt whether the 'carriage' to which his 'valued readers have had to entrust themselves meets every requirement'. It certainly does not meet them: for modern man travels a lot faster if he is not sitting in this Straussian carriage – or more correctly: he was travelling a lot faster long before this Straussian carriage existed. So if it be true that the celebrated 'minority that cannot be ignored' of which and in whose name Strauss speaks really 'sets great store by consistency', then they must be just as dissatisfied with Strauss the carriage-builder as we are with Strauss the logician.

But let us forget about the logician: perhaps the book really is well formed artistically, and conforms to the laws of beauty even if it does not possess a well-thought-out logical plan. And it is only now, after determining that he has not borne himself as a scientific, orderly minded and systematizing scholar, that we arrive at the question whether Strauss is a good writer.

Perhaps he conceived it as his task, not so much to frighten people away from the 'old faith', as to lure them to the new philosophy of life by depicting it in cheerful and lively colours. If he thought of scholars and the educated as his first readers, he must have realized from his own experience that, while they can be laid low with the heavy artillery of scientific proof, they can never by this means be brought to surrender, though they fall prey all the more readily to lightly clad arts of seductions. 'Lightly clad', and that 'intentionally', is however what Strauss himself calls his book; his public panegyrists also find it and describe it as 'lightly clad', as for example this one does in the following terms: 'The discourse moves forward in a pleasing rhythm and handles the art of demonstration with playful ease when it is engaged critically against what is old, as it does no less when it seductively prepares and presents to both undemanding and experienced palates the new things it brings. The arrangement of such manifold and dissimilar material, where everything is to be touched on but nothing pursued at length, is well thought out; the transitions from one subject to another are especially skilful, and even more admirable, perhaps, is the dexterity with which uncomfortable things are pushed aside or buried in silence.' The senses of such panegyrists are, as is apparent here too, alert not so much to what an author *can* do as to what he *wants* to do. What Strauss wants to do, however, is betrayed most clearly in his emphatic and not wholly innocent recommendation of a Voltairean gracefulness in the service of which he could have learned those 'lightly clad' arts of which his panegyrist speaks – supposing, that is, that virtue can be taught and a pedant can ever become a dancer.

Who cannot harbour reservations when for example he reads these words of Strauss's on Voltaire (p. 219): 'as a philosopher Voltaire is not original, it is true, but in the main an elaborator of English researches: yet he proves to be altogether a master of his material, which with incomparable dexterity he illuminates from all sides and thereby, without being strictly methodical, satisfies the demands of thoroughness'. All the negative traits are in keeping: no one will maintain that as a philosopher Strauss is original or strictly methodical; the question is whether we will also acknowledge that he is a 'master of his material' or concede to him 'incomparable dexterity'. The confession that the work is 'intentionally lightly clad' allows us to guess that incomparable dexterity was at any rate intended.

Not to build a temple or a dwelling, but to set down a summer-house surrounded with horticulture – that was our architect's dream. It almost seems, indeed, that even that mysterious feeling for the cosmos was intended mainly as a means of aesthetic effect, like a view of an irrational element, the sea for instance, from within an elegant and rational terrace. The walk through the first section – that is to say, through the theological catacombs with their obscurity and their convoluted and baroque ornamentation – was again only an aesthetic means of emphasizing by contrast the purity, brightness and rationality of the section entitled 'What is our conception of the world?': for immediately after that walk in the gloom and glimpse of distant irrational windings, we enter a hall with a fanlight; it receives us with cheerful sobriety, there are celestial charts and mathematical figures on the walls and it is filled with scientific apparatus and cupboards lined with skeletons, stuffed monkeys and anatomical specimens. But we do not wholly recover our good humour until we pass through this hall and enter the full domestic ease and comfort of the occupants of our summer-house; we discover them with their women and children engaged with their newspapers and common-place chatter about politics, we listen for a time as they discuss marriage and universal suffrage, capital punishment and workers' strikes, and it seems to us impossible that the rosary of public opinion could be told more quickly. Finally we are also to be convinced of the classical taste of those who dwell here: a brief visit to the library and the music-room discloses, as expected, that the best books lie on the shelves and the most celebrated pieces of music on the music-stands; they even play us something, and if it was supposed to be Haydn's music at least Haydn was not to blame if it sounded like Riehl's music for the home. In the meantime, the master of the house has had occasion to state that he is in entire agreement with Lessing, also with Goethe, though excluding the second part of *Faust*. Finally the summer-house owner commends himself, and expresses the view that those he disagrees with are beyond help and not yet ripe for his point of view; whereupon he offers us his carriage, with the polite reservation that he cannot guarantee it will answer to all our requirements; the stones on his carriageways are, moreover, newly scattered and we might be much buffeted about. Our Epicurean garden god then takes his leave of us with the incomparable dexterity he had recognized and commended in Voltaire.

Who could now doubt this incomparable dexterity? We recognize the master of his material, the lightly clad horticulturalist is unmasked; and still we hear the voice of the classic author: 'As a writer I refuse to be a philistine, I refuse! I refuse! I want to be Voltaire, the German Voltaire! and best of all the French Lessing too!'

We have betrayed a secret: our Master does not always know who he would prefer to be, Voltaire or Lessing, but wants at no price to be a philistine; if possible, he would like to be both, Lessing *and* Voltaire – that it might be fulfilled which was written: 'he had no character whatever: whenever he wanted a character he always had to assume one'.

10

If we have understood Strauss the confessor correctly, he himself is a true philistine with a narrow, dried-up soul and with sober and scholarly requirements: and yet no one would be angrier at being called a philistine than David Strauss the writer. He would approve if one called him headstrong, rash, malicious, foolhardy; but he would be most pleased of all to be compared with Lessing or Voltaire, since they were certainly not philistines. In his search to procure this pleasure he is often undecided whether he ought to imitate the bold dialectical impetuosity of Lessing or whether it might not be better to comport himself as a satyr-like free-spirited elder in the manner of Voltaire. Whenever he sits down to write he always composes his features as though he were about to have his portrait painted: sometimes he makes his face resemble Lessing's, sometimes Voltaire's. When we read his praise of the Voltairean style (p. 217), he seems to be expressly admonishing the present for not having long since recognized what it possesses in the modern Voltaire: 'the merits of his style', Strauss says, 'are everywhere the same: simple naturalness, transparent clarity, lively flexibility, pleasing charm. Warmth and emphasis are not wanting where they are needed; hatred of pomposity and affectation came from Voltaire's innermost nature; just as when, on the other hand, passion and impetuosity lowered the tone of his discourse, the fault lay not with the stylist but with the human being in him.' To judge from this, Strauss is well aware of the significance of *simplicity of style*: it has always been the mark of genius, which also possesses the privilege of expressing itself simply, naturally and with naivety. It therefore betrays no common ambition when an author chooses a simple style: for, although many will see what such an author would like to be taken for, there are nonetheless many who are so obliging as to take him for it. But if an author possesses genius he betrays it in more than simplicity and precision of expression: his abundant power plays with his material even when it is difficult and dangerous. Stiff and timid steps will get no one along unfamiliar paths littered with a thousand abysses: the genius, however, runs nimbly along such paths with daring or elegant strides and disdains cautiously to measure his steps.

That the problems Strauss passes in review are serious and dreadful ones, and have been treated as such by the wise of every age, is known to Strauss himself, and yet he calls his book *lightly clad*. Of all the dread and gloomy seriousness of reflection into which one is plunged perforce when faced with the questions of the value of existence and the duties of man there is not the slightest suspicion as our gifted Master goes fluttering past us, 'lightly clad and intentionally so' – more lightly clad, indeed, than is his Rousseau, who, he informs us, denuded his lower half and draped his upper, while Goethe, he says, draped his lower half and denuded his upper. Wholly naive geniuses, it seems, do not drape themselves at all, so perhaps the expression 'lightly clad' is only a euphemism for naked.

Of the goddess truth, the few who have seen her affirm that she has been naked: and perhaps in the eyes of those who have not seen her but accept the word of those few who have, nakedness or lightly-cladness is in itself a proof of truth, even if only circumstantial proof. Merely to suspect that this is the case works to the advantage of an author's ambition: someone sees something naked – 'suppose it should be the truth!' he says to himself, and assumes a more solemn expression than the one he usually wears. But an author has already attained much if he has constrained his reader to regard him more solemnly than he does some other, more heavily clad author. It is the way to one day becoming a 'classic': and Strauss himself tells us that he has 'been accorded the unsought honour of being regarded as a kind of classic prose-writer', that he has thus arrived at the goal of his journey. Strauss the genius runs about the streets as a 'classic' disguised as a lightly clad goddess, and Strauss the philistine is, to employ an original locution of this genius, at all costs to be 'decreed out of fashion' or 'thrown out never to return'.

Alas, the philistine does return, again and again, despite all such decrees and throwings-out! Alas, the face, twisted into a semblance of Voltaire or Lessing, from time to time snaps back into its old, honest, original shape! Alas, the mask of genius all too often falls off, and the Master never wears a more vexed expression, his gestures are never stiffer, than when he has just attempted to imitate the stride of genius and to make his eyes flash with the fire of genius. Ours is a cold clime, and it is precisely because he goes around so lightly clad that he runs the risk of catching cold more often and more gravely than others; that the others then notice all this may be acutely painful, but if he is ever to be cured he will have to submit to the following public diagnosis: There was once a Strauss, a brave, rigorous and austerely clad scholar, whom we found as congenial as anyone who in Germany serves truth seriously and with vigour and knows how to stay within his own limitations; he who is now celebrated by public opinion as David Strauss has become someone else: it may be the fault of the theologians that he has become this someone else; enough, we find the game he now plays with the mask of genius as repellent or ludicrous as we found his former seriousness evocative of seriousness and sympathy. When he now informs us: 'it would also be an act of ingratitude towards *my genius* if I did not rejoice that, beside the gift of unsparing destructive criticism, I have also been granted the innocent pleasure of artistic creativity', it may surprise him to know that despite this self-testimonial there are people who maintain the

47

opposite: firstly, that he has never possessed the gift of artistic creativity, and then that the pleasure he calls 'innocent' is anything but innocent, inasmuch as it gradually undermined a fundamentally vigorous and deep-seated scholarly and critical nature – *that is to say, the genius Strauss actually did possess* – and in the end destroyed it. In an access of unrestrained candour, Strauss himself concedes that he has always 'had his own Merck within him, who cried to him: you must no longer produce such trash, others can do that!' This was the voice of the genuine Straussian genius: and it even tells him how much or how little his latest, innocently lightly clad testament of the modern philistine is worth. Others can do that too! And many could do it better! And those who could do it best, more gifted and richer spirits than Strauss, would, when they had done it, never have produced anything other than – trash.

I believe I have made it clear how I regard Strauss the writer: as an actor who plays at being a genius and classic. Lichtenberg once said: 'The simple style is to be recommended first of all because no honest man subjects what he has to say to artificial elaboration', but that certainly does not mean that the simple manner is a proof of authorial integrity. I could wish that Strauss the writer were more honest, for then he would write better and be less celebrated. Or – if he absolutely must be an actor – I could wish he were a good actor and knew better how to imitate the style of naive genius and the classic. For it remains to be said that Strauss is in fact a bad actor and utterly worthless as a stylist.

11

The reproach that one is not a good writer is softened, to be sure, by the fact that in Germany it is very difficult to become even a mediocre and tolerable writer, and quite astonishingly improbable that one will become a good one. A natural basis is lacking, an artistic evaluation, treatment and cultivation of oral speech. As the expressions 'salon conversation', 'sermon', 'parliamentary oratory', indicate, public speech has in Germany not yet attained to a national style or even to the desire for a style; language has not yet emerged from the stage of naive experimentation; so that there is no unified norm by which the writer may be guided and he thus has a certain right to handle language on his own responsibility: and this must result in that limitless dilapidation of the German language which constitutes the 'language of the present' and which has been described most forcefully by Schopenhauer. 'If this goes on', he once said, 'in the year 1900 the German classics will no longer be comprehensible, since the only language understood will be the shabby jargon of our noble "present" – the basic character of which is impotence.' Already, indeed, German linguistic arbiters and grammarians writing in the most recent journals give the impression that our classics can no longer be valid to us as stylistic models because they employ a large number of words, locutions and syntactical figures which we have lost: for which reason it might seem appropriate to collect together the masterpieces of our present literary celebrities for the purpose of imitating their vocabulary and phraseology, as has in fact been done by Sander in his concise pocket dictionary of infamous language. Here the repellent stylistic monster Gutzkow appears as a classic: and it seems that we have in general to accustom ourselves to a whole new and surprising host of 'classics', among whom the first, or one of the first, is David Strauss – whom we cannot describe in any way other than we have already described him: as a worthless stylist.

Now, it is extremely characteristic of the pseudo-culture of the cultural philistine that he should even appropriate the concept of the classic and the model writer – he who exhibits his strength only in warding off a real, artistically vigorous cultural style and through steadfastness in warding off arrives at a homogeneity of expression which almost resembles a unity of style. How is it possible that, given the limitless experimentation with language everyone is permitted to indulge in, certain individual authors nonetheless discover a universally agreeable tone of voice? What is it really that is here so universally agreeable? Above all a negative quality: the absence of anything offensive – *but anything truly productive is offensive.* – For the greater part of what the German of today reads undoubtedly comprises the newspapers and the magazines that go with them: the language here employed, a ceaseless drip of the same locutions and the same words, imprints itself on his ear, and since he usually reads this literature at times when his wearied mind is in any case little capable of resistance, his ear for language gradually comes to feel at home in this everyday German and is pained when it notices its absence. The manufacturers of these newspapers, however, are, as would be expected from their whole way of life, the most accustomed to the slime of this newspaper language: they have in the strictest sense of the word lost all taste, and the most their tongue can still savour with any kind of pleasure is the totally corrupt and capricious. This explains the *tutti unisono* which, notwithstanding the general debility and sickness, greets every newly invented solecism: such impudent corruptions are an act of revenge on the language for the unbelievable boredom it inflicts upon its day-labourers. I recall having read an appeal 'to the German people' by Berthold Auerbach in which every locution was an un-German distortion and falsification of the language, and which as a whole resembled a soulless mosaic of words stuck together with an international syntax; not to speak of the shamelessly slovenly German with which Eduard Devrient celebrated the memory of Mendelssohn. Thus the solecism – this is the remarkable thing – is felt by our philistines, not as objectionable, but as a stimulating refreshment in the arid and treeless desert of everyday German. But the *truly* productive he does find objectionable. The most modern model author is not merely forgiven his distorted, extravagant or threadbare syntax and his ludicrous neologisms, they are reckoned a merit in him which gives his work piquancy: but woe to the stylist with character who avoids these everyday locutions as seriously and persistently as he does 'the monsters of present-day scribbling hatched out last night', as Schopenhauer puts it. When platitudes, commonplaces and hackneyed and feeble language are the rule, and badness and corruption received as stimulating exceptions, then the forceful, uncommon and beautiful falls into disfavour: so that in Germany there is constantly being repeated the story of the traveller who came to the land of the hunchbacks and was shamefully insulted by its inhabitants because of his supposedly defective physique, until at last a priest had mercy on him and said to the people: 'Rather pity this poor stranger and sacrifice to the gods in gratitude for having adorned you with this stately hump.'

If anyone should compose a grammar of current everyday German and trace the rules which, as an unwritten and unspoken yet compelling imperative, govern everyone's writing-desk, he would encounter some strange notions of style and rhetoric, taken perhaps from recollections of school and enforced Latin exercises, perhaps from reading French writers at whose astonishing crudeness any properly educated Frenchman would have a right to scoff. It seems that, though reputed thorough, the Germans have never yet reflected on these strange notions, under the rule of which more or less every German lives and writes.

Then we have the demand that from time to time a simile or a metaphor should appear, and that the metaphor must be a new one: but to the poor writer's brain new and modern are the same thing, and it now torments itself to draw metaphors from the railway, the telegraph, the steam-engine, the stock exchange, and feels proud of the fact that these similes must be new because they are modern. In Strauss's confessional book we find ample tribute paid to the modern metaphor: he dismisses us with a page-and-a-half long simile drawn from road improvement works, a few pages earlier he compares the world to a machine with its wheels, pistons, hammers and 'soothing oil'. – A meal which starts with champagne (p. 362). Kant as a hydropathic establishment (p. 325). 'The Swiss constitution compares with the English as a watermill compares with a steam-engine, a waltz or a song with a fugue or a symphony' (p. 265). 'In the case of every appeal, the correct succession of tribunals must be adhered to. The intermediate tribunal between the individual and mankind, however, is the nation' (p. 258). 'If we wish to discover whether life in fact exists in an organism that seems to us dead, we usually test it by administering a strong, often painful stimulus, a jab for instance' (p. 141). 'The religious domain in the human soul is like the domain of the Redskin in America' (p. 138). 'To set down the sum total of all the preceding in round numbers at the bottom of the bill' (p. 90). 'The Darwinian theory is like a railway track that has just been marked out . . . where the banners flutter gaily in the wind' (p. 176). It is in this way, namely the most modern way, that Strauss has complied with the philistine demand that from time to time a new metaphor must make an appearance.

Also very widespread is a further demand that didactic statements must be composed in long sentences employing abstractions, while those intended to persuade should preferably be in short little sentences with contrasting forms of expression hopping one after the other. Strauss provides on page 132 a model sentence of the didactic and scholarly kind: inflated to truly Schleiermacherish proportions, it creeps along at the pace of a tortoise: 'That at the earlier stages of religion, instead of a single such Whence there appear many, instead of one God there appears a multiplicity of gods, is, according to this derivation of religion, due to the fact that the various natural forces or conditions of life which arouse in man the feeling of absolute dependence still act upon him in the beginning in all their multifariousness, he has not yet become aware how in regard to his absolute dependence upon them there is no distinction between them, consequently the Whence of this dependence or the Being to which in the last instance they are to be traced back can be only one.' An example of the opposite kind of thing, of the short little sentences and affected vivacity which have so excited some readers they can now mention Strauss only in concert with Lessing, can be found on page 8: 'I am well aware that what I propose to discuss in the following pages is known just as well by countless other people and by some it is known better. Some of them have already spoken out. Should I therefore keep silent? I do not believe so. For we all supplement one another. If another knows many things better than I, perhaps I know a few things better than he; and I have a viewpoint on many things different from the viewpoint of others. So out with it, let me display my colours, that it may be seen whether or not they are genuine.' To be sure, Strauss's style usually maintains a mean between this free-and-easy quick-march and the funereal crawl of the first example: but between two vices there does not always dwell virtue; all too often what dwells there is weakness, lameness and impotence. I was very disappointed, in fact, when I looked through Strauss's book in search of more subtle and wittier traits and expressions; since I had found nothing praiseworthy in the confessor I actually established a heading under which to list such passages, so that I might at least be able to say something in praise of Strauss the writer. I searched and searched but could list nothing. On the other hand, a second list with the heading 'Solecisms, confused similes, obscure abbreviations, tastelessness and affectation' became so full I can venture to reproduce here only a modest selection of the examples I assembled. Perhaps it will reveal precisely what it is that evokes in the contemporary German his belief that Strauss is a great stylist: for here we find curiosities of expression which in the arid dust and desert of the book as a whole offer if not pleasant at any rate painfully stimulating surprises: on encountering such passages we notice, to employ a Straussian metaphor, that at least we are not yet dead by the way we react to these jabs. For the rest of the book displays a total lack of anything whatever offensive, that is to say productive, such as would now be reckoned a positive quality in the classic prose-writer. Extreme sobriety and aridity, a truly starving sobriety, nowadays awakens in the educated masses the unnatural feeling that precisely these are the signs of flourishing health, so that here there apply the words of the author of the *Dialogus de Oratibus*: '*illam ipsam quam iactant sanitatem non firmitate sed ieiunio consequuntur*'.* With instinctive unanimity, they hate all *firmitas* because it bears witness to a healthiness quite different from theirs, and seek to throw suspicion on

---

*illam ipsam quam iactant sanitatem non firmitate sed ieiunio consequuntur: even their health, which they parade, they obtain not through strength but through fasting (Tacitus)

firmitas, on conciseness, on fiery energy of movement, on abundant and delicate play of the muscles. They have agreed together to invert the nature and names of things and henceforth to speak of health where we see weakness, of sickness and tension where we encounter true health. That is how David Strauss comes to be accounted a 'classic'.

If only this sobriety were at least a strictly logical sobriety: but simplicity and rigour in thinking is precisely what these weaklings lack, and in their hands language itself becomes a logical tangle. Just try translating this Straussian style into Latin – which can be done even with Kant, and with Schopenhauer is pleasurable and easy. The reason Strauss's German is altogether unamenable to it is probably not that his German is more German than Kant's or Schopenhauer's, but that his German is confused and illogical while theirs is informed with grandeur and simplicity. He who knows the effort the ancients expended on learning to speak and write, and how the moderns make no such effort, feels, as Schopenhauer once said, a real sense of relief when, having been compelled to wade through a German book like this one, he turns to those other ancient yet ever new languages: 'for with these', he says, 'I have before me a language with fixed rules and a firmly established and faithfully observed grammar and orthography and can devote myself wholly to the thought expressed in it; while with German I am continually distracted by the impudence of the writer seeking to obtrude his own grammatical and orthographical whims and eccentricities: a piece of swaggering folly I find repellent. It is truly an agony to see a fair and ancient language possessing a classical literature mishandled by ignoramuses and asses.'

Thus Schopenhauer's holy wrath cries out to you, so you cannot say you were not warned. But he who absolutely refuses to heed this warning, and insists on continuing in his belief that Strauss is a classic, should, as a final word of advice, be recommended to imitate him. If you do try this, though, it will be at your peril: you will have to pay for it, in your style and, eventually, in your head, that the dictum of Indian wisdom may be fulfilled in you too: 'To gnaw at the horn of a cow is useless and shortens life: you grind down your teeth and yet you get no nourishment.'

12

In conclusion we shall now place before our classic prose-writer the promised collection of examples of his style; perhaps Schopenhauer would give it the title: 'New documents of the shabby jargon of today'; for, if it is any comfort to him, David Strauss may be comforted to be told that nowadays all the world writes as he does, and some people write even worse than he, and that in the country of the blind the one-eyed man is king. Indeed, we concede to him a great deal when we concede to him one eye; we do so, however, because at least Strauss does not write like the most infamous of all corrupters of German, the Hegelians and their deformed offspring. At least he wants to get back out of this swamp and he has partly succeeded, though he is as yet very far from being on firm land; it is still noticeable that in his youth he stuttered Hegelian: something in him became dislocated at that time, some muscle got stretched; his ear became dulled, like the ear of a boy brought up amid the beating of drums, so that thereafter he became deaf to the subtle and mighty laws of sound under whose rule every writer lives who has been strictly trained to follow good models. He therewith lost as a stylist his best possessions and, if he is not to slip back into the Hegelian mud, is condemned to live out his life on the barren and perilous quicksands of newspaper style. Nonetheless he has succeeded in becoming famous for a couple of hours in our time, and perhaps there will be a couple of hours more when it will be remembered that he was once famous; but then night will come and he will be forgotten: and already at this moment, as we inscribe his stylistic sins in the black book, twilight begins to fall on his fame. For he who has sinned against the German language has profaned the mystery of all that is German: through all the confusion and changes of nations and customs, it alone has, as by a metaphysical magic, preserved itself and therewith the German spirit. It alone also guarantees the future of this spirit, provided it does not itself perish at the hands of the present. 'But *Di meliora!** Away, pachyderms, away! This is the German language, in which men have spoken, in which great poets have sung and great thinkers written. Keep your paws off!' –

[*Nietzsche now gives some 70 examples of the kind of language in which* Der alte und neue Glaube *is written and subjects them to a scathing commentary. The faults exposed include grammatical errors of various kinds, offences against good usage, jumbled metaphors, impossible imagery and meaninglessness; and the critique substantiates the charge that Strauss has lost all feeling for German and any clear awareness of the meaning of the words he uses. To attempt to translate Strauss's faulty sentences into English equivalents would be an enjoy-*

---

*Di meliora!: O ye good gods!

able but otherwise senseless exercise in ingenuity; and for the reader who cannot read these sentences in the original German Nietzsche's comments must lose most of their relevence and force. The sensible course would therefore seem to be to omit this passage.]

Herewith I have completed my confession of faith. It is the confession of an individual; and what can such an individual do against all the world, even if his voice is audible everywhere! His judgment would – to leave you with one last genuine feather from the Straussian plumage – be only '*of as much subjective truth as without any objective power of proof*':– is that not so, my dear friends? So continue to be of good cheer! For the time being at least let it rest with your '*of as much . . . as without*'. For the time being? That is to say, for as long as that for which it is always time, and which the present time has more need of than ever, continues to count as untimely – I mean: telling the truth.

2
On the uses and disadvantages of history for life

Foreword

'In any case, I hate everything that merely instructs me without augmenting or directly invigorating my activity.' These words are from Goethe, and they may stand as a sincere *ceterum censeo** at the beginning of our meditation on the value of history. For its intention is to show why instruction without invigoration, why knowledge not attended by action, why history as a costly superfluity and luxury, must, to use Goethe's word, be seriously hated by us – hated because we still lack even the things we need and the superfluous is the enemy of the necessary. We need history, certainly, but we need it for reasons different from those for which the idler in the garden of knowledge needs it, even though he may look nobly down on our rough and charmless needs and requirements. We need it, that is to say, for the sake of life and action, not so as to turn comfortably away from life and action, let alone for the purpose of extenuating the self-seeking life and the base and cowardly action. We want to serve history only to the extent that history serves life: for it is possible to value the study of history to such a degree that life becomes stunted and degenerate – a phenomenon we are now forced to acknowledge, painful though this may be, in the face of certain striking symptoms of our age.

I have striven to depict a feeling by which I am constantly tormented; I revenge myself upon it by handing it over to the public. Perhaps this depiction will inspire someone or other to tell me that he too knows this feeling but that I have not felt it in its pure and elemental state and have certainly not expressed it with the assurance that comes from mature experience. Someone, I say, may perhaps do so: most people, however, will tell me that this feeling is altogether perverse, unnatural, detestable and wholly impermissible, and that by feeling it I have shown myself unworthy of the mighty historical movement which, as is well known, has been in evidence among the Germans particularly for the past two generations. Whatever the case, however, that I should venture a description of my feeling will promote rather than injure general decorum,

*_ceterum censeo_: but I'm of the opinion

since it will offer to many the opportunity of paying compliments to the said movement. And for myself I shall gain something that is worth more to me even than decorum – that is, to be publicly instructed and put right about the character of our own time.

This meditation too is untimely, because I am here attempting to look afresh at something of which our time is rightly proud – its cultivation of history – as being injurious to it, a defect and deficiency in it; because I believe, indeed, that we are all suffering from a consuming fever of history and ought at least to recognize that we are suffering from it. But if Goethe was right to assert that when we cultivate our virtues we at the same time cultivate our faults, and if, as everyone knows, a hypertrophied virtue – such as the historical sense of our age appears to be – can ruin a nation just as effectively as a hypertrophied vice: then there can be no harm in indulging me for this once. And it may partly exonerate me when I give an assurance that the experiences which evoked those tormenting feelings were mostly my own and that I have drawn on the experiences of others only for purposes of comparison; and further, that it is only to the extent that I am a pupil of earlier times, especially the Hellenic, that though a child of the present time I was able to acquire such untimely experiences. That much, however, I must concede to myself on account of my profession as a classicist: for I do not know what meaning classical studies could have for our time if they were not untimely – that is to say, acting counter to our time and thereby acting on our time and, let us hope, for the benefit of a time to come.

1

Consider the cattle, grazing as they pass you by: they do not know what is meant by yesterday or today, they leap about, eat, rest, digest, leap about again, and so from morn till night and from day to day, fettered to the moment and its pleasure or displeasure, and thus neither melancholy nor bored. This is a hard sight for man to see; for, though he thinks himself better than the animals because he is human, he cannot help envying them their happiness – what they have, a life neither bored nor painful, is precisely what he wants, yet he cannot have it because he refuses to be like an animal. A human being may well ask an animal: 'Why do you not speak to me of your happiness but only stand and gaze at me?' The animal would like to answer, and say: 'The reason is I always forget what I was going to say' – but then he forgot this answer too, and stayed silent: so that the human being was left wondering.

But he also wonders at himself, that he cannot learn to forget but clings relentlessly to the past: however far and fast he may run, this chain runs with him. And it is a matter for wonder: a moment, now here and then gone, nothing before it came, again nothing after it has gone, nonetheless returns as a ghost and disturbs the peace of a later moment. A leaf flutters from the scroll of time, floats away – and suddenly floats back again and falls into the man's lap. Then the man says 'I remember' and envies the animal, who at once forgets and for whom every moment really dies, sinks back into night and fog and is extinguished for ever. Thus the animal lives *unhistorically*: for it is contained in the present, like a number without any awkward fraction left over; it does not know how to dissimulate, it conceals nothing and at every instant appears wholly as what it is; it can therefore never be anything but honest. Man, on the other hand, braces himself against the great and ever greater pressure of what is past: it pushes him down or bends him sideways, it encumbers his steps as a dark, invisible burden which he would like to disown and which in traffic with his fellow men he does disown, so as to excite their envy. That is why it affects him like a vision of a lost paradise to see the herds grazing or, in closer proximity to him, a child which, having as yet nothing of the past to shake off, plays in blissful blindness between the hedges of past and future. Yet its play must be disturbed; all too soon it will be called out of its state of forgetfulness. Then it will learn to understand the phrase 'it was': that password which gives conflict, suffering and satiety access to man so as to remind him what his existence fundamentally is – an imperfect tense that can never become a perfect one. If death at last brings the desired forgetting, by that act it at the same time extinguishes the present and all being and therewith sets the seal on the knowledge that being is only an uninterrupted has-been, a thing that lives by negating, consuming and contradicting itself.

If happiness, if reaching out for new happiness, is in any sense what fetters living creatures to life and makes them go on living, then perhaps no philosopher is more justified than the Cynic: for the happiness of the animal, as the perfect Cynic, is the living proof of the rightness of Cynicism. The smallest happiness, if only it is present uninterruptedly and makes happy, is incomparably more happiness than the greatest happiness that comes only as an episode, as it were a piece of waywardness or folly, in a continuum of joylessness, desire and privation. In the case of the smallest or of the greatest happiness, however, it is always the same thing that makes happiness happiness: the ability to forget or, expressed in more scholarly fashion, the capacity to feel *unhistorically* during its duration. He who cannot sink down on the threshold of the moment and forget all the past, who cannot stand balanced like a goddess of victory without growing dizzy and afraid, will never know what happiness is – worse, he will never do anything to make others happy. Imagine the extremest possible example of a man who did not possess the power of forgetting at all and who was thus condemned to see everywhere a state of becoming: such a man would no longer believe in his own being, would no longer believe in himself, would see everything flowing asunder in moving points and would lose himself in this stream of becoming: like a true pupil of Heraclitus, he would in the end hardly dare to raise his finger. Forgetting is essential to action of any kind, just as not only light but darkness too is essential for the life of everything organic. A man who wanted to feel historically through and through would be like one forcibly deprived of sleep, or an animal that had to live only by rumination and ever repeated rumination. Thus: it is possible to live almost without memory, and to live happily moreover, as the animal demonstrates; but it is altogether impossible to *live* at all without forgetting. Or, to express my theme even more simply: *there is a degree of sleeplessness, of rumination, of the historical sense, which is harmful and ultimately fatal to the living thing, whether this living thing be a man or a people or a culture.*

To determine this degree, and therewith the boundary at which the past has to be forgotten if it is not to become the gravedigger of the present, one would have to know exactly how great the *plastic power* of a man, a people, a culture is: I mean by plastic power the capacity to develop out of oneself in one's own way, to transform and incorporate into oneself what is past and foreign, to heal wounds, to replace what has been lost, to recreate broken moulds. There are people who possess so little of this power that they can perish from a single experience, from a single painful event, often and especially from a single subtle piece of injustice, like a man bleeding to death from a scratch; on the other hand, there are those who are so little affected by the worst and most dreadful disasters, and even by their own wicked acts, that they are able to feel tolerably well and be in possession of a kind of clear conscience even in the midst of them or at any rate very soon afterwards. The stronger the innermost roots of a man's nature, the more readily will he be able to assimilate and appropriate the things of the past; and the most powerful and tremendous nature would be characterized by the fact that it would know no boundary at all at which the historical sense began to overwhelm it; it would draw to itself and incorporate into itself all the past, its own and that most foreign to it, and as it were transform it into blood. That which such a nature cannot subdue it knows how to forget; it no longer exists, the horizon is rounded and closed, and there is nothing left to suggest there are people, passions, teachings, goals lying beyond it. And this is a universal law: a living thing can be healthy, strong and fruitful only when bounded by a horizon; if it is incapable of drawing a horizon around itself, and at the same time too self-centred to enclose its own view within that of another, it will pine away slowly or hasten to its timely end. Cheerfulness, the good conscience, the joyful deed, confidence in the future – all of them depend, in the case of the individual as of a nation, on the existence of a line dividing the bright and discernible from the unilluminable and dark; on one's being just as able to forget at the right time as to remember at the right time; on the possession of a powerful instinct for sensing when it is necessary to feel historically and when unhistorically. This, precisely, is the proposition the reader is invited to meditate upon: *the unhistorical and the historical are necessary in equal measure for the health of an individual, of a people and of a culture.*

First of all, there is an observation that everyone must have made: a man's historical sense and knowledge can be very limited, his horizon as narrow as that of a dweller in the Alps, all his judgments may involve injustice and he may falsely suppose that all his experiences are original to him – yet in spite of this injustice and error he will nonetheless stand there in superlative health and vigour, a joy to all who see him; while close beside him a man far more just and instructed than he sickens and collapses because the lines of his horizon are always restlessly changing, because he can no longer extricate himself from the delicate net of his judiciousness and truth for a simple act of will and desire. On the other hand we have observed the animal, which is quite unhistorical, and dwells within a horizon reduced almost to a point, and yet lives in a certain degree of happiness, or at least without boredom and dissimulation; we shall thus have to account the capacity to feel to a certain degree unhistorically as being more vital and more fundamental, inasmuch as it constitutes the foundation upon which alone anything sound, healthy and great, anything truly human, can grow. The unhistorical is like an atmosphere within which alone life can germinate and with the destruction of which it must vanish. It is true that only by imposing limits on this unhistorical element by thinking, reflecting, comparing, distinguishing, drawing conclusions, only through the appearance within that encompassing cloud of a vivid flash of light – thus only through the power of employing the past for the purposes of life and of again introducing into history that which has been done and is gone – did man become man: but with an excess of history man again ceases to exist, and without that envelope of the unhistorical he would never have begun or dared to begin. What deed would man be capable of if he had not first entered into that vaporous region of the unhistorical? Or, to desert this imagery and illustrate by example: imagine a man seized by a vehement passion, for a woman or for a great idea: how different the world has become to him! Looking behind him he seems to himself as though blind, listening around him he hears only a dull, meaningless noise; whatever he does perceive, however, he perceives as he has never perceived before – all is so palpable, close, highly coloured, resounding, as though he apprehended it with all his senses at once. All his valuations are altered and disvalued; there are so many things he is no longer capable of evaluating at all because he can hardly feel them any more: he asks himself why he was for so long the fool of the phrases and opinions of others; he is amazed that his memory revolves unwearyingly in a circle and yet is too weak and weary to take even a single leap out of this circle. It is the condition in which one is the least capable of being just; narrow-minded, ungrateful to the past, blind to dangers, deaf to warnings, one is a little vortex of life in a dead sea of darkness and oblivion: and yet this condition – unhistorical, anti-historical through and through – is the womb not only of the unjust but of every just deed too; and no painter will paint his picture, no general achieve his victory, no people attain its freedom without having first desired and striven for it in an unhistorical condition such as that described. As he who acts is, in Goethe's words, always without a conscience, so is he also always without knowledge; he forgets most things so as to do one thing, he is unjust towards what lies behind him, and he recognizes the rights only of that which is now to come into being and no other rights whatever. Thus he who acts loves his deed infinitely more than it deserves to be loved: and the finest deeds take place in such a superabundance of love that, even if their worth were incalculable in other respects, they must still be unworthy of this love.

If, in a sufficient number of cases, one could scent out and retrospectively breathe this unhistorical atmosphere within which every great historical event has taken place, he might, as a percipient being, raise himself to a *suprahistorical* vantage point such as Niebuhr once described as the possible outcome of historical reflection. 'History, grasped clearly and in detail', he says, 'is useful in one way at least: it enables us to recognize how unaware even the greatest and highest spirits of our human race have been of the chance nature of the form assumed by the eyes through which they see and through which they compel everyone to see – compel, that is, because the intensity of their consciousness is exceptionally great. He who has not grasped this quite definitely and in many instances will be subjugated by the appearance of a powerful spirit who brings to a given form the most impassioned commitment.' We may use the word 'suprahistorical' because the viewer from this vantage point could no longer feel any temptation to go on living or to take part in history; he would have recognized the essential condition of all happenings – this blindness and injustice in the soul of him who acts; he would, indeed, be cured for ever of taking history too seriously, for he would have learned from all men and all experiences, whether among Greeks or Turks, from a single hour of the first or of the nineteenth century, to answer his own question as to how or to what end life is lived. If you ask your acquaintances if they would like to relive the past ten or twenty years, you will easily discover which of them is prepared for this suprahistorical standpoint: they will all answer No, to be sure, but they will have different reasons for answering No. Some may perhaps be consoling themselves: 'but the next twenty will be better'; they are those of whom David Hume says mockingly:

> And from the dregs of life hope to receive
> What the first sprightly running could not give.

Let us call them historical men; looking to the past impels them towards the future and fires their courage to go on living and their hope that what they want will still happen, that happiness lies behind the hill they are advancing towards. These historical men believe that the meaning of existence will come more and more to light in the course of its *process*, and they glance behind them only so that, from the process so far, they can learn to understand the present and to desire the future more vehemently; they have no idea that, despite their preoccupation with history, they in fact think and act unhistorically, or that their occupation with history stands in the service, not of pure knowledge, but of life.

But our question can also be answered differently. Again with a No – but with a No for a different reason: with the No of the suprahistorical man, who sees no salvation in the process and for whom, rather, the world is complete and reaches its finality at each and every moment. What could ten more years teach that the past ten were unable to teach!

Whether the sense of this teaching is happiness or resignation or virtue or atonement, suprahistorical men have never been able to agree; but, in opposition to all historical modes of regarding the past, they are unanimous in the proposition: the past and the present are one, that is to say, with all their diversity identical in all that is typical and, as the omnipresence of imperishable types, a motionless structure of a value that cannot alter and a significance that is always the same. Just as the hundreds of different languages correspond to the same typically unchanging needs of man, so that he who understood these needs would be unable to learn anything new from any of these languages, so the suprahistorical thinker beholds the history of nations and of individuals from within, clairvoyantly divining the original meaning of the various hieroglyphics and gradually even coming wearily to avoid the endless stream of new signs: for how should the unending superfluity of events not reduce him to satiety, over-satiety and finally to nausea! So that perhaps the boldest of them is at last ready to say to his heart, with Giacomo Leopardi:

Nothing lives that is worthy
Thy agitation, and the earth deserves not a sigh.
Our being is pain and boredom and the world is dirt – nothing more.
Be calm.

But let us leave the suprahistorical men to their nausea and their wisdom: today let us rejoice for once in our unwisdom and, as believers in deeds and progress and as honourers of the process, give ourselves a holiday. Our valuation of the historical may be only an occidental prejudice: but let us at least make progress within this prejudice and not stand still! Let us at least learn better how to employ history for the purpose of *life*! Then we will gladly acknowledge that the suprahistorical outlook possesses more wisdom than we do, provided we can only be sure that we possess more life: for then our unwisdom will at any rate have more future than their wisdom will. And in order to leave no doubt as to the meaning of this antithesis of life and wisdom, I shall employ an ancient, tried-and-tested procedure and straightway propound a number of theses.

A historical phenomenon, known clearly and completely and resolved into a phenomenon of knowledge, is, for him who has perceived it, dead: for he has recognized in it the delusion, the injustice, the blind passion, and in general the whole earthly and darkening horizon of this phenomenon, and has thereby also understood its power in history. This power has now lost its hold over him insofar as he is a man of knowledge: but perhaps it has not done so insofar as he is a man involved in life.

History become pure, sovereign science would be for mankind a sort of conclusion of life and a settling of accounts with it. The study of history is something salutary and fruitful for the future only as the attendant of a mighty new current of life, of an evolving culture for example, that is to say only when it is dominated and directed by a higher force and does not itself dominate and direct.

Insofar as it stands in the service of life, history stands in the service of an unhistorical power, and, thus subordinate, it can and should never become a pure science such as, for instance, mathematics is. The question of the degree to which life requires the service of history at all, however, is one of the supreme questions and concerns in regard to the health of a man, a people or a culture. For when it attains a certain degree of excess, life crumbles and degenerates, and through this degeneration history itself finally degenerates too.

2

That life is in need of the services of history, however, must be grasped as firmly as must the proposition, which is to be demonstrated later, that an excess of history is harmful to the living man. History pertains to the living man in three respects: it pertains to him as a being who acts and strives, as a being who preserves and reveres, as a being who suffers and seeks deliverance. This threefold relationship corresponds to three species of history – insofar as it is permissible to distinguish between a *monumental*, an *antiquarian* and a *critical* species of history.

History belongs above all to the man of deeds and power, to him who fights a great fight, who needs models, teachers, comforters and cannot find them among his contemporaries. It belonged thus to Schiller: for our time is so bad, Goethe said, that the poet no longer encounters in the human life that surrounds him a nature he can employ. It is the man of deeds Polybius has in mind when he calls political history the proper preparation for governing a state and the best teacher who, by recalling to us the misfortunes of others, instructs us in how we may steadfastly endure our own changes of fortune. He who has learned to recognize in this the meaning of history is vexed at the sight of inquisitive tourists or pedantic micrologists clambering about on the pyramids of the great eras of the past; where he finds inspiration to imitate or to do better, he does not wish to encounter the idler who, hungry for distraction or excitement, prowls around as though among pictures in a gallery. Among these feeble and hopeless idlers, among those around him who seem active but are in fact merely agitated and bustling, the man of action avoids despair and disgust by turning his gaze backwards and pausing for breath in his march towards the goal. His goal, however, is happiness, perhaps not his own but often that of a nation or of mankind as a whole; he flees from resignation and needs history as a specific against it. Mostly there is no reward beckoning him on, unless it be fame, that is, the expectation of a place of honour in the temple of history, where he in turn can be a teacher, comforter and admonisher to those who come after him. For the commandment which rules over him is: that which in the past was able to expand the concept 'man' and make it more beautiful must exist everlastingly, so as to be able to accomplish this everlastingly. That the great moments in the struggle of the human individual constitute a chain, that this chain unites mankind across the millennia like a range of human mountain peaks, that the summit of such a long-ago moment shall be for me still living, bright and great – that is the fundamental idea of the faith in humanity which finds expression in the demand for a *monumental* history. But it is precisely this demand that greatness shall be everlasting that sparks off the most fearful of struggles. For everything else that lives cries No. The monumental shall not come into existence – that is the counter-word. Apathetic habit, all that is base and petty, filling every corner of the earth and billowing up around all that is great like a heavy breath of the earth, casts itself across the path that greatness has to tread on its way to immortality and retards, deceives, suffocates and stifles it. This path, however, leads through human brains! Through the brains of timorous and shortlived animals which emerge again and again to the same needs and distresses and fend off destruction only with effort and then only for a short time. For they want first of all but one thing: to live, at any cost. Who would associate *them* with that hard relay-race of monumental history through which alone greatness goes on living! And yet again and again there awaken some who, gaining strength through reflecting on past greatness, are inspired with the feeling that the life of man is a glorious thing, and even that the fairest fruit of this bitter plant is the knowledge that in earlier times someone passed through this existence infused with pride and strength, someone else sunk in profound thoughtfulness, a third exhibiting mercy and helpfulness – all of them, however, leaving behind them a single teaching: that he lives best who has no respect for existence. If the common man takes this little span of time with such gloomy earnestness and clings to it so desperately, those few we have just spoken of have known, on their way to immortality and to monumental history, how to regard it with Olympian laughter or at least with sublime mockery; often they descended to their grave with an ironic smile – for what was there left of them to bury! Only the dross, refuse, vanity, animality that had always weighed them down and that was now consigned to oblivion after having for long been the object of their contempt. But one thing will live, the monogram of their most essential being, a work, an act, a piece of rare enlighten-ment, a creation: it will live because posterity cannot do without it. In this transfigured form, fame is something more than the tastiest morsel of our egoism, as Schopenhauer called it: it is the belief in the solidarity and continuity of the greatness of all ages and a protest against the passing away of generations and the transitoriness of things.

Of what use, then, is the monumentalistic conception of the past, engagement with the classic and rare of earlier times, to the man of the present? He learns from it that the greatness that once existed was in any event once *possible* and may thus be possible again; he goes his way with more cheerful step, for the doubt which assailed him in weaker moments, whether he was not perhaps desiring the impossible, has now been banished. Supposing someone believed that it would require no more than a hundred men educated and actively working in a new spirit to do away with the bogus form of culture which has just now become the fashion in Germany, how greatly it would strengthen him to realize that the culture of the Renaissance was raised on the shoulders of just such a band of a hundred men.

And yet – to learn something new straightaway from this example – how inexact, fluid and provisional that comparison would be! How much of the past would have to be overlooked if it was to pro-duce that mighty effect, how violently what is individual in it would have to be forced into a universal mould and all its sharp corners and hard outlines broken up in the interest of conformity! At bottom, indeed, that which was once possible could present itself as a possibility for a second time only if the Pythagoreans were right in believing that when the constellation of the heavenly bodies is repeated the same things, down to the smallest event, must also be repeated on earth: so that whenever the stars stand in a certain relation to one another a Stoic again joins with an Epicurean to murder Caesar, and when they stand in another relation Columbus will again discover America. Only if, when the fifth act of the earth's drama ended, the whole play every time began again from the beginning, if it was certain that the same complex of motives, the same *deus ex machina*, the same catastrophe were repeated at definite intervals, could the man of power venture to desire monumental history in full icon-like *veracity*, that is to say with every individual peculiarity depicted in precise detail: but that will no doubt happen only when the astronomers have again become astrologers. Until that time, monumental history will have no use for that absolute veracity: it will always have to deal in approximations and generalities, in making what is dissimilar look similar; it will always have to diminish the differences of motives and instigations so as to exhibit the *effectus* monumentally, that is to say as something exemplary and worthy of imitation, at the expense of the *causae*: so that, since it as far as possible ignores causes, one might with only slight exaggeration call it a collection of 'effects in themselves', of events which will produce an effect upon all future ages. That which is celebrated at popular festivals, at religious or military anniversaries, is really such an 'effect in itself': it is this which will not let the ambitious sleep, which the brave wear over their hearts like an amulet, but it is not the truly historical *connexus* of cause and effect – which, fully understood, would only demonstrate that the dice-game of chance and the future could never again produce anything exactly similar to what it produced in the past.

As long as the soul of historiography lies in the great *stimuli* that a man of power derives from it, as long as the past has to be described as worthy of imitation, as imitable and possible for a second time, it of course incurs the danger of becoming somewhat distorted, beautified and coming close to free poetic invention; there have been ages, indeed, which were quite incapable of distinguishing between a monumentalized past and a mythical fiction, because precisely the same stimuli can be derived from the one world as from the other. If, therefore, the monumental mode of regarding history *rules* over the other modes – I mean over the antiquarian and critical

– the past itself suffers *harm*: whole segments of it are forgotten, despised, and flow away in an uninterrupted colourless flood, and only individual embellished facts rise out of it like islands: the few personalities who are visible at all have something strange and unnatural about them, like the golden hip which the pupils of Pythagoras supposed they saw on their master. Monumental history deceives by analogies: with seductive similarities it inspires the courageous to foolhardiness and the inspired to fanaticism; and when we go on to think of this kind of history in the hands and heads of gifted egoists and visionary scoundrels, then we see empires destroyed, princes murdered, wars and revolutions launched and the number of historical 'effects in themselves', that is to say, effects without sufficient cause, again augmented. So much as a reminder of the harm that monumental history can do among men of power and achievement, whether they be good men or evil: what, however, is it likely to do when the impotent and indolent take possession of it and employ it!

Let us take the simplest and most frequent example. Imagine the inartistic natures, and those only weakly endowed, armoured and armed by a monumentalist history of the artists: against whom will they now turn their weapons? Against their arch-enemies, the strong artistic spirits, that is to say against those who alone are capable of learning from that history in a true, that is to say life-enhancing sense, and of transforming what they have learned into a more elevated practice. Their path will be barred, their air darkened, if a half-understood monument to some great era of the past is erected as an idol and zealously danced around, as though to say: 'Behold, this is true art: pay no heed to those who are evolving and want something new!' This dancing mob appears to possess even the privilege of determining what is 'good taste': for the creative man has always been at a disadvantage compared with those who have only looked on and taken no part themselves; just as the public house politician has at all times been cleverer, more judicious and more prudent than the statesman who actually rules. But if one goes so far as to employ the popular referendum and the numerical majority in the domain of art, and as it were compels the artist to defend himself before the forum of the aesthetically inactive, then you can take your oath on it in advance that he will be condemned: not in spite of the fact that his judges have solemnly proclaimed the canon of monumental art (that is to say, the art which, according to the given definition, has at all times 'produced an effect'), but precisely *because* they

71

have: while any art which, because contemporary, is not yet monumental, seems to them unnecessary, unattractive and lacking in the
authority conferred by history. On the other hand, their instincts tell
them that art can be slain by art: the monumental is never to be
repeated, and to make sure it is not they invoke the authority which
the monumental derives from the past. They are connoisseurs of art
because they would like to do away with art altogether; they pose as
physicians, while their basic intent is to mix poisons; they develop
their taste and tongue as they do so as to employ this spoiled taste as
an explanation of why they so resolutely reject all the nourishing
artistic food that is offered them. For they do not desire to see new
greatness emerge: their means of preventing it is to say 'Behold,
greatness already exists!' In reality, they are as little concerned about
this greatness that already exists as they are about that which is
emerging: their lives are evidence of this. Monumental history is the
masquerade costume in which their hatred of the great and powerful
of their own age is disguised as satiated admiration for the great and
powerful of past ages, and muffled in which they invert the real
meaning of that mode of regarding history into its opposite; whether
they are aware of it or not, they act as though their motto were: let the
dead bury the living.

Each of the three species of history which exist belongs to a certain
soil and a certain climate and only to that: in any other it grows into a
devastating weed. If the man who wants to do something great has
need of the past at all, he appropriates it by means of monumental
history; he, on the other hand, who likes to persist in the familiar and
the revered of old, tends the past as an antiquarian historian; and
only he who is oppressed by a present need, and who wants to throw
off this burden at any cost, has need of critical history, that is to say a
history that judges and condemns. Much mischief is caused through
the thoughtless transplantation of these plants: the critic without
need, the antiquary without piety, the man who recognizes greatness
but cannot himself do great things, are such plants, estranged from
their mother soil and degenerated into weeds.

3

History thus belongs in the second place to him who preserves and
reveres – to him who looks back to whence he has come, to where he
came into being, with love and loyalty; with this piety he as it were
gives thanks for his existence. By tending with care that which has

existed from of old, he wants to preserve for those who shall come into existence after him the conditions under which he himself came into existence – and thus he serves life. The possession of ancestral goods changes its meaning in such a soul: *they* rather possess *it*. The trivial, circumscribed, decaying and obsolete acquire their own dignity and inviolability through the fact that the preserving and revering soul of the antiquarian man has emigrated into them and there made its home. The history of his city becomes for him the history of himself; he reads its walls, its towered gate, its rules and regulations, its holidays, like an illuminated diary of his youth and in all this he finds again himself, his force, his industry, his joy, his judgment, his folly and vices. Here we lived, he says to himself, for here we are living; and here we shall live, for we are tough and not to be ruined overnight. Thus with the aid of this 'we' he looks beyond his own individual transitory existence and feels himself to be the spirit of his house, his race, his city. Sometimes he even greets the soul of his nation across the long dark centuries of confusion as his own soul; an ability to feel his way back and sense how things were, to detect traces almost extinguished, to read the past quickly and correctly no matter how intricate its palimpsest may be – these are his talents and virtues. Endowed with these talents and virtues Goethe stood before Erwin von Steinbach's monumental work; in the storm of his feelings the historical clouds which veiled the time between them were rent apart: it was his recognition, at first sight, of the German work of art 'exerting its power through a strong, rough German soul'. It was the same tendency which directed the Italians of the Renaissance and reawoke in their poets the genius of ancient Italy to a 'wonderful new resounding of the primeval strings', as Jakob Burckhardt puts it. But this antiquarian sense of veneration of the past is of the greatest value when it spreads a simple feeling of pleasure and contentment over the modest, rude, even wretched conditions in which a man or a nation lives; Niebuhr, for example, admits with honourable candour that on moor and heathland, among free peasants who possess a history, he can live contented and never feel the want of art. How could history serve life better than when it makes the less favoured races and peoples contented with their own homeland and its customs, and restrains them from roving abroad in search of something they think more worth having and engaging in battles for it? Sometimes this clinging to one's own environment and companions, one's own toilsome customs, one's own bare mountainside, looks like obstinacy and ignorance – yet it is a very salutary ignorance and one most calculated to further the interests of the community: a fact of which anyone must be aware who knows the dreadful consequences of the desire for expeditions and adventures, especially when it seizes whole hordes of nations, and who has seen from close up the condition a nation gets into when it has ceased to be faithful to its own origins and is given over to a restless, cosmopolitan hunting after new and ever newer things. The feeling antithetical to this, the contentment of the tree in its roots, the happiness of knowing that one is not wholly accidental and arbitrary but grown out of a past as its heir, flower and fruit, and that one's existence is thus excused and, indeed, justified – it is this which is today usually designated as the real sense of history.

This notwithstanding, such a condition is certainly not one in which a man would be most capable of resolving the past into pure knowledge; so that here too, as in the case of monumental history, we perceive that, as long as the study of history serves life and is directed by the vital drives, the past itself suffers. To employ a somewhat free metaphor: the tree is aware of its roots to a greater degree than it is able to see them; but this awareness judges how big they are from the size and strength of its visible branches. If, however, the tree is in error as to this, how greatly it will be in error regarding all the rest of the forest around it! – for it knows of the forest only that in it which obstructs or favours it and nothing beside. The antiquarian sense of a man, a community, a whole people, always possesses an extremely restricted field of vision; most of what exists it does not perceive at all, and the little it does see it sees much too close up and isolated; it cannot relate what it sees to anything else and it therefore accords everything it sees equal importance and therefore to each individual thing too great importance. There is a lack of that discrimination of value and that sense of proportion which would distinguish between the things of the past in a way that would do true justice to them; their measure and proportion is always that accorded them by the backward glance of the antiquarian nation or individual.

This always produces one very imminent danger: everything old and past that enters one's field of vision at all is in the end blandly taken to be equally worthy of reverence, while everything that does not approach this antiquity with reverence, that is to say everything new and evolving, is rejected and persecuted. Thus even the Greeks tolerated the hieratic style in their plastic arts beside the free and great; later, indeed, they did not merely tolerate the elevated nose and the frosty smile but even made a cult of it. When the senses of a people harden in this fashion, when the study of history serves the life of the past in such a way that it undermines continuing and especially higher life, when the historical sense no longer conserves life but mummifies it, then the tree gradually dies unnaturally from the top downwards to the roots – and in the end the roots themselves usually perish too. Antiquarian history itself degenerates from the moment it is no longer animated and inspired by the fresh life of the present. Its piety withers away, the habit of scholarliness continues without it and rotates in egoistic self-satisfaction around its own axis. Then there appears the repulsive spectacle of a blind rage for collecting, a restless raking together of everything that has ever existed. Man is encased in the stench of must and mould; through the antiquarian approach he succeeds in reducing even a more creative disposition, a nobler desire, to an insatiable thirst for novelty, or rather for antiquity and for all and everything; often he sinks so low that in the end he is content to gobble down any food whatever, even the dust of bibliographical minutiae.

But even when this degeneration does not take place, when antiquarian history does not lose the foundation in which alone it must be rooted if it is to benefit life, sufficient dangers remain should it grow too mighty and overpower the other modes of regarding the past. For it knows only how to *preserve* life, not how to engender it; it always undervalues that which is becoming because it has no instinct for divining it – as monumental history, for example, has. Thus it hinders any firm resolve to attempt something new, thus it paralyses the man of action who, as one who acts, will and must offend some piety or other. The fact that something has grown old now gives rise to the demand that it be made immortal; for when one considers all that such an antiquity – an ancient custom of the ancestors, a religious belief, an inherited political privilege – has experienced during the course of its existence, how great a sum of piety and reverence on the part of individuals and generations, then it must seem arrogant or even wicked to replace such an antiquity with a novelty and to set against such a numerical accumulation of acts of piety and reverence the single unit of that which is evolving and has just arrived.

Here it becomes clear how necessary it is to mankind to have, beside the monumental and antiquarian modes of regarding the past, a *third* mode, the *critical*: and this, too, in the service of life. If he is to live, man must possess and from time to time employ the strength to break up and dissolve a part of the past: he does this by bringing it before the tribunal, scrupulously examining it and finally condemning it; every past, however, is worthy to be condemned – for that is the nature of human things: human violence and weakness have always played a mighty role in them. It is not justice which here sits in judgment; it is even less mercy which pronounces the verdict: it is life alone, that dark, driving power that insatiably thirsts for itself. Its sentence is always unmerciful, always unjust, because it has never proceeded out of a pure well of knowledge; but in most cases the sentence would be the same even if it were pronounced by justice itself. 'For all that exists is *worthy* of perishing. So it would be better if nothing existed.' It requires a great deal of strength to be able to live and to forget the extent to which to live and to be unjust is one and the same thing. Luther himself once opined that the world existed only through a piece of forgetful negligence on God's part: for if God had foreseen 'heavy artillery' he would not have created the world. Sometimes, however, this same life that requires forgetting demands a temporary suspension of this forgetfulness; it wants to be clear as to how unjust the existence of anything – a privilege, a caste, a dynasty, for example – is, and how greatly this thing deserves to perish. Then its past is regarded critically, then one takes the knife to its roots, then one cruelly tramples over every kind of piety. It is always a dangerous process, especially so for life itself: and men and ages which serve life by judging and destroying a past are always dangerous and endangered men and ages. For since we are the out-come of earlier generations, we are also the outcome of their aber-rations, passions and errors, and indeed of their crimes; it is not possible wholly to free oneself from this chain. If we condemn these aberrations and regard ourselves as free of them, this does not alter the fact that we originate in them. The best we can do is to confront our inherited and hereditary nature with our knowledge of it, and through a new, stern discipline combat our inborn heritage and inplant in ourselves a new habit, a new instinct, a second nature, so that our first nature withers away. It is an attempt to give oneself, as it were *a posteriori*, a past in which one would like to originate in oppo-sition to that in which one did originate: – always a dangerous attempt because it is so hard to know the limit to denial of the past and because second natures are usually weaker than first. What hap-pens all too often is that we know the good but do not do it, because we also know the better but cannot do it. But here and there a victory is nonetheless achieved, and for the combatants, for those who employ critical history for the sake of life, there is even a noteworthy consolation: that of knowing that this first nature was once a second nature and that every victorious second nature will become a first.

4

These are the services history is capable of performing for life; every man and every nation requires, in accordance with its goals, energies and needs, a certain kind of knowledge of the past, now in the form of monumental, now of antiquarian, now of critical history: but it does not require it as a host of pure thinkers who only look on at life, of knowledge-thirsty individuals whom knowledge alone will satisfy and to whom the accumulation of knowledge is itself the goal, but always and only for the ends of life and thus also under the domination and supreme direction of these ends. That this is the natural relationship of an age, a culture, a nation with its history – evoked by hunger, regulated by the extent of its need, held in bounds by its inherent plastic powers – that knowledge of the past has at all times been desired only in the service of the future and the present and not for the weakening of the present or for depriving a vigorous future of its roots: all this is simple, as the truth is simple, and will at once be obvious even to him who has not had it demonstrated by historical proof.

And now let us quickly take a look at our own time! We are startled, we shy away: where has all the clarity, all the naturalness and purity of this relationship between life and history gone? in what restless and exaggerated confusion does this problem now swell before our eyes! Does the fault lie with us, who observe it? Or has the constellation of life and history really altered through the interposition of a mighty, hostile star between them? Let others show that we have seen falsely: for our part we shall say what we think we see. And what we see is certainly a star, a gleaming and glorious star interposing itself, the constellation really has been altered – *by science, by the demand that history should be a science*. Now the demands of life alone no longer reign and exercise constraint on knowledge of the past: now all the frontiers have been torn down and all that has ever been rushes upon mankind. All perspectives have been shifted back to the beginning of all becoming, back into infinity. Such an immense spectacle as the science of universal becoming, history, now displays

77

has never before been seen by any generation; though it displays it, to be sure, with the perilous daring of its motto: *fiat veritas, pereat vita.* *

Let us now picture the spiritual occurrence introduced into the soul of modern man by that which we have just described. Historical knowledge streams in unceasingly from inexhaustible wells, the strange and incoherent forces its way forward, memory opens all its gates and yet is not open wide enough, nature travails in an effort to receive, arrange and honour these strange guests, but they themselves are in conflict with one another and it seems necessary to constrain and control them if one is not oneself to perish in their conflict. Habituation to such a disorderly, stormly and conflict-ridden household gradually becomes a second nature, though this second nature is beyond question much weaker, much more restless, and thoroughly less sound than the first. In the end, modern man drags around with him a huge quantity of indigestible stones of knowledge, which then, as in the fairy tale, can sometimes be heard rumbling about inside him. And in this rumbling there is betrayed the most characteristic quality of modern man: the remarkable antithesis between an interior which fails to correspond to any exterior and an exterior which fails to correspond to any interior – an antithesis unknown to the peoples of earlier times. Knowledge, consumed for the greater part without hunger for it and even counter to one's needs, now no longer acts as an agent for transforming the outside world but remains concealed within a chaotic inner world which modern man describes with a curious pride as his uniquely characteristic 'subjectivity'. It is then said that one possesses content and only form is lacking; but such an antithesis is quite improper when applied to living things. This precisely is why our modern culture is not a living thing: it is incomprehensible without recourse to that antithesis; it is not a real culture at all but only a kind of knowledge of culture; it has an idea of and feeling for culture but no true cultural achievement emerges from them. What actually inspires it and then appears as a visible act, on the other hand, often signifies not much more than an indifferent convention, a pitiful imitation or even a crude caricature. Cultural sensibility then lies quietly within, like a snake that has swallowed rabbits whole and now lies in the sun and avoids all unnecessary movement. The inner process is now the thing itself, is what actually constitutes 'culture'.

*fiat veritas, pereat vita: let truth prevail though life perish

Anyone observing this has only one wish, that such a culture should not perish of indigestion. Imagine, for example, a Greek observing such a culture: he would perceive that for modern man 'educated' and 'historically educated' seem so to belong together as to mean one and the same thing and to differ only verbally. If he then said that one can be very educated and yet at the same time altogether uneducated historically, modern men would think they had failed to hear him aright and would shake their heads. That celebrated little nation of a not so distant past – I mean these same Greeks – during the period of their greatest strength kept a tenacious hold on their unhistorical sense; if a present-day man were magically transported back to that world he would probably consider the Greeks very 'uncultured' – whereby, to be sure, the secret of modern culture, so scrupulously hidden, would be exposed to public ridicule: for we moderns have nothing whatever of our own; only by replenishing and cramming ourselves with the ages, customs, arts, philosophies, religions, discoveries of others do we become anything worthy of notice, that is to say, walking encyclopaedias, which is what an ancient Greek transported into our own time would perhaps take us for. With encyclopaedias, however, all the value lies in what is contained within, in the content, not in what stands without, the binding and cover; so it is that the whole of modern culture is essentially subjective: on the outside the bookbinder has printed some such thing as 'Handbook of subjective culture for outward barbarians'. This antithesis of inner and outer, indeed, makes the exterior even more barbaric than it would be if a rude nation were only to develop out of itself in accordance with its own uncouth needs. For what means are available to nature for overcoming that which presses upon it in too great abundance? One alone: to embrace it as lightly as possible so as quickly to expel it again and have done with it. From this comes a habit of no longer taking real things seriously, from this arises the 'weak personality' by virtue of which the real and existent makes only a slight impression; one becomes ever more negligent of one's outer appearance and, provided the memory is continually stimulated by a stream of new things worth knowing which can be stored tidily away in its coffers, one finally widens the dubious gulf between content and form to the point of complete insensibility to barbarism. The culture of a people as the antithesis to this barbarism was once, and as I think with a certain justice, defined as unity of artistic style in all the expressions of the life of a people; this definition should not be misunderstood in the sense of implying an

79

antithesis between barbarism and *fine* style; what is meant is that a people to whom one attributes a culture has to be in all reality a single living unity and not fall wretchedly apart into inner and outer, content and form. He who wants to strive for and promote the culture of a people should strive for and promote this higher unity and join in the destruction of modern bogus cultivatedness for the sake of a true culture; he should venture to reflect how the health of a people undermined by the study of history may be again restored, how it may rediscover its instincts and therewith its honesty.

I may as well speak directly of ourselves, we Germans of the present day who are more afflicted than other nations by that weakness of personality and that contradiction between form and content. Form generally counts with us as a convention, as a vestment and disguise, and it is therefore, if not exactly hated, at any rate not loved; it would be even more correct to say that we have an extraordinary fear of the word 'convention' and, no doubt, also of the thing. It was this fear which led the German to desert the school of France: he wanted to become more natural and thereby more German. But this 'thereby' seems to have been a miscalculation: escaped from the school of convention, he then let himself go in whatever manner his fancy happened to suggest to him, and at bottom did no more than imitate in a slovenly and half-forgetful way what he had formerly imitated with scrupulous care and often with success. So it is that, compared with past ages, we dwell even today in a carelessly inaccurate copy of French convention: a fact to which all our comings and goings, conversations, clothing and habitations bear witness. We thought we were retreating into naturalness, but what we were really doing was letting ourselves go and electing for ease and comfort and the smallest possible degree of self-discipline. Take a stroll through a German city – compared with the distinct national qualities displayed in foreign cities, all the conventions here are negative ones, everything is colourless, worn out, badly copied, negligent, everyone does as he likes but what he likes is never forceful and well considered but follows the rules laid down first by universal haste, then by the universal rage for ease and comfort. A garment which costs no intelligence to design and no time to put on, that is to say a garment borrowed from abroad and imitated in the most easygoing way possible, at once counts with the Germans as a contribution to German national dress. The sense of form is rejected without the slightest misgiving – for we possess the *sense of the content*: for the

Germans are, after all, celebrated for their profound subjectivity.

But this subjectivity also carries with it a celebrated danger: the content itself, of which it is assumed that it cannot be seen from without, may occasionally evaporate; from without, however, neither its former presence nor its disappearance will be apparent at all. But however far from this danger we may imagine the German people to be, the foreigner will still be to some extent justified in maintaining that our subjectivity is too feeble and disorganized to produce an outward effect and endow itself with a form. The subjectivity of the Germans can be receptive to an exceptional degree: serious, powerful, profound, and perhaps even richer than that of other nations; but as a whole it remains weak because all these beautiful threads are not wound together into a powerful knot: so that the visible act is not the act and self-revelation of the totality of this subjectivity but only a feeble or crude attempt on the part of one or other of these threads to pose as being the whole. That is why the German cannot be judged by his actions and why as an individual he is still completely hidden even after he has acted. As is well known, he has to be assessed according to his thoughts and feelings, and these he nowadays expresses in his books. If only it were not precisely these books which, now more than ever before, lead us to doubt whether that celebrated subjectivity really does still reside in its inaccessible little temple; it is a dreadful thought that one day they might disappear and all that would be left to signalize the German would be his arrogantly clumsy and meekly slovenly exterior: almost as dreadful as if that hidden subjectivity were sitting in there falsified and painted over and had become an actor if not something worse. This, at any rate, is what Grillparzer, as an independent observer, seems to have gathered from his experience in the theatre. 'We feel in abstractions', he says, 'we hardly know any longer how feeling really expresses itself with our contemporaries; we show them performing actions such as they no longer perform nowadays. Shakespeare has ruined all of us moderns.'

This is a single case and perhaps it has been generalized too hastily: but how fearful it would be if such a generalization were justified, if a host of individual cases should crowd in upon the observer; how desolating it would be to have to say: we Germans feel in abstractions, we have all been ruined by history – a proposition which would destroy at its roots all hope of a future national culture: for any such hope grows out of the belief in the genuineness and immediacy of German feeling, out of the belief in a sound and whole subjectivity. What is there left to hope for or believe in if the source of hope and belief is muddied, if subjectivity has learned to make leaps, to dance, to paint itself, to express itself in abstractions and with calculation and gradually to lose itself! And how should the great productive spirit continue to endure among a people no longer secure in a unified subjectivity and which falls asunder into the cultivated with a miseducated and misled subjectivity on the one hand and the uncultivated with an inaccessible subjectivity on the other! How should that spirit endure if unity of feeling among the people has been lost, and if, moreover, it knows that this feeling is falsified and retouched precisely among that part of the people which calls itself the cultured part and lays claim to possession of the national artistic conscience? Even if here and there an individual's taste and judgment has grown more subtle and sublimated, that is no advantage to *him*: he is racked by the knowledge that he has to speak as it were to a sect and is no longer needed in the body of his nation. Perhaps he now prefers to bury his treasure rather than suffer the disgust of being presumptuously patronized by a sect while his heart is full of pity for all. The instinct of the nation no longer comes out to meet him; it is useless for him to stretch out his arms towards them in longing. What is there now left to this spirit but to turn his inspired hatred against that constraint, against the barriers erected in the so-called culture of his nation, so as to condemn what to him, as a living being and one productive of life, is destructive and degrading: thus he exchanges a profound insight into his destiny for the divine joys of creation and construction, and ends as a solitary man of knowledge and satiated sage. It is the most painful of spectacles: he who beholds it will know a sacred compulsion: here, he says to himself, I must render aid, that higher unity in the nature and soul of a people must again be created, that breach between inner and outer must again vanish under the hammer-blows of necessity. But what weapons can he employ? What does he have but, again, his profound insight: propagating it and sowing it with full hands he hopes to implant a need: and out of a vigorous need there will one day arise a vigorous deed. And so as to leave no doubt of the source of my example of that need, that necessity, that perception, let me say expressly that it is for *German unity* in that highest sense that we strive, and strive more ardently than we do for political reunification, *the unity of German spirit and life after the abolition of the antithesis of form and content, of subjectivity and convention.* –

The oversaturation of an age with history seems to me to be hostile and dangerous to life in five respects: such an excess creates that contrast between inner and outer which we have just discussed, and thereby weakens the personality; it leads an age to imagine that it possesses the rarest of virtues, justice, to a greater degree than any other age; it disrupts the instincts of a people, and hinders the individual no less than the whole in the attainment of maturity; it implants the belief, harmful at any time, in the old age of mankind, the belief that one is a latecomer and epigone; it leads an age into a dangerous mood of irony in regard to itself and subsequently into the even more dangerous mood of cynicism: in this mood, however, it develops more and more a prudent practical egoism through which the forces of life are paralyzed and at last destroyed.

And now back to our first proposition: modern man suffers from a weakened personality. As the Roman of the imperial era became un-Roman in relation to the world which stood at his service, as he lost himself in the flood of foreigners which came streaming in and degenerated in the midst of the cosmopolitan carnival of gods, arts and customs, so the same must happen to modern man who allows his artists in history to go on preparing a world exhibition for him; he has become a strolling spectator and has arrived at a condition in which even great wars and revolutions are able to influence him for hardly more than a moment. The war is not even over before it is transformed into a hundred thousand printed pages and set before the tired palates of the history-hungry as the latest delicacy. It seems that the instrument is almost incapable of producing a strong and full note, no matter how vigorously it is played: its tones at once die away and in a moment have faded to a tender historical echo. Expressed morally: you are no longer capable of holding on to the sublime, your deeds are shortlived explosions, not rolling thunder. Though the greatest and most miraculous event should occur – it must nonetheless descend, silent and unsung, into Hades. For art flees away if you immediately conceal your deeds under the awning of history. He who wants to understand, grasp and assess in a moment that before which he ought to stand long in awe as before an incomprehensible sublimity may be called reasonable, but only in the sense in which Schiller speaks of the rationality of the reasonable man: there are things he does not see which even a child sees, there are things he does not hear which even a child hears, and these things are precisely the most important things: because he does not understand these things, his understanding is more childish than the child and more simple than simplicity – and this in spite of the many cunning folds of his parchment scroll and the virtuosity of his fingers in unravelling the entangled. The reason is that he has lost and destroyed his instincts and, having lost his trust in the 'divine animal', he can no longer let go the reins when his reason falters and his path leads him through deserts. Thus the individual grows fainthearted and unsure and dares no longer believe in himself: he sinks into his own subjective depths, which here means into the accumulated lumber of what he has learned but which has no outward effect, of instruction which does not become life. If one watches him from outside, one sees how the expulsion of the instincts by history has transformed man almost into mere *abstractis* and shadows: no one dares to appear as he is, but masks himself as a cultivated man, as a scholar, as a poet, as a politician. If, believing all this to be in earnest and not a mere puppet-play – for they all affect earnestness – one takes hold of these masks, one suddenly has nothing but rags and tatters in one's hands. That is why one should no longer let oneself be deceived, that is why one should order them: 'Off with your coats or be what you seem!' It can no longer be borne that everyone of a noble seriousness should become a Don Quixote, since he has better things to do than to buffet about with such false realities. But he must nonetheless keep a sharp lookout, whenever he encounters a mask cry his 'Halt! Who goes there?' and tear the mask from its face. Strange! One would think that history would encourage men to be *honest* – even if only honest fools; and hitherto this has indeed been its effect, only now it is no longer! Historical education and the identical bourgeois coat rule at the same time. While the 'free personality' has never before been commended so volubly, there are no personalities to be seen, let alone free personalities – nothing but anxiously muffled up identical people. Individuality has withdrawn within: from without it has become invisible; a fact which leads one to ask whether indeed there could be causes without effects. Or is a race of eunuchs needed to watch over the great historical world-harem? Pure objectivity would certainly characterize such a race. For it almost seems that the task is to stand guard over history to see that nothing comes out of it except more history, and certainly no real events! – to take care that history does not make any personality 'free', that is to say truthful towards itself, truthful towards others, in both word and deed. It is only through such truthfulness that the distress, the inner misery, of modern man will come to light, and that, in place of that anxious concealment through convention and masquerade, art and religion, true ancillaries, will be able to combine to implant a culture which corresponds to real needs and does not, as present-day universal education teaches it to do, deceive itself as to these needs and thereby become a walking lie.

In an age which suffers from this universal education, to what an unnatural, artificial and in any case unworthy state must the most truthful of all sciences, the honest naked goddess philosophy, be reduced! In such a world of compelled external uniformity it must remain the learned monologue of the solitary walker, the individual's chance capture, the hidden secret of the chamber, or the harmless chatter of academic old men and children. No one dares venture to fulfil the philosophical law in himself, no one lives philosophically with that simple loyalty that constrained a man of antiquity to bear himself as a Stoic wherever he was, whatever he did, once he had affirmed his loyalty to the Stoa. All modern philosophizing is political and official, limited by governments, churches, academies, customs and the cowardice of men to the appearance of scholarship; it sighs 'if only' or knows 'there once was' and does nothing else. Within a historical culture philosophy possesses no rights if it wants to be more than a self-restrained knowing which leads to no action; if modern man had any courage or resolution at all, if he were not merely a subjective creature even in his enmities, he would banish philosophy; as it is, he contents himself with modestly concealing its nudity. One may think, write, print, speak, teach philosophy – to that point more or less everything is permitted; only in the realm of action, of so-called life, is it otherwise: there only one thing is ever permitted and everything else simply impossible: thus will historical culture have it. Are there still human beings, one then asks oneself, or perhaps only thinking-, writing- and speaking-machines?

Goethe once said of Shakespeare: 'No one despised outward costume more than he; he knew very well the inner human costume, and here all are alike. They say he hit off the Romans admirably; but I don't find it so, they are all nothing but flesh-and-blood Englishmen, but they are certainly human beings, human from head to foot, and the Roman toga sits on them perfectly well.' Now I ask whether it would be possible to represent our contemporary men of letters, popular figures, officials or politicians as Romans; it simply would not work, because they are not human beings but only

flesh-and-blood compendia and as it were abstractions made concrete. If they possess a character of their own it is buried so deep it
cannot get out into the light of day: if they are human beings they are
so only to him 'who explores the depths'. To anyone else they are
something different, not men, not gods, not animals, but creations
of historical culture, wholly structure, image, form without
demonstrable content and, unhappily, ill-designed form and, what
is more, uniform. And so let my proposition be understood and
pondered: *history can be borne only by strong personalities, weak ones are
utterly extinguished by it*. The reason is that history confuses the feelings
and sensibility when these are not strong enough to assess the past
by themselves. He who no longer dares to trust himself but involuntarily asks of history 'How ought I to feel about this?' finds that his
timidity gradually turns him into an actor and that he is playing a
role, usually indeed many roles and therefore playing them badly
and superficially. Gradually all congruity between the man and his
historical domain is lost; we behold pert little fellows associating
with the Romans as though they were their equals: and they root and
burrow in the remains of the Greek poets as though these too were
corpora for their dissection and were as *vilia* as their own literary *corpora*
may be.* Suppose one of them is engaged with Democritus, I always
feel like asking: why not Heraclitus? Or Philo? Or Bacon? Or
Descartes? – or anyone else. And then: why does it have to be a
philosopher? Why not a poet or an orator? And: why a Greek at all,
why not an Englishman or a Turk? Is the past not big enough for you
to be able to find nothing except things in comparison with which
you cut so ludicrous a figure? But, as I have said, this is a race of
eunuchs, and to a eunuch one woman is like another, simply a
woman, woman in herself, the eternally unapproachable – and it is
thus a matter of indifference what they do so long as history itself is
kept nice and 'objective', bearing in mind that those who want to
keep it so are for ever incapable of making history themselves. And
since the eternally womanly will never draw you upward, you draw it
down to you and, being neuters, take history too for a neuter.† But
so that it shall not be thought that I am seriously comparing history

---

vilia corpora: vile bodies
†Alludes to the closing lines of Goethe's *Faust II*: 'Das Ewig-Weibliche/Zieht uns
hinan'. Nietzsche often alludes to the phrase, always in an ironic-humorous tone: he
failed, I think, to discover any meaning in it.

with the eternally womanly, I should like to make it clear that, on the contrary, I regard it rather as the eternally manly: though, to be sure, for those who are 'historically educated' through and through it must be a matter of some indifference whether it is the one or the other: for they themselves are neither man nor woman, nor even hermaphrodite, but always and only neuters or, to speak more cultivatedly, the eternally objective.

If the personality is emptied in the manner described and has become eternally subjectless or, as it is usually put, objective, nothing can affect it any longer; good and right things may be done, as deeds, poetry, music: the hollowed-out cultivated man at once looks beyond the work and asks about the history of its author. If he has already several other works behind him, he is at once obliged to have explained to him the previous and possible future progress of his development, he is at once compared with other artists, criticized as to his choice of subject and his treatment of it, dissected, carefully put together again, and in general admonished and set on the right path. The most astonishing thing may come to pass – the host of the historically neutral is always there ready to supervise the author of it even while he is still far off. The echo is heard immediately: but always as a 'critique', though the moment before the critic did not so much as dream of the possibility of what has been done. The work never produces an effect but only another 'critique'; and the critique itself produces no effect either, but again only a further critique. There thus arises a general agreement to regard the acquisition of many critiques as a sign of success, of few or none as a sign of failure. At bottom, however, even given this kind of 'effect' everything remains as it was: people have some new thing to chatter about for a while, and then something newer still, and in the meantime go on doing what they have always done. The historical culture of our critics will no longer permit any effect at all in the proper sense, that is an effect on life and action: their blotting-paper at once goes down even on the blackest writing, and across the most graceful design they smear their thick brush-strokes which are supposed to be regarded as corrections: and once again that is the end of that. But their critical pens never cease to flow, for they have lost control of them and instead of directing them are directed by them. It is precisely in this immoderation of its critical outpourings, in its lack of self-control, in that which the Romans call *impotentia*, that the modern personality betrays its weakness.

6

But let us leave this weakness behind; and let us turn to a much celebrated strength of modern man with the question, a painful one to be sure, as to whether on account of his well-known historical 'objectivity' he has a right to call himself strong, that is to say *just*, and just in a higher degree than men of other ages. Is it true that this objectivity originates in an enhanced need and demand for justice? Or is it an effect of quite different causes and only appears to originate in a desire for justice? Does it perhaps seduce one to a harmful, because all too flattering, prejudice as to the virtues of modern man? – Socrates considered that to delude oneself that one possesses a virtue one does not possess is an illness bordering on madness: and such a delusion is certainly more dangerous than the opposite illusion of being the victim of a fault or a vice. For in the latter case it is at any rate possible one will become better; the former delusion, however, makes a man or an age daily worse – which in the present instance means more unjust.

In truth, no one has a greater claim to our veneration than he who possesses the drive to and strength for justice. For the highest and rarest virtues are united and concealed in justice as in an unfathomable ocean that receives streams and rivers from all sides and takes them into itself. The hand of the just man who is empowered to judge no longer trembles when it holds the scales; he sets weight upon weight with inexorable disregard of himself, his eye is unclouded as it sees the scales rise and fall, and his voice is neither harsh nor tearful when he pronounces the verdict. If he were a cold demon of knowledge, he would spread about him the icy atmosphere of a dreadful suprahuman majesty which we would have to fear, not revere: but that he is a human being and yet nonetheless tries to ascend from indulgent doubt to stern certainty, from tolerant mildness to the imperative 'you must', from the rare virtue of magnanimity to the rarest of all virtues, justice; that he resembles that demon but is from the start only a poor human being; and above all that he has every moment to atone for his humanity and is tragically consumed by an impossible virtue – all this sets him on a solitary height as the most *venerable* exemplar of the species man; for he desires truth, not as cold, ineffectual knowledge, but as a regulating and punishing judge; truth, not as the egoistic possession of the individual, but as the sacred right to overturn all the boundary-stones of egoistic possessions; in a word, truth as the judgment of humanity and not, for instance, as the prey joyfully seized by the individual huntsman. Only insofar as the truthful man possesses the unconditional will to justice is there anything great in that striving for truth which is everywhere so thoughtlessly glorified: a whole host of the most various drives – curiosity, flight from boredom, envy, vanity, the desire for amusement, for example – can be involved in the striving for truth, though in reality they have nothing whatever to do with truth, which has its roots in justice. Thus the world seems to be full of those who 'serve truth', yet the virtue of justice is rarely present, even more rarely recognized and almost always mortally hated: while on the other hand the horde of those who only appear virtuous is at all times received with pomp and honour. The truth is that few serve truth because few possess the pure will to justice, and of these few only a few also possess the strength actually to be just. To possess only the will is absolutely not enough: and the most terrible sufferings sustained by mankind have proceeded precisely from those possessing the drive to justice but lacking the power of judgment; which is why nothing would promote the general wellbeing more mightily than to sow the seeds of correct judgment as widely as possible, so that the fanatic would be distinguished from the judge and the blind desire to be a judge from the conscious ability to judge. But where could a means of implanting the power of judgment be found! –man will always remain in doubt and trepidation whether, when truth and justice are spoken of, it is a fanatic or a judge who is speaking to them. That is why they must be forgiven if they have always extended an especially cordial welcome to those 'servants of truth' who possess neither the will nor the power to judge and set themselves the task of seeking 'pure, self-subsistent' knowledge or, more clearly, truth that eventuates in nothing. There are very many truths that are a matter of complete indifference; there are problems whose just solution does not demand even an effort, let alone a sacrifice. In this region of indifference and absence of danger a man may well succeed in becoming a cold demon of knowledge: and nonetheless, even if in favourable times whole cohorts of scholars and inquirers are transformed into such demons – it will always fortunately be possible that such an age will suffer from a lack of a stern and great sense of justice, that is, of the noblest centre of the so-called drive to truth.

Now picture to yourself the historical virtuoso of the present day: is he the justest man of his time? It is true he has developed in himself such a tenderness and susceptibility of feeling that nothing human is alien to him; the most various ages and persons continue to sound in kindred notes on the strings of his lyre: he has become a passive sounding-board whose reflected tones act upon other similar sounding-boards: until at last the whole air of an age is filled with the confused humming of these tender and kindred echoes. Yet it seems to me as though only the harmonics of the original historical note are audible: the solidity and power of the original can no longer be divined in the shrill and bubble-thin vibrations of these strings. The original note recalled actions, distress, terrors; this note lulls us and makes of us tame spectators; it is as though the 'Eroica' Symphony had been arranged for two flutes for the entertainment of drowsy opium-smokers. Through this we are already in a position to assess how these virtuosi will stand in regard to modern man's supreme claim to a higher and purer sense of justice; this virtue never has anything pleasing about it, knows no delicious tremors, is harsh and dread-inspiring. In comparison, how low even magnanimity stands in the scale of the virtues, and magnanimity is itself possessed by only a few rare historians! Many more of them attain only to tolerance, to allowing validity to what they cannot deny happened, to explaining away and extenuating, on the correct assumption that the inexperienced will interpret the mere absence of abrasiveness and harsh condemnation of the past as evidence of a just disposition. But only superior strength can judge, weakness is obliged to tolerate if it is not to make a hypocritical pretence of strength and turn justice sitting in judgment into an actor. There still remains a dreadful species of historian, efficient, severe and honest of character but narrow of mind; the will to be just is there, as is the pathos attending the office of judge: but all their verdicts are false, for approximately the same reason as the verdicts of ordinary court juries are false. How improbable it thus is that there should be an abundance of talent for history! Quite apart from the disguised egoists and partymen who employ an air of objectivity in furtherance of their crooked game. And quite apart also from those wholly thoughtless people who when they write history do so in the naive belief that all the popular views of precisely their own age are the right and just views and that to write in accord with the views of their age is the same thing as being just; a belief in which every religion dwells and about which in the case of religions no further comment is needed. These naive historians call the assessment of the opinions and deeds of the past according to the everyday standards of the present moment 'objectivity': it is here they discover the canon of all truth; their task is to adapt the past to contemporary triviality. On the other hand, they

90

call all historiography 'subjective' that does not accept these popular standards as canonical.

And may an illusion not creep into the word objectivity even in its highest interpretation? According to this interpretation, the word means a condition in the historian which permits him to observe an event in all its motivations and consequences so purely that it has no effect at all on his own subjectivity: it is analogous to that aesthetic phenomenon of detachment from personal interest with which a painter sees in a stormy landscape with thunder and lightning, or a rolling sea, only the picture of them within him, the phenomenon of complete absorption in the things themselves: it is a superstition, however, that the picture which these things evoke in a man possessing such a disposition is a true reproduction of the empirical nature of the things themselves. Or is it supposed that at this moment the things as it were engrave, counterfeit, photograph themselves by their own action on a purely passive medium?

This would be mythology, and bad mythology at that: and it is forgotten, moreover, that that moment is precisely the strongest and most spontaneous moment of creation in the depths of the artist, a moment of composition of the highest sort, the outcome of which may be an artistically true painting but cannot be an historically true one. To think of history objectively in this fashion is the silent work of the dramatist; that is to say, to think of all things in relation to all others and to weave the isolated event into the whole: always with the presupposition that if a unity of plan does not already reside in things it must be implanted into them. Thus man spins his web over the past and subdues it, thus he gives expression to his artistic drive – but not to his drive towards truth or justice. Objectivity and justice have nothing to do with one another. A historiography could be imagined which had in it not a drop of common empirical truth and yet could lay claim to the highest degree of objectivity. Indeed, Grillparzer ventures to declare: 'What is history but the way in which the spirit of man apprehends *events impenetrable to him*; unites things when God alone knows whether they belong together; substitutes something comprehensible for what is incomprehensible; imposes his concept of purpose from without upon a whole which, if it possesses a purpose, does so only inherently; and assumes the operation of chance where a thousand little causes have been at work. All human beings have at the same time their own individual necessity, so that millions of courses run parallel beside one another in straight or crooked lines, frustrate or advance one another, strive forwards or backwards, and thus assume for one another the character of chance, and so, quite apart from the influence of the occurrences of nature, make it impossible to establish any all-embracing necessity prevailing throughout all events.' But it is exactly this kind of necessity that is supposed to be brought to light as the result of that 'objective' view of things! This is a presupposition which, if enunciated by an historian as an article of faith, would assume a very strange shape; Schiller is quite clear as to the purely subjective nature of this assumption when he says of the historian: 'one phenomenon after another begins to forsake the realm of blind chance and limitless freedom and to take its place as a fitting member of a harmonious whole – *which whole is, of course, present only in his imagination*'. But what is one to make of this assertion, hovering as it does between tautology and nonsense, by one celebrated historical virtuoso: 'the fact of the matter is that all human actions are subject to the mighty and irresistible direction of the course of things, though it may often not be apparent'? Such a proposition is not, as it might perhaps seem, enigmatic wisdom in the shape of plain foolishness, as when Goethe's court gardener says 'Nature may let itself be forced but it cannot be compelled', or in the fairground placard reported by Swift: 'Here can be seen the biggest elephant in the world except itself.' For how are human actions and the course of things to be distinguished from one another? It seems to me in general that historians such as the one we have just quoted cease to instruct as soon as they begin to generalize and then reveal the weakness they feel in the dark obscurities they employ. In other sciences the generalizations are the most important thing, inasmuch as they contain the laws: but if such propositions as that quoted are intended to count as laws, then one must object that in that case the work of the historiographer is wasted; for whatever truth remains in such propositions after the obscurities referred to have been removed is something completely familiar and even trivial; for it will be obvious to everyone through every kind of experience down to the very smallest. To incommode whole nations and expend years of wearisome toil on it, however, is merely to pile experiment upon experiment long after the law intended to be extracted from them has been amply demonstrated: a senseless excess of experimentation which has in fact plagued the natural sciences since the time of Zöllner. If the value of a drama lay solely in its conclusion, the drama itself would be merely the most wearisome and indirect way possible of reaching this goal; and so I hope that the significance of history will not be thought to lie in its general propositions, as if these were the flower and fruit of the whole endeavour, but that its value will be seen to consist in its taking a familiar, perhaps commonplace theme, an everyday melody, and composing inspired variations on it, enhancing it, elevating it to a comprehensive symbol, and thus disclosing in the original theme a whole world of profundity, power and beauty.

For this, however, there is required above all great artistic facility, creative vision, loving absorption in the empirical data, the capacity to imagine the further development of a given type – in any event, objectivity is required, but as a positive quality. So often objectivity is only a phrase. Instead of the outwardly tranquil but inwardly flashing eye of the artist there is the affectation of tranquillity; just as a lack of feeling and moral strength is accustomed to disguise itself as incisive coldness and detachment. In certain cases banality of ideas, the everyday wisdom which seems calm and tranquil only because it is tedious, ventures to pose as that artistic condition in which the subject becomes silent and wholly imperceptible. What is then preferred is that which produces no emotion at all and the driest phrase is the right phrase. One goes so far, indeed, as to believe that he to whom a moment of the past *means nothing at all* is the proper man to describe it. This is frequently the relationship between classicists and the Greeks they study: they mean nothing to one another – a state of affairs called 'objectivity'! It is precisely where the highest and rarest is to be represented that this ostentatious indifference becomes most infuriating – for it is the *vanity* of the historian which is responsible for it. Such authors incline one to agree with the proposition that a man possesses vanity to the degree that he lacks understanding. No, at any rate be honest! Do not seek the appearance of justice if you are not called to the dreadful vocation of the just man. As though it were the task of every age to have to be just towards everything that has ever existed! It could even be said that ages and generations never do have the right to judge previous ages and generations: such an uncomfortable mission falls only to individuals, and these of the rarest kind. Who compels you to judge? And, moreover – test yourself to see whether you could be just if you wanted to be! As judge, you must stand higher than he who is to be judged; whereas all you are is subsequent to him. The guests who come last to table have to be content with the last places: and do you want the first? Then at least perform some high and great deed; perhaps then they really will make room for you, even if you do come last.

If you are to venture to interpret the past you can do so only out of the fullest exertion of the vigour of the present: only when you put forth your noblest qualities in all their strength will you divine what is worth knowing and preserving in the past. Like to like! Otherwise you will draw the past down to you. Do not believe historiography that does not spring from the head of the rarest minds; and you will know the quality of a mind when it is obliged to express something universal or to repeat something universally known: the genuine historian must possess the power to remint the universally known into something never heard of before, and to express the universal so simply and profoundly that the simplicity is lost in the profundity and the profundity in the simplicity. No one can be a great historian, an artist and a shallow-pate at the same time: on the other hand, one should not underrate the workmen who sift and carry merely because they can certainly never become great historians; but even less should one confuse them with them, but regard them rather as the necessary apprentices and handymen in the service of the master: much as the French used, with greater naivety than is possible to a German, to speak of the *historiens de M. Thiers*. These workmen are gradually to become great scholars, but cannot for that reason ever be masters. A great scholar and a great shallowpate – these two go rather better under one hat.

To sum up: history is written by the experienced and superior man. He who has not experienced greater and more exalted things than others will not know how to interpret the great and exalted things of the past. When the past speaks it always speaks as an oracle: only if you are an architect of the future and know the present will you understand it. The extraordinary degree and extent of the influence exercised by Delphi is nowadays explained principally by the fact that the Delphic priests had an exact knowledge of the past; now it would be right to say that only he who constructs the future has a right to judge the past. If you look ahead and set yourself a great goal, you at the same time restrain that rank analytical impulse which makes the present into a desert and all tranquillity, all peaceful growth and maturing almost impossible. Draw about yourself the fence of a great and comprehensive hope, of a hope-filled striving. Form within yourself an image to which the future shall correspond, and forget the superstition that you are epigones. You will have enough to ponder and to invent when you reflect on the life of the future; but do not ask of history that it should show you the How? and the Wherewith? to this life. If, on the other hand, you acquire a living knowledge of the history of great men, you will learn from it a supreme commandment: to become mature and to flee from that paralyzing upbringing of the present age which sees its advantage in preventing your growth so as to rule and exploit you to the full while you are still immature. And if you want biographies, do not desire those which bear the legend 'Herr So-and-So and his age', but those upon whose title-page there would stand 'a fighter against his age'. Satiate your soul with Plutarch and when you believe in his heroes dare at the same time to believe in yourself. With a hundred such men – raised in this unmodern way, that is to say become mature and accustomed to the heroic – the whole noisy sham-culture of our age could now be silenced for ever. –

7

When the historical sense reigns *without restraint*, and all its consequences are realized, it uproots the future because it destroys illusions and robs the things that exist of the atmosphere in which alone they can live. Historical justice, even when it is genuine and practised with the purest of intentions, is therefore a dreadful virtue because it always undermines the living thing and brings it down: its judgment is always annihilating. If the historical drive does not also contain a drive to construct, if the purpose of destroying and clearing is not to allow a future already alive in anticipation to raise its house on the ground thus liberated, if justice alone prevails, then the instinct for creation will be enfeebled and discouraged. A religion, for example, which is intended to be transformed into historical knowledge under the hegemony of pure historical justice, a religion which is intended to be understood through and through as an object of science and learning, will when this process is at an end also be found to have been destroyed. The reason is that historical verification always brings to light so much that is false, crude, inhuman, absurd, violent that the mood of pious illusion in which alone anything that wants to live can live necessarily crumbles away: for it is only in love, only when shaded by the illusion produced by love, that is to say in the unconditional faith in right and perfection, that man is creative. Anything that constrains a man to love less than unconditionally has severed the roots of his strength: he will wither away, that is to say become dishonest. In producing this effect, history is the antithesis of art: and only if history can endure to be transformed into a work of art will it perhaps be able to preserve instincts or even evoke them. Such a historiography would, however, be altogether contrary to the analytical and inartistic tendencies of our time, which would indeed declare it false. But a history which, lacking the direction of an inner drive to construct, does nothing but destroy, in the long run denaturizes its instruments: for such men destroy illusions and 'he who destroys the illusions in himself and others is punished by nature, the cruellest tyrant'. For a good length of time, it is true, one can occupy oneself with history in a perfectly innocent and harmless way, as though it were merely an occupation like any other; recent theology especially seems to have entered into partnership with history out of pure innocence, and even now it almost refuses to see that, probably much against its will, it has thereby placed itself in the service of the Voltairean *écrasez*.* No one should suppose that this development conceals a powerful new constructive instinct – unless, that is, one is to regard the so-called Protestant Union† as the work of a new religion, and perhaps the jurist Holtzendorf (the editor and prefacer of the even more problematical Protestant Bible) as John the Baptist at the river Jordan. For some time yet the Hegelian philosophy still smouldering in older heads may assist in propagating this innocence, perhaps by teaching one how to distinguish the 'idea of Christianity' from its manifold imperfect 'phenomenal forms' and even to convince oneself that it is the 'preferred tendency of the idea' to reveal itself in ever purer forms, and at last in its purest, most transparent, indeed hardly visible form, in the brains of the contemporary *theologus liberalis vulgaris*. But when he hears these purest-of-the-pure Christians speaking of earlier impure Christians the impartial auditor often has the impression that what is being spoken of is not Christianity at all but – well, what are we to think? When we find the 'greatest theologian of the century'‡ characterizing Christianity as the religion which can 'discover itself in all existing and in several other barely possible religions', and when the 'true church' is supposed to be that which 'becomes a flowing mass, where there are no contours, where every part is now here, now there, and everything blends peacefully together' – again, what are we to think?

What one can learn in the case of Christianity – that under the influence of a historical treatment it has become denaturized, until a

---

*'Voltairean *écrasez*': alludes to Voltaire's motto 'écrasez l'infame!' – destroy the infamous thing (i.e. the Church).

†Protestant Union: the military alliance formed between 1608 and 1621 by the Protestant princes of Germany.

‡'greatest theologian of the century': Schleiermacher (see glossary).

completely historical, that is to say just treatment resolves it into pure knowledge about Christianity and thereby destroys it – can be studied in everything else that possesses life: that it ceases to live when it is dissected completely, and lives a painful and morbid life when one begins to practise historical dissection upon it. There are people who believe that German music could have a transforming and reforming effect on the Germans: they are angered, and consider it an injustice against the most vigorous part of our culture, when they see such men as Mozart and Beethoven already engulfed by all the learned dust of biography and compelled by the torture-instruments of historical criticism to answer a thousand impertinent questions. Does it not mean its premature death, or at least paralysis, when that, the living effects of which are not yet exhausted, is subjected to curious investigation of the countless minutiae of its life and works, and when problems of knowledge are sought where one ought to learn to live and forget all problems? Imagine a couple of these modern biographers transported to the birthplace of Christianity or of the Lutheran Reformation; their sober, pragmatic curiosity would have exactly sufficed to render any *actio in distans* impossible: just as the most wretched little animal can prevent the mightiest oak-tree from coming into existence by eating the acorn. All living things require an atmosphere around them, a mysterious misty vapour; if they are deprived of this envelope, if a religion, an art, a genius is condemned to revolve as a star without atmosphere, we should no longer be surprised if they quickly wither and grow hard and unfruitful. It is the same with all great things, 'which never succeed without some illusion', as Hans Sachs says in the *Meistersinger*.

But every nation, too, indeed every human being that wants to become *mature* requires a similar enveloping illusion, a similar protective and veiling cloud; nowadays, however, maturity as such is hated because history is held in greater honour than life. There is, indeed, rejoicing that now 'science is beginning to dominate life': that condition may, possibly, be attained; but life thus dominated is not of much value because it is far less *living* and guarantees far less life for the future than did a former life dominated not by knowledge but by instinct and powerful illusions. But the present age is, as aforesaid, supposed to be an age, not of whole, mature and harmonious personalities, but of labour of the greatest possible common utility. That means, however, that men have to be adjusted to the purposes of the age so as to be ready for employment as soon as possible: they must labour in the factories of the general good before they are mature, indeed so that they shall not become mature – for this would be a luxury which would deprive the 'labour market' of a great deal of its workforce. Some birds are blinded so that they may sing more beautifully; I do not think the men of today sing more beautifully than their grandfathers, but I know they have been blinded. The means, the infamous means used to blind them, however, is *too bright, too sudden, too varying light*. The young man is swept along through all the millennia: youths who understand nothing of war, diplomatic action, commercial policy are thought fit to be introduced to political history. But as the youth races through history, so do we modern men race through art galleries and listen to concerts. We feel that one thing sounds different from another, that one thing produces a different effect from another: increasingly to lose this sense of strangeness, no longer to be very much surprised at anything, finally to be pleased with everything – that is then no doubt called the historical sense, historical culture. To speak without euphemism: the mass of the influx is so great, the strange, barbaric and violent things that press upon the youthful soul do so with such overwhelming power that its only refuge is in an intentional stupidity. Where there has been a stronger and more subtle awareness, another emotion has no doubt also appeared: disgust. The young man has become so homeless and doubts all concepts and all customs. He now knows: every age is different, it does not matter what you are like. In melancholy indifference he lets opinion after opinion pass him by and he understands how Hölderlin felt when he read Diogenes Laertius on the lives and teachings of the Greek philosophers: 'I have again found here what I have often before discovered, that the transitoriness and changeableness of human thoughts and systems strike me as being almost more tragic than the destinies which alone are usually called real.' No, to be so overwhelmed and bewildered by history is, as the ancients demonstrate, not at all necessary for youth, but in the highest degree dangerous to it, as the moderns demonstrate. But now notice the actual student of history, the heir of an enfeeblement already visible almost before he has ceased to be a boy. He has acquired the 'methods' for doing work of his own, the right technique and the noble bearing of the master; a wholly isolated little chapter of the past has fallen victim to his astuteness and the methods he has learned; he has already produced, indeed to use a prouder word, he has 'created' something, he has now become an active servant of truth and a lord in the universal empire of history. If already as a boy he was 'ripe', now he is over-ripe: one needs only to shake him and wisdom comes clattering down into one's lap; but the wisdom is rotten and there is a worm in every apple. Believe me: if men are to labour and be useful in the factory of science before they are mature, science will soon be ruined just as effectively as the slaves thus employed too early. I regret the need to make use of the jargon of the slave-owner and employer of labour to describe things which in themselves ought to be thought of as free of utility and raised above the necessities of life; but the words 'factory', 'labour market', 'supply', 'making profitable', and whatever auxiliary verbs egoism now employs, come unbidden to the lips when one wishes to describe the most recent generation of men of learning. Sterling mediocrity grows even more mediocre, science ever more profitable in the economic sense. Actually our most recent men of learning are wise on one point, and on that they are, I admit, wiser than anyone has ever been, but on all other points they are infinitely different – to use a cautious expression – from any man of learning of the old stamp. This notwithstanding, they demand honours and advantages for themselves, as though the state and public opinion were duty bound to accept the new coins as being of equal value to the old. The carters have made a contract with one another and by restamping themselves as geniuses have decreed that genius is superfluous; probably a later age will see that their buildings are carted together, not constructed. Those who unwearyingly repeat the modern call to battle and sacrifice 'Division of labour! Fall in!' must for once be told in round and plain terms: if you want to push science forward as quickly as possible you will succeed in destroying it as quickly as possible; just as a hen perishes if it is compelled to lay eggs too quickly. Science has certainly been pushed forward at an astonishing speed over the past decades: but just look at the men of learning, the exhausted hens. They are in truth not 'harmonious' natures; they can only cackle more than ever because they lay eggs more often: though the eggs, to be sure, have got smaller and smaller (though the books have got thicker and thicker). As the final and most natural outcome we have the universally admired 'popularization' (together with 'feminization' and 'infantization') of science, that is to say the infamous trimming of the coat of science to fit the body of the 'general public' – to employ a cutting expression for an activity suited to tailors. Goethe saw this as a misuse of science and demanded that the sciences should affect the outside world only through *enhanced practical application*. The older generation of men of learning, moreover, had good grounds for regarding such a misuse as difficult and burdensome: it is on equally good grounds that the younger generation finds it easy, for, except in the case of a tiny corner of knowledge, they themselves are very much 'general public' and share its needs. They have only to sit at their ease for once and they are able to open to the curiosity of this general populace even the little realm of their own special study. This relaxation is afterwards called 'the man of learning modestly condescending to his people': while in reality the man of learning has, to the extent that he is not a man of learning but one of the mob, descended only to his own level. Create for yourselves the concept of a 'people': it could never be too exalted or too noble a concept. If you thought well of the people you would show them compassion and would guard against offering them your historical aqua fortis as a refreshing draught of life. But in your hearts you despise them, for you cannot bring yourself seriously to care about their future, and your behaviour is that of practical pessimists, by which I mean men directed by a presentiment of coming disaster and therefore sluggishly indifferent to the wellbeing of others and to your own as well. If only the ground will go on bearing *us*! And if it ceases to bear us, that too is very well: – that is their feeling and thus they live an *ironic* existence.

8

It may seem strange, though it ought not to seem self-contradictory, when I ascribe a kind of *ironic self-awareness* to an age accustomed to break into such loud and innocent rejoicing at its historical culture, and say that it is infused with a presentiment that there is really nothing to rejoice about and a fear that all the merriment of historical knowledge will soon be over and done with. Goethe presented to us a comparable enigma in regard to the individual personality in his noteworthy account of Newton: he discovers at the foundation (or, more correctly, at the highest point) of his being 'a troubled presentiment that he is in error', the momentary expression, as it were, of a superior consciousness that has attained to a certain ironical overview of his inherent nature. So it is that we find in precisely the greatest and more highly developed historical men a suppressed consciousness, often amounting to a general scepticism, of how great an absurdity and superstition it is to believe that the education of a nation has to be as preponderantly historical as it is now; for precisely the most vigorous nations, vigorous in deeds and works, lived differently from this and raised their children differently. But that absurdity and superstition is suited to us – so runs the sceptical objection – to us, the latecomers, the last pale offspring of mightier and happier races, to us who are the fulfilment of Hesiod's prophesy that men would one day be born already grey-haired and that as soon as he saw that sign Zeus would eradicate this race. Historical culture is indeed a kind of inborn grey-hairedness, and those who bear its mark from childhood must instinctively believe in the *old age of mankind*: to age, however, there pertains an appropriate senile occupation, that of looking back, of reckoning up, of closing accounts, of seeking consolation through remembering what has been, in short historical culture. But the human race is a tough and persistent thing and will not permit its progress – forwards or backwards – to be viewed in terms of millennia, or indeed hardly in terms of hundreds of millennia; that is to say, it will not be viewed as a whole *at all* by that infinitesimal atom, the individual man. What is there in a couple of thousand years (or in other words the space of 34 consecutive generations of 60 years each) which permits us to speak of the 'youth' of mankind at the beginning and the 'old age' of mankind at the end? Is there not concealed in this paralysing belief that humanity is already declining a misunderstanding of a Christian theological idea inherited from the Middle Ages, the idea that the end of the world is coming, that we are fearfully awaiting the Last Judgment? Is the increasing need for historical judgment not that same idea in a new dress, as though our age, being the ultimate age, were empowered to exercise over all the past that universal judgment which Christian belief never supposed would be pronounced by men but by 'the Son of Man'? In earlier times this '*memento mori*' addressed to mankind as a whole as well as to individual men was an ever-painful goad and as it were the high point of medieval learning and conscience. Its modern antithesis, '*memento vivere*', is, to speak frankly, still a somewhat modest little sound rather than a full-throated one, and has something almost dishonest about it. For mankind continues to treasure its *memento mori* and reveals the fact through its universal need for history: knowledge, its mightiest wing-beats notwithstanding, has not been able to soar aloft, a profound sense of hopelessness remains and has assumed that historical colouring with which all higher education and culture is now saddened and darkened. A religion which of all the hours of a man's life holds the last to be the most important, which prophesies an end to

101

all life on earth and condemns all who live to live in the fifth act of a tragedy, may well call forth the profoundest and noblest powers, but it is inimical to all new planting, bold experimentation, free aspiration; it resists all flight into the unknown because it loves and hopes for nothing there: it allows what is becoming to force its way up only with reluctance, and then when the time is ripe it sacrifices it or sets it aside as a seducer to existence, as a liar as to the value of existence. What the Florentines did when, under the influence of Savonarola's preaching, they made that celebrated holocaust of paintings, manuscripts, mirrors and masks, Christianity would like to do to every culture which stimulates continued striving and bears that *memento vivere* as its motto; and if it proves impossible to do this in a blunt and direct manner, that is to say by force, it nonetheless achieves its aim by allying itself with historical culture, usually without the latter's knowledge moreover, and speaking henceforth through its mouth rejects with a shrug everything still coming into being and smothers it in the awareness of being a latecomer and epigone, in short of being born grey-haired. Austere and profoundly serious reflection on the worthlessness of all that has occurred, on the ripeness of the world for judgment, is dissipated into the sceptical attitude that it is at any rate as well to know about all that has occurred, since it is too late to do anything better. Thus the historical sense makes its servants passive and retrospective; and almost the only time the sufferer from the fever of history becomes active is when this sense is in abeyance through momentary forgetfulness – though even then, as soon as the act is finished he at once dissects it, prevents it from producing any further effects by analysing it, and finally skins it for the purpose of 'historical study'. In this sense we are still living in the Middle Ages and history is still disguised theology: just as the reverence with which the unlearned laity treat the learned class is inherited from the reverence with which it treated the clergy. What one formerly gave to the church one now gives, though more sparingly, to learning: but that one gives at all is an effect of the church's former influence – the modern spirit, as is well known, is somewhat niggardly and unskilled in the noble virtue of generosity.

Perhaps this observation will not be very acceptable, perhaps as unacceptable as my derivation of our excess of history from the medieval *memento mori* and the hopelessness in regard to all coming ages of human existence which Christianity bears in its heart. If so, you might try to replace this explanation, which I offer only with some hesitation, with a better one; for the origin of historical culture

– its quite radical conflict with the spirit of any 'new age', any 'modern awareness' – this origin *must* itself be known historically, history *must* itself resolve the problem of history, knowledge *must* turn its sting against itself – this threefold *must* is the imperative of the 'new age', supposing this age really does contain anything new, powerful, original and promising more life. Or is it actually the case that we Germans – to leave the Romance nations out of account – must always be no more than 'heirs' in all the higher affairs of culture, because that is all we *can* ever be; a proposition once memorably expressed by Wilhelm Wackernagel: 'We Germans are a nation of heirs, with all our higher knowledge, even with our beliefs, no more than heirs of the world of antiquity; even those hostile to it continually breathe the immortal spirit of classical culture beside the spirit of Christianity, and if anyone succeeded in excluding these two elements from the atmosphere which surrounds the inner world of man there would not be much left to prolong a life of the spirit.' And even if we Germans were really no more than heirs – to be able to look upon such a culture as *that* as our rightful inheritance would make the appellation 'heirs' the greatest and proudest possible: yet we would nonetheless be obliged to ask whether it really was our eternal destiny to be *pupils of declining antiquity*: at some time or other we might be permitted gradually to set our goal higher and more distant, some time or other we ought to be allowed to claim credit for having developed the spirit of Alexandrian-Roman culture so nobly and fruitfully – among other means through our universal history – that we might now as a reward be permitted to set ourselves the even mightier task of striving to get behind and beyond this Alexandrian world and boldly to seek our models in the original ancient Greek world of greatness, naturalness and humanity. *But there we also discover the reality of an essentially unhistorical culture and one which is nonetheless, or rather on that account, an inexpressibly richer and more vital culture.* Even if we Germans were in fact nothing but successors – we could not be anything greater or prouder than successors if we had appropriated such a culture and were the heirs and successors of that.

What I mean by this – and it is all I mean – is that the thought of being epigones, which can often be a painful thought, is also capable of evoking great effects and grand hopes for the future in both an individual and in a nation, provided we regard ourselves as the heirs and successors of the astonishing powers of antiquity and see in this our honour and our spur. What I do not mean, therefore, is that we should live as pale and stunted late descendants of strong races coldly prolonging their life as antiquarians and gravediggers. Late descendants of that sort do indeed live an ironic existence: annihilation follows at the heels of the limping gait of their life; they shudder at it when they rejoice in the past, for they are embodied memory yet their remembrance is meaningless if they have no heirs. Thus they are seized by the troubled presentiment that their life is an injustice, since there will be no future life to justify it.

But suppose we imagine these antiquarian latecomers suddenly exchanging this painfully ironic modesty for a state of shamelessness; suppose we imagine them announcing in shrill tones: the race is now at its zenith, for only now does it possess knowledge of itself, only now has it revealed itself to itself – we should then behold a spectacle through which, as in a parable, the enigmatic significance for German culture of a certain very celebrated philosophy would be unriddled. I believe there has been no dangerous vacillation or crisis of German culture this century that has not been rendered more dangerous by the enormous and still continuing influence of this philosophy, the Hegelian. The belief that one is a latecomer of the ages is, in any case, paralysing and depressing: but it must appear dreadful and devastating when such a belief one day by a bold inversion raises this latecomer to godhood as the true meaning and goal of all previous events, when his miserable condition is equated with a completion of world-history. Such a point of view has accustomed the Germans to talk of a 'world-process' and to justify their own age as the necessary result of this world-process; such a point of view has set history, insofar as history is 'the concept that realizes itself', 'the dialectics of the spirit of the peoples' and the 'world-tribunal', in place of the other spiritual powers, art and religion, as the sole sovereign power.

History understood in this Hegelian fashion has been mockingly called God's vicissitudes on earth, though the god referred to has been created only by the history. This god, however, became transparent and comprehensible to himself within the Hegelian craniums and has already ascended all the dialectically possible steps of his evolution up to this self-revelation: so that for Hegel the climax and terminus of the world-process coincided with his own existence in Berlin. Indeed, he ought to have said that everything that came after him was properly to be considered merely as a musical coda to the world-historical rondo or, even more properly, as superfluous. He did not say it: instead he implanted into the generation thoroughly leavened by him that admiration for the 'power of history' which in practice transforms every moment into a naked admiration for success and leads to an idolatry of the factual: which idolatry is now generally described by the very mythological yet quite idiomatic expression 'to accommodate oneself to the facts'. But he who has once learned to bend his back and bow his head before the 'power of history' at last nods 'Yes' like a Chinese mechanical doll to every power, whether it be a government or public opinion or a numerical majority, and moves his limbs to the precise rhythm at which any 'power' whatever pulls the strings. If every success is a rational necessity, if every event is a victory of the logical or the 'idea' – then down on your knees quickly and do reverence to the whole stepladder of 'success'! What, are there no longer any living mythologies? What, the religions are dying out? Just behold the religion of the power of history, regard the priests of the mythology of the idea and their battered knees! Is it too much to say that all the virtues now attend on this new faith? Or is it not selflessness when the historical man lets himself be emptied until he is no more than an objective sheet of plate glass? Is it not magnanimity when, by worshipping in every force the force itself, one renounces all force of one's own in Heaven and upon earth? Is it not justice always to hold the scales of the powers in one's hands and to watch carefully to see which tends to be the stronger and heavier? And what a school of decorum is such a way of contemplating history! To take everything objectively, to grow angry at nothing, to love nothing, to understand everything, how soft and pliable that makes one; and even if someone raised in this school should for once get publicly angry, that is still cause for rejoicing, for one realizes it is intended only for artistic effect, it is *ira* and *studium* and yet altogether *sine ira et studio.**

How obsolete and old-fashioned my objections to this complex of mythology and virtue are! But I must out with them, even though they excite laughter. I would say therefore: history always inculcates: 'there was once', morality: 'you ought not to' or 'you ought not to have'. Thus history amounts to a compendium of factual immorality. How far astray he would go who regarded history as being at the same time the judge of this factual immorality! Morality is offended, for example, by the fact that a Raphael had to die at thirty-six: such a being ought not to die. If, in the face of this, you wanted to come to

---

ira: anger; *studium*: zeal; *sine ira et studio*: without anger and without zeal

the aid of history as apologists of the factual, you would say: he had expressed everything that was in him, had he lived longer he would have produced only a repetition of the beauty he had created already, and so forth. In that way you become Devil's advocates: you make success, the factual, into your idol, while in reality the factual is always stupid and has at all times resembled a calf rather than a god. As apologists of history you have, moreover, ignorance as a prompter: for it is only because you do not know what such a *natura naturans** as Raphael is that you are not incensed to know that it once was but will never be again. We have recently been informed that, with his eighty-two years, Goethe outlived himself: yet I would gladly exchange a couple of Goethe's 'outlived' years for whole cartloads of fresh modern lifetimes, so as to participate in such conversations as Goethe conducted with Eckermann and thus be preserved from all and any up-to-date instruction from the legionaries of the moment. In relation to such dead men, how few of the living have a right to live at all! That the many are alive and those few live no longer is nothing but a brute truth, that is to say an incorrigible stupidity, a blunt 'thus it is' in opposition to morality's 'it ought not to be thus'. Yes, in opposition to morality! For speak of any virtue you will, of justice, magnanimity, bravery, of the wisdom and sympathy of man – in every case it becomes a virtue through rising against that blind power of the factual and tyranny of the actual and by submitting to laws that are not the laws of the fluctuations of history. It always swims against the tide of history, whether by combating its passions as the most immediate stupid fact of its existence or by dedicating itself to truthfulness as falsehood spins its glittering web around it. If history in general were nothing more than 'the world-system of passion and error', mankind would have to read it as Goethe advised his readers to read *Werther*: as if it called to them 'be a man and do not follow after me!' Fortunately, however, it also preserves the memory of the great fighters *against history*, that is to say against the blind power of the actual, and puts itself in the pillory by exalting precisely these men as the real historical natures who bothered little with the 'thus it is' so as to follow 'thus it shall be' with a more cheerful pride. Not to bear their race to the grave, but to found a new generation of this race – that is what impels them ceaselessly forward: and even if they themselves are late-born – there is a way of living which will

---

**natura naturans*: Spinoza's term for God under the aspect of creating nature, as opposed to created nature – as the cause of all things.

make them forget it – coming generations will know them only as first-born.

9

Is our age perhaps such a first-born? – The vehemence of its historical sense is so great and is expressed in so universal and altogether unrestrained a manner, that future ages will in fact count it a first-born at any rate in this respect – assuming, that is, that there will be any *future ages* in the cultural sense. But it is precisely this fact which evokes in us a grave doubt. Close beside the pride of modern man there stands his ironic view of himself, his awareness that he has to live in an historicizing, as it were a twilight mood, his fear that his youthful hopes and energy will not survive into the future. Here and there one goes further, into *cynicism*, and justifies the course of history, indeed the entire evolution of the world, in a manner especially adapted to the use of modern man, according to the cynical canon: as things are they had to be, as men now are they were bound to become, none may resist this inevitability. The pleasant feeling produced by this kind of cynicism is the refuge of him who cannot endure the ironical state; and the last decade has, moreover, made him a present of one of its fairest inventions, a full and rounded phrase to describe this cynicism: it calls his way of living in the fashion of the age and wholly without reflection 'the total surrender of the personality to the world-process'. The personality and the world-process! The world-process and the personality of the flea! If only one were not compelled everlastingly to hear the hyperbole of hyperboles, the word 'world, world, world' – when one ought more honestly to speak of 'man, man, man'! Heirs of the Greeks and Romans? of Christianity? To these cynics that seems nothing; but heirs of the world-process! Summit and target of the world-process! Meaning and solution of all the riddles of evolution come to light in modern man, the ripest fruit of the tree of knowledge! – that I call an ecstatic feeling of pride; it is by this sign that one can recognize the first-born of all ages, even though they may have also come last. Contemplation of history has never flown so far, not even in dreams; for now the history of mankind is only the continuation of the history of animals and plants; even in the profoundest depths of the sea the universal historian still finds traces of himself as living slime; gazing in amazement, as at a miracle, at the tremendous course mankind has already run, his gaze trembles at that even more astonishing miracle, modern man himself, who is capable of surveying this course. He stands high and proud upon the pyramid of the world-process; as he lays the keystone of his knowledge at the top of it he seems to call out to nature all around him: 'We have reached the goal, we are the goal, we are nature perfected.'

Overproud European of the nineteenth century, you are raving! Your knowledge does not perfect nature, it only destroys your own nature. Compare for once the heights of your capacity for knowledge with the depths of your incapacity for action. It is true you climb upon the sunbeams of knowledge up to Heaven, but you also climb down to chaos. Your manner of moving, that of climbing upon knowledge, is your fatality; the ground sinks away from you into the unknown; there is no longer any support for your life, only spider's threads which every new grasp of knowledge tears apart. – But enough of this seriousness, since it is also possible to view the matter more cheerfully.

The madly thoughtless shattering and dismantling of all foundations, their dissolution into a continual evolving that flows ceaselessly away, the tireless unspinning and historicizing of all there has ever been by modern man, the great cross-spider at the node of the cosmic web – all this may concern and dismay moralists, artists, the pious, even statesmen; *we* shall for once let it cheer us by looking at it in the glittering magic mirror of a *philosophical parodist* in whose head the age has come to an ironical awareness of itself, and has done so with a clarity which (to speak Goethean) 'amounts to infamy'. Hegel once taught us: 'when the spirit changes direction, we philosophers too are there': our age changed direction, to self-irony, and behold! E. von Hartmann too was there and indited his celebrated philosophy of the unconscious, or – to speak more clearly – his philosophy of unconscious irony. We have seldom read a merrier invention or a more philosophical piece of roguery than this of Hartmann; whoever is not enlightened by it as to the nature of *becoming*, not inwardly cleared out and set in order, indeed, in regard to that matter, is truly ripe and ready for becoming a has-been. The beginning and goal of the world-process, from the first stab of consciousness to its being hurled back into nothingness, together with an exact description of the task of our generation within this world-process, all presented direct from that cleverly discovered well of inspiration, the unconscious, and gleaming with apocalyptic light, all so deceptively mimicking straight-faced earnestness as though it were a genuine serious philosophy and not only a joke philosophy – such a production marks its creator as one of the first philosophical parodists of all time; let us therefore sacrifice on his altar, let us sacrifice to him, the discoverer of a true universal medicine, a lock of hair – to steal one of Schleiermacher's terms for expressing admiration. For what medicine could be more efficacious against excess of historical culture than Hartmann's parody of world-history?

Expressed without the rhetoric, what Hartmann proclaims to us from the smokey tripod of unconscious irony amounts to this: he tells us it would be quite sufficient, for our time to be exactly as it is, to bring about, eventually, a condition in which people would find this existence intolerable: which we truly believe. This dreadful ossification of our age, this restless rattling of the bones – such as David Strauss has naively described to us as the fairest factuality – is justified by Hartmann, not only from behind, *ex causis efficientibus*, but even from in front, *ex causa finali*; the rogue illumines our age with the light of the Last Day, and it turns out that our age is a very fine one, especially for him who wants to suffer as acutely as possible from the indigestibility of life and for whom therefore that Last Day cannot come quickly enough. It is true that Hartmann calls the time of life mankind is now approaching its 'years of manhood': but by this he means the happy condition in which all that is left is 'solid mediocrity', art is that which 'perhaps offers entertainment to the Berlin businessman of an evening', in which 'the age no longer requires genius, because it would mean casting pearls before swine or because the age has advanced beyond the stage appropriate to geniuses to a more important one' – to a stage of social evolution, that is to say, at which every worker, 'having a workday which leaves him adequate leisure for intellectual training, leads a comfortable existence'. Rogue of rogues, you give voice to the longings of contemporary mankind: but you likewise know the spectre that will stand at the end of these years of manhood as an outcome of that intellectual training in solid mediocrity – disgust. Things are already in a visibly sorry state, but they will get very much sorrier, 'the Anti-Christ is visibly extending his influence wider and wider' – but that is how it *must* be, that is what it *must* come to, for the road we have taken can lead only to disgust with all existence. 'Let us therefore press the world-process vigorously forward as workers in the vineyard of the Lord, for it is the process alone that can lead to redemption!'

The vineyard of the Lord! The process! Redemption! Who cannot see and hear in this how historical culture, which knows only the word 'becoming', is here deliberately disguising itself as a parodistic deformity, how from behind a grotesque mask it utters the most mischievous nonsense about itself? For what does this last roguish summons to the workers in the vineyard really demand of them? What work are they to press vigorously forward? Or, to put the question differently: what does the historically cultivated man, the modern fanatic of the process swimming and drowning in the stream of becoming, have left to do if he is one day to harvest that disgust we have spoken of, the most exquisite grape of the vineyard? – He has to do nothing but go on living as he has lived hitherto, go on loving what he has loved hitherto, go on hating what he has hated hitherto, and go on reading the newspapers he has read hitherto; for him there is only one sin – to live differently from the way in which he has hitherto lived. How he has hitherto lived, however, is recorded for us in giant monumental characters on that celebrated page which has sent the whole contemporary cultured rabble into ecstasies because they see in them their own justification blazing forth in apocalyptic light. For what the unconscious parodist demands of each individual is 'the total surrender of the personality to the world-process for the sake of its goal, world-redemption'; or even more clearly: 'affirmation of the will to live is proclaimed as for the present the only right course; for only in a total surrender to life and its sorrows, and not in a cowardly renunciation and withdrawal, is anything to be achieved for the world-process', 'the striving for denial of the individual will is as foolish and useless as, indeed even more foolish than, suicide'. 'The thinking reader will understand without further elucidation what shape a practical philosophy erected on these principles would assume, and that such a philosophy can embody, not a sundering from life, but only the fullest reconciliation with it.'

The thinking reader will understand; and one could misunderstand Hartmann? And how unspeakably amusing it is that he should be misunderstood! Are the contemporary Germans a very refined people? A worthy Englishman finds them lacking in 'delicacy of perception', and ventures indeed to say: 'in the German mind there does seem to be something splay, something blunt-edged, unhandy and infelicitous' – would the great German parodist contradict this? It is true that, according to him, we are approaching 'that ideal condition in which the human race creates its history with full conscious awareness': but we are patently still far from that perhaps even more ideal condition in which mankind can read Hartmann's book with full conscious awareness. If they ever do so, no man will ever again utter the words 'world-process' without smiling; for they will call to mind the time when Hartmann's parodistic gospel was listened to, absorbed, attacked, revered, propagated and canonized with all the simple honesty of the 'German mind', indeed with 'the wry earnestness of the owl', as Goethe puts it. But the world must get on, that ideal condition will not be created by dreaming, it must be fought and struggled for, and the path to redemption from that owlish earnestness lies only through cheerfulness. The time will come when one will prudently refrain from all constructions of the world-process or even of the history of man; a time when one will regard not the masses but individuals, who form a kind of bridge across the turbulent stream of becoming. These individuals do not carry forward any kind of process but live contemporaneously with one another; thanks to history, which permits such a collaboration, they live as that republic of genius of which Schopenhauer once spoke; one giant calls to another across the desert intervals of time and, undisturbed by the excited chattering dwarfs who creep about beneath them, the exalted spirit-dialogue goes on. It is the task of history to be the mediator between them and thus again and again to inspire and lend the strength for the production of the great man. No, the *goal of humanity* cannot lie in its end but only *in its highest exemplars*.

Our comedian has, of course, a different point of view, and with that admirable dialectic which is as genuine as its admirers are admirable he tells us: 'The concept of evolution is not compatible with ascribing to the world-process an infinite duration in the past, since then every conceivable evolution must have already been run through, which is not the case (oh rogue!); so likewise we cannot concede to the process an infinite duration in the future; both would annul the concept of evolution towards a goal (rogue again!) and would make the world-process resemble the Danaides' water-jugs. The complete victory of the logical over the illogical (oh rogue of rogues!) must, however, coincide with the temporal end of the world-process, the Last Day.' No, you alert and mocking spirit, as long as the illogical reigns as it does today, as long, for example, as one can speak of the 'world-process' as you speak of it and gain universal applause, the Last Day is still far off: for it is still too cheerful on this earth, many illusions still flourish, for example the illusion your contemporaries harbour about you, we are not yet ready to be hurled back into your nothingness: for we believe that it will be even merrier here once people have begun to understand you, you misunderstood reader of the unconscious. If, however, disgust should nonetheless come with power, as you have prophesied to your readers, if your account of your present and future should turn out to be right – and no one has despised them with such disgust as you have – then I am quite willing to vote with the majority, in the form proposed by you, that next Saturday night punctually at twelve o'clock the world shall perish; and our decree shall conclude: from tomorrow there shall be no more time and the newspapers shall appear no more. But perhaps our decree will have no effect: in that event, though, we shall at least have time to perform a fine experiment. We shall take a pair of scales and place Hartmann's unconscious on one of them and Hartmann's world-process on the other. There are people who believe they will weigh exactly the same: for in each of them there would lie an equally bad expression and an equally good joke. – Once Hartmann's joke has been understood, Hartmann's expression 'world-process' will be of no use except as a joke. It has, in fact, for long been high time that the excesses of the historical sense, the immoderate revelling in the process at the expense of being and life, the senseless displacement of all perspectives, were assaulted by all the militia satirical malice can summon; and it shall always be said in praise of the philosopher of the unconscious that he was the first to feel how ludicrous the idea of the 'world-process' is and to make others feel it even more strongly by the singular earnestness of his presentation of it. To what end the 'world' exists, to what end 'mankind' exists, ought not to concern us at all for the moment except as objects of humour: for the presumptuousness of the little human worm is the funniest thing at present on the world's stage; on the other hand, do ask yourself why you, the individual, exist, and if you can get no other answer try for once to justify your existence as it were *a posteriori* by setting before yourself an aim, a goal, a 'to this end', an exalted and noble 'to this end'. Perish in pursuit of this and only this – I know of no better aim of life than that of perishing, *animae magnae prodigus*,* in pursuit of the great and the impossible. If, on the other hand, the doctrines of sovereign becoming, of the fluidity of all concepts, types and species, of the lack of any cardinal distinction between man and animal – doctrines which I consider true but deadly – are thrust upon the people for another generation with the rage for instruction that has by now become normal, no one should be surprised if the people perishes of petty egoism, ossification and greed, falls apart and ceases to be a people; in its place

---

animae magnae prodigus: careless of life

systems of individualist egoism, brotherhoods for the rapacious exploitation of the non-brothers, and similar creations of utilitarian vulgarity may perhaps appear in the arena of the future. To prepare the way for these creations all one has to do is to go on writing history from the standpoint of the *masses* and seeking to derive the laws which govern it from the needs of these masses, that is to say from the laws which move the lowest mud- and clay-strata of society. The masses seem to me to deserve notice in three respects only: first as faded copies of great men produced on poor paper with worn-out plates, then as a force of resistance to great men, finally as instruments in the hands of great men; for the rest, let the Devil and statistics take them! What, can statistics prove that there are laws in history? Laws? They certainly prove how vulgar and nauseatingly uniform the masses are: but are the effects of inertia, stupidity, mimicry, love and hunger to be called laws? Well, let us suppose they are: that, however, only goes to confirm the proposition that so far as there are laws in history the laws are worthless and the history is also worthless. But the kind of history at present universally prized is precisely the kind that takes the great mass-drives for the chief and weightiest facts of history and regards great men as being no more than their clearest expression, as it were bubbles visible on the surface of the flood. Greatness is, under this supposition, the product of the masses, which is to say order is the product of chaos; and it is only natural that in the end the hymn of praise is sung to the masses that produce it. That which has moved these masses for any length of time and has become what is called 'a power in history' is then accorded the name 'great'. But is that not a quite deliberate confusion of quantity with quality? When the rude masses have found some idea or other, a religious idea for instance, to their liking, strenuously defended it and dragged it along with them for centuries, then and only then is the inventor and founder of this idea to be called great. But why! The noblest and most exalted things make no effect whatever on the masses; the historical success of Christianity, its power in history, its tenacity and durability, happily proves nothing with respect to the greatness of its founder, for if it did it would be evidence against him: between him and that historical success there lies a very dark and earthy stratum of passion, error, thirst for power and honour, of the continuing strength of the *imperium romanum*, a stratum from which Christianity acquired the earthly residue and taste which made possible its continuance in this world and bestowed upon it as it were its tenability. Greatness ought not to depend on success: Demosthenes possessed greatness though he had no success. The purest and truest adherents of Christianity have always hindered and called into question its worldly success and so-called 'power in history' rather than promoted them; for they were accustomed to place themselves outside the 'world' and had no regard for the 'process of the Christian idea'; for which reason they have as a rule remained wholly unknown and anonymous to history. Expressed in Christian terms: the Devil is the regent of this world and the lord of success and progress: in all the powers in history he is the actual power, and that is essentially how it will always remain – even though the fact may be painful to the ears of an age accustomed to the idolization of success and power in history. For it is an age that is practised in bestowing new names on things and has even rebaptized the Devil. It is indeed the hour of a great peril: mankind seems near to discovering that the egoism of individuals, groups or the masses has at all times been the lever of the movements of history; at the same time, however, this discovery has caused no perturbation of any kind, but on the contrary it has now been decreed: egoism shall be our god. In this new faith one is now setting to work with the clearest deliberation to erect the history of the future on the foundation of egoism: only it is to be a more prudent egoism than heretofore, an egoism which imposes certain restraints upon itself so as to ensure its endurance, an egoism which studies history precisely so as to become acquainted with that earlier imprudent egoism. In the course of this study it has been learned that a quite special role in the founding of the world-system of egoism devolves upon the state: it has to be the patron of all the prudent egoisms so as to protect them with its military and police forces against the terrifying outbreaks to which imprudent egoism is liable. It is to the same end that history – the evolutionary history of animal and man – is carefully inculcated into the dangerous, because imprudent, masses and working classes: one knows that a grain of historical culture is capable of breaking down dull and rude instincts and desires or of leading them into the path of a refined egoism. *In summa*: mankind is now, in the words of E. von Hartmann, 'with a thoughtful eye to the future taking into consideration a practical domestic establishment in the earthly homeland'. The same writer calls this period the 'manhood of mankind', and thereby mocks at that which is now called 'man' as though what is understood by this word were simply the sober self-seeker; just as he likewise prophesies an old-age to follow this period of manhood, though again he clearly means only to mock at our contemporary grey-beards: for he

speaks of the mature contemplativeness with which they '
the dissolute sufferings of their life's course and grasp ho
the goals for which they had hitherto supposed they were ͻ
No, a manhood of cunning and historically cultivated egoism
followed by an old-age which clings to life with repulsive greed and
lack of dignity, and then by a final act in which the

> Last scene of all,
> That ends this strange, eventful history,
> Is second childishness, and mere oblivion,
> Sans teeth, sans eyes, sans taste, sans every thing.*

Whether our lives and culture are threatened by these dissolute,
toothless and tasteless greybeards or by Hartmann's so-called 'men',
let us in the face of both of them hold on with our teeth to the rights
of our *youth* and never weary in our youth of defending the future
against these iconoclasts who would wreck it. In this struggle,
however, we shall have to discover a particularly unpleasant fact: *that
the excesses of the historical sense from which the present day suffers are
deliberately furthered, encouraged and – employed.*

They are employed, however, against youth, so as to train them up
to that mature manhood which is striven for everywhere; they are
employed so as to break the natural repugnance of youth by a
scientific-magical illumination of that manly-unmanly egoism
which transfigures it. We know, indeed, what history can do when it
gains a certain ascendancy, we know it only too well: it can cut off the
strongest instincts of youth, its fire, defiance, unselfishness and love,
at the roots, damp down the heat of its sense of justice, suppress or
regress its desire to mature slowly with the counter-desire to be
ready, useful, fruitful as quickly as possible, cast morbid doubt on its
honesty and boldness of feeling; indeed, it can even deprive youth of
its fairest privilege, of its power to implant in itself the belief in a
great idea and then let it grow to an even greater one. A certain excess
of history can do all this, we have seen it do it: and it does it by continually shifting horizons and removing a protective atmosphere
and thus preventing man from feeling and acting *unhistorically*. From
an infinite horizon he then returns to himself, to the smallest egoistic
enclosure, and there he must grow withered and dry: probably he
attains to cleverness, never to wisdom. He 'listens to reason', calcu-
lates and accommodates himself to the facts, keeps calm, blinks and

*From *As You Like It*, Act II Scene vii.

115

knows how to seek his own or his party's advantage in the advantage and disadvantage of others; he unlearns unnecessary modesty and thus step by step becomes the Hartmannesque 'man' and then 'greybeard'. But that is what he is *supposed* to become, precisely that is the sense of the cynical demand for the 'total surrender of the personality to the world-process' – for the sake of its goal, world-redemption, as that rogue, E. von Hartmann, assures us. Well, the will and goal of these Hartmannesque 'men' and 'greybeards' can hardly be precisely world-redemption: though the world would certainly be more redeemed if it were redeemed from these men and greybeards. For then there would come the empire of youth. –

10

Mindful of this situation in which *youth* finds itself I cry Land! Land! Enough and more than enough of the wild and erring voyage over strange dark seas! At last a coast appears in sight: we must land on it whatever it may be like, and the worst of harbours is better than to go reeling back into a hopeless infinity of scepticism. Let us only make land; later on we shall find good harbours right enough, and make the landfall easier for those who come after us.

This voyage was perilous and exciting. How far we still are from the quiet contemplativeness with which we first watched our ship put out. In pursuit of the perils of history we have found ourselves most acutely exposed to them; we ourselves bear visibly the traces of those sufferings which afflict contemporary mankind as a result of an excess of history, and I have no wish to conceal from myself that, in the immoderation of its criticism, in the immaturity of its humanity, in its frequent transitions from irony to cynicism, from pride to scepticism, the present treatise itself reveals its modern character, a character marked by weakness of personality. And yet I trust in the inspirational force which, in the absence of genius, powers my vessel, I trust that *youth* has led me aright when it now *compels me to protest at the historical education of modern man* and when I demand that man should above all learn to live and should employ history only in *the service of the life he has learned to live.* One has to be young to understand this protest; indeed, in view of the premature greybeardedness of our present-day youth one can hardly be young enough if one is to grasp what is here really being protested against. An example will help to make clear what I mean. It is hardly more than a century ago that there awoke in some young people in Germany a natural instinct for what we call poetry. Is it supposed that the generations before them and contemporary with them had failed even to mention that art, even though it was strange to them? The opposite is, of course, the case: they reflected, wrote and argued about 'poetry' with great vigour, producing words about words about words as they did so. This awakening to life of a word did not imply the death of those who awoke it; in a certain sense they are still living, for if, as Gibbon says, it requires only time, though a great deal of time, for a world to perish, so it requires only time, though in Germany, the 'land of gradualness', it requires very much more time, for a false idea to perish. Nonetheless, there are now perhaps a hundred more people than there were a hundred years ago who know what poetry is; perhaps a hundred years hence there will be a further hundred who by then will also have learned what culture is and that the Germans have up to now possessed no culture, however much they may talk and puff themselves up about it. To these people the Germans' universal contentment with their 'culture' will appear as incredible and silly as the once acclaimed classicism of Gottsched or Ramler's reputation as the German Pindar appear to us. They will perhaps think that this culture has been only a kind of knowledge about culture, and false and superficial knowledge at that. False and superficial, that is, because one endured the contradiction between life and knowledge and completely failed to see what characterized the culture of genuinely cultured peoples: that culture can grow and flourish only out of life; while among the Germans it was stuck on like a paper flower or poured over like icing-sugar, and was thus condemned to remain forever deceitful and unfruitful. The education of German youth, however, proceeds from precisely this false and unfruitful conception of culture: its goal, viewed in its essence, is not at all the free cultivated man but the scholar, the man of science, and indeed the most speedily employable man of science, who stands aside from life so as to know it unobstructedly; its result, observed empirically, is the historical-aesthetic cultural philistine, the precocious and up-to-the-minute babbler about state, church and art, the man who appreciates everything, the insatiable stomach which nonetheless does not know what honest hunger and thirst are. That an education with this goal and this result is an anti-natural one is apprehensible only to one who has not yet been fully processed by it; it is apprehensible only to the instinct of youth, for youth still possesses that instinct of nature which remains intact until artificially and forcibly shattered by this education. He who wants, on the con-

trary, to shatter this education has to help youth to speak out, he has
to light the path their unconscious resistance has hitherto taken with
the radiance of concepts and transform it to a conscious and loudly
vocal awareness. But how can he achieve so strange a goal?

Above all by destroying a superstition: the belief in the *necessity* of
this educational operation. The usual view is that our present highly
disagreeable reality is the only one in any way possible. Examine
with this in mind the literature of our higher school and educational
system over the past decades: one will see with angry astonishment
that, all the varying proposals and vehement contentions notwithstanding, the actual objective of education is everywhere
thought of as being the same; that the outcome of education hitherto,
the production of the 'educated man' as he is at present understood,
is unhesitatingly assumed to be the necessary and rational foundation of all future education. The uniform canon is that the young
man has to start with a knowledge of culture, not even with a
knowledge of life and even less with life and experience itself. And
this knowledge of culture is instilled into the youth in the form of historical knowledge; that is to say, his head is crammed with a tremendous number of ideas derived from a highly indirect knowledge of
past ages and peoples, not from direct observation of life. His desire
to experience something himself and to feel evolving within him a
coherent living complex of experiences of his own – such a desire is
confused and as it were made drunk by the illusory promise that it is
possible to sum up in oneself the highest and most noteworthy
experiences of former ages, and precisely the greatest of former ages,
in a few years. It is exactly the same crazy method as that which leads
our young painters into picture-galleries instead of into the
workshop of a master and before all into the unique workshop of the
unique master, nature. As though one could appropriate the arts
and sciences of past times, the actual yield of their life's experience,
by taking a fleeting stroll through the gallery of history! As though
life itself were not a craft which must be learned from the ground up
and practised remorselessly if it is not to eventuate in mere babblers
and bunglers! –

Plato considered it necessary that the first generation of his new
society (in the perfect state) should be educated with the aid of a
mighty *necessary lie*: the children were to be taught to believe that they
had all formerly dwelt asleep under the earth, where they had been
kneaded into shape by nature's workman. Impossible to rebel

against a past of this sort! Impossible to go against the work of the gods! It was to count as an inviolable law of nature: he who is born a philosopher has gold in his body, he who is born a soldier has only silver, he who is born a worker has iron and bronze. As it is impossible to blend these metals together, Plato explained, so it should be impossible ever to mingle or confound the order of castes; belief in the *aeterna veritas* of this order is the foundation of the new education and therewith of the new state. – Now, this is how the modern German believes in the *aeterna veritas* of his system of education, of his kind of culture: and yet this belief would crumble away, as the Platonic state would have crumbled away, if the necessary lie were for once countered with a *necessary truth*: the truth that the German possesses no culture because his education provides no basis for one. He wants the flower without the root and the stem: consequently he wants it in vain. That is the simple truth, a coarse and unpleasant truth, truly a necessary truth.

It is in this necessary truth, however, that *our first generation* must be educated; they will certainly suffer the most from it, for through it they will have to educate themselves, and in opposition to themselves moreover, to a new custom and nature and out of an old and first nature and custom: so that they could say to themselves in old Spanish: *Defienda me Dios de my*, God guard me from myself, that is to say from the nature already educated into me. It must taste this truth drop by drop, like a fierce and bitter medicine, and each one of this generation must overcome himself to the extent of being able to say of himself what he would find it easier to endure if it were said of an entire age: we are without culture, more, we are ruined for living, for right and simple seeing and hearing, for happily seizing what is nearest and most natural to us, and do not yet possess even the basis of a culture, because we are not even convinced we have genuine life in us. Fragmented and in pieces, dissociated almost mechanically into an inner and an outer, sown with concepts as with dragon's teeth, bringing forth conceptual dragons, suffering from the malady of words and mistrusting any feeling of our own which has not yet been stamped with words: being such an unliving and yet uncannily active concept- and word-factory, perhaps I still have the right to say of myself *cogito, ergo sum*, but not *vivo, ergo cogito*. Empty 'being' is granted me, but not full and green 'life'; the feeling that tells me I exist warrants to me only that I am a thinking creature, not that I am a living one, not that I am an *animal* but at most a *cogital*. Only give me life, then I will create a culture for you out of it! – Thus cries each individual of this generation and all those individuals will recognize one another from this cry. Who is to give them this life?

No god and no man: only their own *youth*: unchain this and you will therewith have liberated life. For life was only lying hidden, in prison, it has not yet withered away and died – ask yourselves if it has!

But it is sick, this unchained life, and needs to be cured. It is sick with many illnesses and not only with the memory of its chains – what chiefly concerns us here is that it is suffering from the *malady of history*. Excess of history has attacked life's plastic powers, it no longer knows how to employ the past as a nourishing food. The evil is dreadful, and yet! if youth did not possess nature's clairvoyant gift no one would know it is an evil or that a paradise of health has been lost. This same youth, however, also divines with the curative instinct of this same nature how this paradise is to be regained; it knows the medicine and balsam against the malady of history, against excess of history: but what is this medicine called?

Now, one must not be surprised to find that it is called by the names of poisons: the antidote to the historical is called – *the unhistorical and the suprahistorical*. And with these names we return to the beginning of our reflections and to its meditative calm.

With the word 'the unhistorical' I designate the art and power of *forgetting* and of enclosing oneself within a bounded *horizon*; I call 'suprahistorical' the powers which lead the eye away from becoming towards that which bestows upon existence the character of the eternal and stable, towards *art* and *religion*. *Science* – for it is science which would here speak of poisons – sees in these two forces hostile forces: for science considers the only right and true way of regarding things, that is to say the only scientific way, as being that which sees everywhere things that have been, things historical, and nowhere things that are, things eternal; it likewise lives in a profound antagonism towards the eternalizing powers of art and religion, for it hates forgetting, which is the death of knowledge, and seeks to abolish all limitations of horizon and launch mankind upon an infinite and unbounded sea of light whose light is knowledge of all becoming.

If only man could live in it! As cities collapse and grow desolate when there is an earthquake and man erects his house on volcanic land only in fear and trembling and only briefly, so life itself caves in and grows weak and fearful when the *concept-quake* caused by science robs man of the foundation of all his rest and security, his belief in the enduring and eternal. Is life to dominate knowledge and science, or is knowledge to dominate life? Which of these two forces is the higher and more decisive? There can be no doubt: life is the higher, the dominating force, for knowledge which annihilated life would have annihilated itself with it. Knowledge presupposes life and thus has in the preservation of life the same interest as any creature has in its own continued existence. Thus science requires superintendence and supervision; a *hygiene of life* belongs close beside science and one of the clauses of this hygiene would read: the unhistorical and the suprahistorical are the natural antidotes to the stifling of life by the historical, by the malady of history. It is probable that we who suffer from the malady of history will also have to suffer from the antidotes. But that we suffer from them is no evidence against the correctness of the chosen treatment.

And here I recognize the mission of that *youth* I have spoken of, that first generation of fighters and dragon-slayers which will precede a happier and fairer culture and humanity without itself having more than a presentiment of this future happiness and beauty. This youth will suffer from both the sickness and the antidotes: and nonetheless it will believe itself entitled to boast of a more robust health and in general a more natural nature than its predecessors, the cultivated 'man' and 'greybeard' of the present. Its mission, however, is to undermine the concepts this present has of 'health' and 'culture' and to excite mockery and hatred against these hybrid monsters of concepts; and the sign that guarantees the superior robustness of its own health shall be that this youth can itself discover no concept or slogan in the contemporary currency of words and concepts to describe its own nature, but is only aware of the existence within it of an active power that fights, excludes and divides and of an ever more intense feeling of life. One may assert that this youth does not yet possess culture – but for what youth would this constitute a reproach? One may point to its coarseness and immoderation – but it is not yet old or wise enough to moderate its claims; above all, it does not need hypocritically to defend a finished culture and it enjoys all the consolations and privileges that go with youth, especially the privilege of courageous, unreflecting honesty and the inspiring consolation of hope.

Of these hopeful young people I know that they understand all these generalities from close personal experience and will translate them into a teaching intended for themselves; the others may for the moment perceive only covered dishes that might well be empty: until one day they behold with surprise that the dishes are full and that attacks, demands, life-drives, passions have lain mingled and pressed together in these generalities and that they could not lie thus concealed for very long. Leaving these doubters to time, which brings all things to light, I turn in conclusion to that company of the hopeful to tell them in a parable of the course and progress of their cure, their delivery from the malady of history, and therewith their own history, up to the point at which they will be sufficiently healthy again to study history and, to the ends of life, to employ the past in its three senses, namely monumental or antiquarian or critical. At that point they will be more ignorant than the 'cultivated' people of this present, for they will have unlearned many things and even have lost all desire so much as to glance at that which these cultivated people want to know most of all; from the point of view of these cultivated people, their distinguishing marks are precisely their 'unculture', their indifference and reserve towards much that is of high repute, even towards much that is good. But at this end-point of their cure they will have become *human* again and have ceased to be merely aggregates of humanlike qualities – that is something! That is something to hope for! Do your hearts not laugh when you hope, you hopeful young people?

And how can we attain that goal? you will ask. At the beginning of a journey towards that goal, the god of Delphi cries to you his oracle: 'Know yourself.' It is a hard saying: for that god 'conceals nothing and says nothing, but only indicates, as Heraclitus has said. What does he indicate to you?

There were centuries during which the Greeks found themselves faced by a danger similar to that which faces us: the danger of being overwhelmed by what was past and foreign, of perishing through 'history'. They never lived in proud inviolability: their 'culture' was, rather, for a long time a chaos of foreign, Semitic, Babylonian, Lydian, Egyptian forms and ideas, and their religion truly a battle of all the gods of the East: somewhat as 'German culture' and religion is now a struggling chaos of all the West and of all past ages. And yet, thanks to that Apollonian oracle, Hellenic culture was no mere aggregate. The Greeks gradually learned *to organize the chaos* by following the Delphic teaching and thinking back to themselves, that is, to their real needs, and letting their pseudo-needs die out. Thus they again took possession of themselves; they did not long remain the overburdened heirs and epigones of the entire Orient; after hard struggle with themselves and through protracted application of that oracle, they even became the happiest enrichers and augmenters of the treasure they had inherited and the first-born and models of all future cultured nations.

This is a parable for each one of us: he must organize the chaos within him by thinking back to his real needs. His honesty, the strength and truthfulness of his character, must at some time or other rebel against a state of things in which he only repeats what he has heard, learns what is already known, imitates what already exists; he will then begin to grasp that culture can be something other than a *decoration of life*, that is to say at bottom no more than dissimulation and disguise; for all adornment conceals that which is adorned. Thus the Greek conception of culture will be unveiled to him – in antithesis to the Roman – the conception of culture as a new and improved *physis*, without inner and outer, without dissimulation and convention, culture as a unanimity of life, thought, appearance and will. Thus he will learn from his own experience that it was through the higher force of their *moral* nature that the Greeks achieved victory over all other cultures, and that every increase in truthfulness must also assist to promote *true* culture: even though this truthfulness may sometimes seriously damage precisely the kind of cultivatedness now held in esteem, even though it may even be able to procure the downfall of an entire merely decorative culture.

3
Schopenhauer
as educator

A traveller who had seen many lands and peoples and several of the earth's continents was asked what quality in men he had discovered everywhere he had gone. He replied: 'They have a tendency to laziness.' To many it will seem that he ought rather to have said: 'They are all timid. They hide themselves behind customs and opinions.' In his heart every man knows quite well that, being unique, he will be in the world only once and that no imaginable chance will for a second time gather together into a unity so strangely variegated an assortment as he is: he knows it but he hides it like a bad conscience – why? From fear of his neighbour, who demands conventionality and cloaks himself with it. But what is it that constrains the individual to fear his neighbour, to think and act like a member of a herd, and to have no joy in himself? Modesty, perhaps, in a few rare cases. With the great majority it is indolence, inertia, in short that tendency to laziness of which the traveller spoke. He is right: men are even lazier than they are timid, and fear most of all the inconveniences with which unconditional honesty and nakedness would burden them. Artists alone hate this sluggish promenading in borrowed fashions and appropriated opinions and they reveal everyone's secret bad conscience, the law that every man is a unique miracle; they dare to show us man as he is, uniquely himself to every last movement of his muscles, more, that in being thus strictly consistent in uniqueness he is beautiful, and worth regarding, and in no way tedious. When the great thinker despises mankind, he despises its laziness: for it is on account of their laziness that men seem like factory products, things of no consequence and unworthy to be associated with or instructed. The man who does not wish to belong to the mass needs only to cease taking himself easily; let him follow his conscience, which calls to him: 'Be your self! All you are now doing, thinking, desiring, is not you yourself.'

Every youthful soul hears this call day and night and trembles when he hears it; for the idea of its liberation gives it a presentiment of the measure of happiness allotted it from all eternity – a happiness to which it can by no means attain so long as it lies fettered by the chains of fear and convention. And how dismal and senseless life can be without this liberation! There exists no more repulsive and desolate creature in the world than the man who has evaded his genius and who now looks furtively to left and right, behind him and all about him. In the end such a man becomes impossible to get hold of, since he is wholly exterior, without kernel, a tattered, painted bag of clothes, a decked-out ghost that cannot inspire even fear and certainly not pity. And if it is true to say of the lazy that they kill time, then it is greatly to be feared that an era which sees its salvation in public opinion, that is to say private laziness, is a time that really will be killed: I mean that it will be struck out of the history of the true liberation of life. How reluctant later generations will be to have anything to do with the relics of an era ruled, not by living men, but by pseudo-men dominated by public opinion; for which reason our age may be to some distant posterity the darkest and least known, because least human, portion of human history. I go along the new streets of our cities and think how, of all these gruesome houses which the generation of public opinion has built for itself, not one will be standing in a hundred years' time, and how the opinions of these house-builders will no doubt by then likewise have collapsed. On the other hand, how right it is for those who do not feel themselves to be citizens of this time to harbour great hopes; for if they were citizens of this time they too would be helping to kill their time and so perish with it – while their desire is rather to awaken their time to life and so live on themselves in this awakened life.

But even if the future gave us no cause for hope – the fact of our existing at all in this here-and-now must be the strongest incentive to us to live according to our own laws and standards: the inexplicable fact that we live precisely today, when we had all infinite time in which to come into existence, that we possess only a shortlived today in which to demonstrate why and to what end we came into existence now and at no other time. We are responsible to ourselves for our own existence; consequently we want to be the true helmsman of this existence and refuse to allow our existence to resemble a mindless act of chance. One has to take a somewhat bold and dangerous line with this existence: especially as, whatever happens, we are bound to lose it. Why go on clinging to this clod of earth, this way of life, why pay heed to what your neighbour says? It is so parochial to bind oneself to views which are no longer binding even a couple of hundred miles away. Orient and Occident are chalk-lines drawn before us to fool our timidity. I will make an attempt to attain freedom, the youthful soul says to itself; and is it to be hindered in this by the fact that two nations happen to hate and fight one another, or that two continents are separated by an ocean, or that all around it a religion is taught which did not yet exist a couple of thousand years ago. All that is not you, it says to itself. No one can construct for you the bridge upon which precisely you must cross the stream of life, no one but you yourself alone. There are, to be sure, countless paths and bridges and demi-gods which would bear you through this stream; but only at the cost of yourself: you would put yourself in pawn and lose yourself. There exists in the world a single path along which no one can go except you: whither does it lead? Do not ask, go along it. Who was it who said: 'a man never rises higher than when he does not know whither his path can still lead him'?*

But how can we find ourselves again? How can man know himself? He is a thing dark and veiled; and if the hare has seven skins, man can slough off seventy times seven and still not be able to say: 'this is really you, this is no longer outer shell'. Moreover, it is a painful and dangerous undertaking thus to tunnel into oneself and to force one's way down into the shaft of one's being by the nearest path. A man who does it can easily so hurt himself that no physician can cure him. And, moreover again, what need should there be for it, since everything bears witness to what we are, our friendships and enmities, our glance and the clasp of our hand, our memory and that which we do not remember, our books and our handwriting. This, however, is the means by which an inquiry into the most important aspect can be initiated. Let the youthful soul look back on life with the question: what have you truly loved up to now, what has drawn your soul aloft, what has mastered it and at the same time blessed it? Set up these revered objects before you and perhaps their nature and their sequence will give you a law, the fundamental law of your own true self. Compare these objects one with another, see how one completes, expands, surpasses, transfigures another, how they constitute a stepladder upon which you have clambered up to yourself as you are now; for your true nature lies, not concealed deep within you, but immeasurably high above you, or at least above that which you usually take yourself to be. Your true educators and formative teachers reveal to you what the true basic material of your being is, something in itself ineducable and in any case difficult of access, bound and paralysed: your educators can be only your liberators.

*Oliver Cromwell, as quoted by Cardinal de Retz in his *Memoirs*.

And that is the secret of all culture: it does not provide artificial limbs, wax noses or spectacles – that which can provide these things is, rather, only sham education. Culture is liberation, the removal of all the weeds, rubble and vermin that want to attack the tender buds of the plant, an outstreaming of light and warmth, the gentle rustling of nocturnal rain, it is imitation and worship of nature where nature is in her motherly and merciful mood, it is the perfecting of nature when it deflects her cruel and merciless assaults and turns them to good, and when it draws a veil over the expressions of nature's step-motherly mood and her sad lack of understanding.

Certainly there may be other means of finding oneself, of coming to oneself out of the bewilderment in which one usually wanders as in a dark cloud, but I know of none better than to think on one's true educators. And so today I shall remember one of the teachers and taskmasters of whom I can boast, *Arthur Schopenhauer* – and later on I shall recall others.

2

If I am to describe what an event my first glance at Schopenhauer's writings was for me, I must dwell for a moment on an idea which used to come to me in my youth more pressingly, and more frequently, than perhaps any other. When in those days I roved as I pleased through wishes of all kinds, I always believed that at some time fate would take from me the terrible effort and duty of educating myself: I believed that, when the time came, I would discover a philosopher to educate me, a true philosopher whom one could follow without any misgiving because one would have more faith in him than one had in oneself. Then I asked myself: what would be the principles by which he would educate you? – and I reflected on what he might say about the two educational maxims which are being hatched in our time. One of them demands that the educator should quickly recognize the real strength of his pupil and then direct all his efforts and energy and heat at them so as to help that one virtue to attain true maturity and fruitfulness. The other maxim, on the contrary, requires that the educator should draw forth and nourish *all* the forces which exist in his pupil and bring them to a harmonious relationship with one another. But should he who has a decided inclination to be a goldsmith for that reason be forcibly compelled to study music? Is one to agree that Benvenuto Cellini's father was right continually to force him to play the 'dear little horn' – 'that accursed

piping', as his son called it? In the case of such strong and definite
talents one would not agree: so could it perhaps be that that maxim
advocating a harmonious development should be applied only to
more mediocre natures in which, though there may reside a con-
geries of needs and inclinations, none of them amounts to very
much taken individually? But where do we discover a harmonious
whole at all, a simultaneous sounding of many voices in one nature,
if not in such men as Cellini, men in whom everything, knowledge,
desire, love, hate, strives towards a central point, a root force, and
where a harmonious system is constructed through the compelling
domination of this living centre? And so perhaps these two maxims
are not opposites at all? Perhaps the one simply says that man should
have a centre and the other that he should also have a periphery?
That educating philosopher of whom I dreamed would, I came to
think, not only discover the central force, he would also know how to
prevent its acting destructively on the other forces: his educational
task would, it seemed to me, be to mould the whole man into a living
solar and planetary system and to understand its higher laws of
motion.

In the meantime I still lacked this philosopher, and I tried this one
and that one; I discovered how wretched we modern men appear
when compared with the Greeks and Romans even merely in the
matter of a serious understanding of the tasks of education. With the
need for this in one's heart one can run through all Germany,
especially its universities, and fail to find what one is seeking; for
many far simpler and more basic desires are still unfulfilled there.
Anyone who seriously wanted to train in Germany as an orator, for
example, or intended to enter a school for writers, would find that
school nowhere; it seems not to have been realized that speaking
and writing are arts which cannot be acquired without the most careful
instruction and arduous apprenticeship. Nothing, however, displays the arrogant self-satisfaction of our contemporaries more
clearly or shamefully than their half niggardly, half thoughtless
undemandingness in regard to teachers and educators. What will
not suffice, even among our noblest and best-instructed families,
under the name of family tutor; what a collection of antiques and
eccentrics is designated a grammar school and not found wanting;
what are we not content with for a university – what leaders, what
institutions, in comparison with the difficulty of the task of educating
a man to be a man! Even the much admired way in which our German
men of learning set about their scientific pursuits reveals above all

131

that they are thinking more of science than they are of mankind, that they have been trained to sacrifice themselves to it like a legion of the lost, so as in turn to draw new generations on to the same sacrifice. If it is not directed and kept within bounds by a higher maxim of education, but on the contrary allowed to run wilder and wilder on the principle 'the more the better', traffic with science is certainly as harmful to men of learning as the economic principle of *laissez faire* is to the morality of whole nations. Who is there that still remembers that the education of the scholar is an extremely difficult problem, if his humanity is not to be sacrificed in the process – and yet this difficulty is plainly obvious when one regards the numerous examples of those who through an unthinking and premature devotion to science have become crookbacked and humped. But there is an even weightier witness to the absence of all higher education, weightier and more perilous and above all much more common. If it is at once obvious why an orator or a writer cannot now be educated in these arts – because there are no educators for them –; if it is almost as obvious why a scholar must now become distorted and contorted – because he is supposed to be educated by science, that is to say by an inhuman abstraction – then one finally asks oneself: where are we, scholars and unscholarly, high placed and low, to find the moral exemplars and models among our contemporaries, the visible epitome of morality for our time? What has become of any reflection on questions of morality – questions that have at all times engaged every more highly civilized society? There is no longer any model or any reflection of any kind; what we are in fact doing is consuming the moral capital we have inherited from our forefathers, which we are incapable of increasing but know only how to squander; in our society one either remains silent about such things or speaks of them in a way that reveals an utter lack of acquaintance with or experience of them and that can only excite revulsion. Thus it has come about that our schools and teachers simply abstain from an education in morality or make do with mere formalities: and virtue is a word that no longer means anything to our teachers or pupils, an old-fashioned word that makes one smile – and it is worse if one does not smile, for then one is being a hypocrite.

The explanation of this spiritlessness and of why all moral energy is at such a low ebb is difficult and involved; but no one who considers the influence victorious Christianity had on the morality of our ancient world can overlook the reaction of declining Christianity upon our own time. Through the exaltedness of its ideal, Christianity excelled the moral systems of antiquity and the naturalism that resided in them to such a degree that this naturalism came to excite apathy and disgust; but later on, when these better and higher ideals, though now known, proved unattainable, it was no longer possible to return to what was good and high in antique virtue, however much one might want to. It is in this oscillation between Christianity and antiquity, between an imitated or hypocritical Christian morality and an equally despondent and timid revival of antiquity, that modern man lives, and does not live very happily; the fear of what is natural he has inherited and the renewed attraction of this naturalness, the desire for a firm footing somewhere, the impotence of his knowledge that reels back and forth between the good and the better, all this engenders a restlessness, a disorder in the modern soul which condemns it to a joyless unfruitfulness. Never have moral educators been more needed, and never has it seemed less likely they would be found; in the times when physicians are required the most, in times of great plagues, they are also most in peril. For where are the physicians for modern mankind who themselves stand so firmly and soundly on their feet that they are able to support others and lead them by the hand? A certain gloominess and torpor lies upon even the finest personalities of our time, a feeling of ill-humour at the everlasting struggle between dissimulation and honesty which is being fought out within them, a lack of steady confidence in themselves – whereby they become quite incapable of being signposts and at the same time taskmasters for others.

It was thus truly roving through wishes to imagine I might discover a true philosopher as an educator who could raise me above my insufficiencies insofar as these originated in the age and teach me again to be *simple* and *honest* in thought and life, that is to say to be untimely, that word understood in the profoundest sense; for men have now become so complex and many-sided they are bound to become dishonest whenever they speak at all, make assertions and try to act in accordance with them.

It was in this condition of need, distress and desire that I came to know Schopenhauer.

I am one of those readers of Schopenhauer who when they have read one page of him know for certain they will go on to read all the pages and will pay heed to every word he ever said. I trusted him at once and my trust is the same now as it was nine years ago. Though this is a foolish and immodest way of putting it, I understand him as though it were for me he had written. Thus it is that I have never discovered any paradox in him, though here and there a little error; for what are paradoxes but assertions which carry no conviction because their author himself is not really convinced of them and makes them only so as to glitter and seduce and in general cut a figure. Schopenhauer never wants to cut a figure: for he writes for himself and no one wants to be deceived, least of all a philosopher who has made it a rule for himself: deceive no one, not even yourself! Not even with the pleasant sociable deception which almost every conversation entails and which writers imitate almost unconsciously; even less with the conscious deception of the orator and by the artificial means of rhetoric. Schopenhauer, on the contrary, speaks with himself: or, if one feels obliged to imagine an auditor, one should think of a son being instructed by his father. It is an honest, calm, goodnatured discourse before an auditor who listens to it with love. We are lacking such writers. The speaker's powerful sense of wellbeing embraces us immediately he begins to speak; we feel as we do on entering the high forest, we take a deep breath and acquire that sense of wellbeing ourselves. We feel that here we shall always find a bracing air; here there is a certain inimitable unaffectedness and naturalness such as is possessed by men who are within themselves masters of their own house, and a very rich house at that: in contrast to those writers who surprise themselves most when they for once say something sensible and whose style therefore acquires something restless and unnatural. Schopenhauer's voice reminds us just as little of the scholar whose limbs are naturally stiff and whose chest is narrow and who therefore goes about with awkward embarrassment or a strutting gait; while on the other hand Schopenhauer's rough and somewhat bear-like soul teaches us not so much to feel the absence of the suppleness and courtly charm of good French writers as to disdain it, and no one will discover in him that imitated, as it were silver-plated pseudo-Frenchness in which German writers so much indulge. Schopenhauer's way of expressing himself reminds me here and there a little of Goethe, but otherwise he recalls no German model at all. For he understands how to express the profound with simplicity, the moving without rhetoric, the strictly scientific without pedantry: and from what German could he have learned this? He is also free of the over-subtle, over-supple and – if I may be allowed to say so – not very German style that characterizes Lessing: which is a great merit in him, for Lessing is the most seductive of all German writers of prose. And, to say without more ado the highest thing I can say in regard to his style, I cannot do better than quote a sentence of his own: 'a philosopher must be very honest not to call poetry or rhetoric to his aid'. That there is something called honesty and that it is even a virtue belongs, I know, in the age of public opinion to the private opinions that are forbidden; and thus I shall not be praising Schopenhauer but only characterizing him if I repeat: he is honest even as a writer; and so few writers are honest that one ought really to mistrust anyone who writes. I know of only one writer whom I would compare with Schopenhauer, indeed set above him, in respect of honesty: Montaigne. That such a man wrote has truly augmented the joy of living on this earth. Since getting to know this freest and mightiest of souls, I at least have come to feel what he felt about Plutarch: 'as soon as I glance at him I grow a leg or a wing.'* If I were set the task, I could endure to make myself at home in the world with him.

Schopenhauer has a second quality in common with Montaigne, as well as honesty: a cheerfulness that really cheers. *Aliis laetus, sibi sapiens.*† For there are two very different kinds of cheerfulness. The true thinker always cheers and refreshes, whether he is being serious or humorous, expressing his human insight or his divine forbearance; without peevish gesturing, trembling hands, tearfilled eyes, but with certainty and simplicity, courage and strength, perhaps a little harshly and valiantly but in any case as a victor: and this it is – to behold the victorious god with all the monsters he has combated – that cheers one most profoundly. The cheerfulness one sometimes encounters in mediocre writers and bluff and abrupt thinkers, on the other hand, makes us feel miserable when we read it: the effect produced upon me, for example, by David Strauss's cheerfulness. One feels downright ashamed to have such cheerful contemporaries, because they compromise our time and the people in it before posterity. This kind of cheerful thinker simply does not see the sufferings and the monsters he purports to see and combat; and his cheerfulness is vexing because he is deceiving us: he wants to make us believe that a victory has been fought and won. For at bottom there is cheerfulness only where there is a victory; and this applies to the works of true thinkers just as much as it does to any work of art. Let its content be as dreadful and as serious as the problem of life itself: the work will produce a depressing and painful effect only if

---

*A misunderstanding of Montaigne's assertion: 'Je ne le puis si peu accointer que je n'en tire cuisse ou aisle', which Florio translates as: 'He can no sooner come in my sight but I pull some leg or wing from him.'

†*Aliis laetus, sibi sapiens*: cheerful for others, wise for himself

the semi-thinker and semi-artist has exhaled over it the vapour of his inadequacy; while nothing better or happier can befall a man than to be in the proximity of one of those victors who, precisely because they have thought most deeply, must love what is most living and, as sages, incline in the end to the beautiful. They speak truly, they do not stammer, and do not chatter about what they have heard; they are active and live truly and not the uncanny masquerade men are accustomed to live: which is why in their proximity we for once feel human and natural and might exclaim with Goethe: 'How glorious and precious a living thing is! how well adapted to the conditions it lives in, how true, how full of being!'*

I am describing nothing but the first, as it were physiological, impression Schopenhauer produced upon me, that magical out-pouring of the inner strength of one natural creature on to another that follows the first and most fleeting encounter; and when I subse-quently analyse that impression I discover it to be compounded of three elements, the elements of his honesty, his cheerfulness and his steadfastness. He is honest because he speaks and writes to himself and for himself, cheerful because he has conquered the hardest task by thinking, and steadfast because he has to be. His strength rises straight and calmly upwards like a flame when there is no wind, imperturbably, without restless wavering. He finds his way every time before we have so much as noticed that he has been seeking it; as though compelled by a law of gravity he runs on ahead, so firm and agile, so inevitably. And whoever has felt what it means to dis-cover among our tragelaphine men† of today a whole, complete, self-moving, unconstrained and unhampered natural being will understand my joy and amazement when I discovered Schopenhauer: I sensed that in him I had discovered that educator and philosopher I had sought for so long. But I had discovered him only in the form of a book, and that was a great deficiency. So I strove all the harder to see through the book and to imagine the living man whose great tes-tament I had to read and who promised to make his heirs only those who would and could be more than merely his readers: namely his sons and pupils.

3

I profit from a philosopher only insofar as he can be an example. That he is capable of drawing whole nations after him through this

*From the *Italienische Reise*, 9 October 1786.
†From 'Tragelaphen-Menschheit' (meaning 'horned beast').

example is beyond doubt; the history of India, which is almost the history of Indian philosophy, proves it. But this example must be supplied by his outward life and not merely in his books – in the way, that is, in which the philosophers of Greece taught, through their bearing, what they wore and ate, and their morals, rather than by what they said, let alone by what they wrote. How completely this visible philosophical life is lacking in Germany! where the body is only just beginning to liberate itself long after the spirit seems to have been liberated; and yet it is only an illusion that a spirit can be free and independent if this achieved sovereignty – which is at bottom creative sovereignty over oneself – is not demonstrated anew from morn till night through every glance and every gesture. Kant clung to his university, submitted himself to its regulations, retained the appearance of religious belief, endured to live among colleagues and students: so it is natural that his example has produced above all university professors and professorial philosophy. Schopenhauer had little patience with the scholarly castes, separated himself from them, strove to be independent of state and society – this is his example, the model he provides – to begin with the most superficial things. But many stages in the liberation of the philosophical life are still unknown among the Germans, though they will not always be able to remain unknown. Our artists are living more boldly and more honestly; and the mightiest example we have before us, that of Richard Wagner, shows how the genius must not fear to enter into the most hostile relationship with the existing forms and order if he wants to bring to light the higher order and truth that dwells within him. 'Truth', however, of which our professors speak so much, seems to be a more modest being from which no disorder and nothing extraordinary is to be feared: a self-contented and happy creature which is continually assuring all the powers that be that no one needs to be the least concerned on its account; for it is, after all, only 'pure knowledge'. Thus what I was trying to say is that the philosopher in Germany has more and more to unlearn how to be 'pure knowledge': and it is to precisely that end that Schopenhauer as a human being can serve as an example.

It is, however, nothing less than a miracle that he was able to become this human example: for he was pressed upon, from within and without, by the most tremendous dangers which would have crushed or shattered any weaker being. It seems to me there was a strong probability that Schopenhauer the human being would perish and at best leave behind 'pure knowledge': but this too only at best; most probably neither human being nor knowledge would remain.

An Englishman recently described the most general danger facing uncommon men who live in a society tied to convention: 'Such alien characters at first become submissive, then melancholic, then ill and finally they die. A Shelley would not have been able to live in England, and a race of Shelleys would have been impossible.'* Our Hölderlin and Kleist, and who knows who else besides, were ruined by their uncommonness and could not endure the climate of so-called German culture; and only natures of iron, such as Beethoven, Goethe, Schopenhauer and Wagner are able to stand firm. But these too exhibit many of the effects of the wearying struggle they have had to engage in: they breathe heavily and their voice can easily become too loud. A practised diplomat who had seen and spoken with Goethe only now and then told his friends: 'Voilà un homme, qui a eu de grands chagrins!' – which Goethe translated as: 'There is another one who has had a hard time of it!' and added: 'If the traces of the sufferings we have endured and the deeds we have carried through cannot be expunged from our faces, it is no wonder if everything that remains of us and of our endeavours bears the same impress.' And this is the Goethe whom our cultural philistines point to as the happiest of Germans, so as to demonstrate that it must therefore be possible to be happy among them – with the implication that anyone who feels unhappy and solitary among them has only himself to blame. It is from this proposition that they derive and give practical expression to their cruel dogma that if a person is a solitary it must be because he harbours a secret guilt. Now, poor Schopenhauer had such a secret guilt on his conscience, namely that of valuing his philosophy more than his contemporaries; and he was, moreover, unhappily aware, precisely from the case of Goethe, that if he was to save his philosophy from perishing he had at any cost to defend it against the indifference of his contemporaries; for there exists a species of inquisitorial censorship in which, according to Goethe, the Germans are very skilled; it is called: unbreakable silence. And it had achieved at any rate this much: the greater part of the first edition of his chief work had to be reduced to waste paper. The threatening danger that his great deed would be undone simply through indifference created in him a terrible, barely controllable

---

*Quoted, possibly from memory for it is not entirely accurate, from Walter Bagehot's *Physics and Politics*. Bagehot refers to New England, not England.

agitation; not a single adherent of any note appeared. It makes us sad to see him hunting for the slightest sign that he was not utterly unknown; and his loud, too loud, triumphing when he did finally acquire readers (*'legor et legar'*)* has something painfully moving in it. All the traits he exhibits that are not those of the great philosopher are those of the suffering human being fearful for the safety of his noblest possessions; thus he is tormented by fear of losing his modest income and then perhaps being unable still to maintain his pure and truly antique attitude towards philosophy; thus he often failed in his many attempts to establish firm and sympathetic friendships and was repeatedly obliged to return with a downcast eye to his faithful dog. He was a total solitary; he had not a single companion truly of his own kind to console him – and between one and none there lies, as always between something and nothing, an infinity. No one who possesses true friends knows what true solitude is, even though he have the whole world around him for his enemies. – Ah, I well understand that you do not know what solitude is. Where there have been powerful societies, governments, religions, public opinions, in short wherever there has been tyranny, there the solitary philosopher has been hated; for philosophy offers an asylum to a man into which no tyranny can force its way, the inward cave, the labyrinth of the heart: and that annoys the tyrants. There the solitaries conceal themselves: but there too lurks their greatest danger. These people who have fled inward for their freedom also have to live outwardly, become visible, let themselves be seen; they are united with mankind through countless ties of blood, residence, education, fatherland, chance, the importunity of others; they are likewise presupposed to harbour countless opinions simply because these are the ruling opinions of the time; every gesture which is not clearly a denial counts as agreement; every motion of the hand that does not destroy is interpreted as approval. They know, these solitaries, free in spirit, that they continually seem other than what they think: while they desire nothing but truth and honesty, they are encompassed by a net of misunderstandings; and however vehemently they may desire, they cannot prevent a cloud of false opinions, approximations, half-admissions, indulgent silence, erroneous interpretation from gathering about their actions. Because of this a cloud of melancholy gathers on their brows; for such as these it is more hateful than death itself to be forced to present a semblance to the world;

---

*legor et legar: I am read, I shall be read

and their perpetual bitter resentment of this constraint fills them
with volcanic menace. From time to time they revenge themselves
for their enforced concealment and compelled restraint. They
emerge from their cave wearing a terrifying aspect; their words and
deeds are then explosions and it is possible for them to perish by
their own hand. This was the dangerous way in which Schopenhauer
lived. It is precisely such natures as he who want love, who need
companions before whom they can venture to be as simple and open
as they are before themselves and in whose presence they can cease
to suffer the torment of silence and dissimulation. If you remove
these companions you create an increasingly dangerous condition;
Heinrich von Kleist perished of not being loved, and the most terrible
antidote to uncommon men is to drive them so deep into themselves
that when they re-emerge it is always as a volcanic eruption. Yet there
will always be demi-gods who can endure to live, and live victoriously,
under such terrible conditions; and if you want to hear their lonely
song, listen to the music of Beethoven.

This was the first danger in whose shadow Schopenhauer grew up:
isolation. The second was despair of the truth. This danger attends
every thinker who sets out from the Kantian philosophy, provided
he is a vigorous and whole man in suffering and desire and not a
mere clattering thought- and calculating-machine. Now we all know
very well the shameful implications of this presupposition; it seems
to me, indeed, that Kant has had a living and life-transforming
influence on only a very few men. One can read everywhere, I know,
that since this quiet scholar produced his work a revolution has
taken place in every domain of the spirit; but I cannot believe it. For I
cannot see it in those men who would themselves have to be
revolutionized before a revolution could take place in any whole
domain whatever. If Kant ever should begin to exercise any wide
influence we shall be aware of it in the form of a gnawing and dis-
integrating scepticism and relativism; and only in the most active
and noble spirits who have never been able to exist in a state of doubt
would there appear instead that undermining and despair of all
truth such as Heinrich von Kleist for example experience as the
effect of the Kantian philosophy. 'Not long ago', he writes in his
moving way, 'I became acquainted with the Kantian philosophy –
and I now have to tell you of a thought I derived from it, which I feel
free to do because I have no reason to fear it will shatter you so profoundly and painfully as it has me. – We are unable to decide
whether that which we call truth really is truth, or whether it only

140

appears to us to be. If the latter, then the truth we assemble here is nothing after our death, and all endeavour to acquire a possession which will follow us to the grave is in vain. – If the point of this thought does not penetrate your heart, do not smile at one who feels wounded by it in the deepest and most sacred part of his being. My one great aim has failed me and I have no other.'* When, indeed, will men again feel in this natural Kleistian fashion, when will they again learn to assess the meaning of a philosophy in the 'most sacred part' of their being? And yet this must be done if we are to understand what, after Kant, Schopenhauer can be to us – namely the leader who leads us from the heights of sceptical gloom or criticizing renunciation up to the heights of tragic contemplation, to the nocturnal sky and its stars extended endlessly above us, and who was himself the first to take his path. His greatness lies in having set up before him a picture of life as a whole, in order to interpret it as a whole; while even the most astute heads cannot be dissuaded from the error that one can achieve a more perfect interpretation if one minutely investigates the paint with which this picture is produced and the material upon which it is painted; perhaps with the result that one concludes that it is a quite intricately woven canvas with paint upon it which is chemically inexplicable. To understand the picture one must divine the painter – that Schopenhauer knew. Nowadays, however, the whole guild of the sciences is occupied in understanding the canvas and the paint but not the picture; one can say, indeed, that only he who has a clear view of the picture of life and existence as a whole can employ the individual sciences without harm to himself, for without such a regulatory total picture they are threads that nowhere come to an end and only render our life more confused and labyrinthine. Schopenhauer is, as I said, great in that he pursues this picture as Hamlet pursues the ghost, without letting himself be led aside, as scholars are, or becoming enmeshed in abstract scholasticism, as is the fate of rabid dialecticians. The study of quarter-philosophers is enticing only so as to recognize that they make at once for the places in the edifices of great philosophies where scholarly for and against, where brooding, doubting, contradicting are permitted, and that they thereby elude the challenge of every great philosophy, which as a whole always says only: this is the picture of all life, and learn from it the meaning of your own life. And the reverse: only read your own life and comprehend from it

*Letter to Wilhelmine von Zenge, 22 March 1801.

the hieroglyphics of universal life. And this is how Schopenhauer's philosophy should also always be interpreted at first: individually, by the individual only for himself, so as to gain insight into his own want and misery, into his own limitedness, so as then to learn the nature of his antidotes and consolations: namely, sacrifice of the ego, submission to the noblest ends, above all to those of justice and compassion. He teaches us to distinguish between those things that really promote human happiness and those that only appear to do so: how neither riches nor honours nor erudition can lift the individual out of the profound depression he feels at the valuelessness of his existence, and how the striving after these valued things acquires meaning only through an exalted and transfiguring overall goal: to acquire power so as to aid the evolution of the *physis* and to be for a while the corrector of its follies and ineptitudes. At first only for yourself, to be sure; but through yourself in the end for everyone. It is true that this is a striving which by its nature leads towards resignation: for what and how much is amenable to any kind of improvement at all, in the individual or in the generality!

If we apply these words to Schopenhauer, we touch on the third and most characteristic danger in which he lived and which lay concealed in the whole structure and skeleton of his being. Every human being is accustomed to discovering in himself some limitation, of his talent or of his moral will, which fills him with melancholy and longing; and just as his feeling of sinfulness makes him long for the saint in him, so as an intellectual being he harbours a profound desire for the genius in him. This is the root of all true culture; and if I understand by this the longing of man to be *reborn* as saint and genius, I know that one does not have to be a Buddhist to understand this myth. Where we discover talent devoid of that longing, in the world of scholars or that of the so-called cultivated, we are repelled and disgusted by it; for we sense that, with all their intellect, such people do not promote an evolving culture and the procreation of genius – which is the goal of all culture – but hinder it. It is a state of petrifaction, equivalent in value to that routine, cold and self-laudatory virtuousness which is also farthest, and keeps itself far, from true saintliness. Now, Schopenhauer's nature contained a strange and extremely dangerous dualism. Few thinkers have felt with a comparable intensity and certainty that genius moved within them; and his genius promised him the highest – that there would be no deeper furrow than that which his ploughshare was digging in the ground of modern mankind. Thus he knew half his nature to be satisfied, its desires stilled, sure of its strength; thus he victoriously fulfilled his calling with greatness and dignity. In the other half there dwelt a burning longing; we comprehend it when we hear that he turned away with a pained expression from the picture of the great founder of *la Trappe*,* Rancé, with the words: 'That is a matter of grace.' For the genius longs more deeply for sainthood because from his watchtower he has seen farther and more clearly than other men, down into the reconciliation of knowledge with being, over into the domain of peace and denial of the will, across to the other coast of which the Indians speak. But precisely here is the miracle: how inconceivably whole and unbreakable must Schopenhauer's nature have been if it could not be destroyed even by this longing and yet was not petrified by it! What that means, each will understand according to what and how much he is: and none of us will ever fully understand it.

The more one reflects on the three dangers just described, the more surprising it becomes that Schopenhauer should have defended himself against them with such vigour and emerged from the battle in such good shape. He bore many scars and open wounds, it is true; and he had acquired a disposition that may perhaps seem a little too astringent and sometimes also too pugnacious. But even the greatest of men cannot attain to his own ideal. That Schopenhauer can offer us a model is certain, all these scars and blemishes notwithstanding. One might say, indeed, that that in his nature which was imperfect and all too human brings us closer to him in a human sense, for it lets us see him as a fellow sufferer and not only in the remote heights of a genius.

Those three constitutional dangers that threatened Schopenhauer threaten us all. Each of us bears a productive uniqueness within him as the core of his being; and when he becomes aware of it, there appears around him a strange penumbra which is the mark of his singularity. Most find this something unendurable, because they are, as aforesaid, lazy, and because a chain of toil and burdens is suspended from this uniqueness. There can be no doubt that, for the singular man who encumbers himself with this chain, life witholds almost everything – cheerfulness, security, ease, honour – that he desired of it in his youth; solitude is the gift his fellow men present to him; let him live where he will, he will always find there the desert and the cave. Let him see to it that he does not become subjugated,

---

la Trappe: monastery from which the Trappist order takes its name.

that he does not become depressed and melancholic. And to that end let him surround himself with pictures of good and brave fighters, such as Schopenhauer was. But the second danger which threatened Schopenhauer is not altogether rare, either. Here and there a man is equipped by nature with mental acuteness, his thoughts like to do the dialectical double-step; how easy it is, if he carelessly lets go the reins of his talent, for him to perish as a human being and to lead a ghostly life in almost nothing but 'pure knowledge'; or, grown accustomed to seeking the for and against in all things, for him to lose sight of truth altogether and then be obliged to live without courage or trust, in denial and doubt, agitated and discontented, half hopeful, expecting to be disappointed: 'No dog would go on living like this!'* The third danger is that of petrifaction, in the moral or the intellectual sphere; a man severs the bonds that tied him to his ideal; he ceases to be fruitful, to propagate himself, in this or that domain; in a cultural sense he becomes feeble or useless. The uniqueness of his being has become an indivisible, uncommunicating atom, an icy rock. And thus one can be reduced to ruin by this uniqueness just as well as by the fear of it, by oneself as well as by surrender of oneself, by longing as well as by petrifaction: and to live at all means to live in danger.

Besides these constitutional dangers to which Schopenhauer would have been exposed in whatever century he had lived, there are also dangers which arose from his *age*; and this distinction between constitutional dangers and those proceeding from the age he lived in is essential for an understanding of what is exemplary and educative in Schopenhauer's nature. Let us think of the philosopher's eye resting upon existence: he wants to determine its value anew. For it has been the proper task of all great thinkers to be lawgivers as to the measure, stamp and weight of things. How it must obstruct him if the mankind most immediate to him is a feeble and worm-eaten fruit! How much allowance he has to make for the valuelessness of his time if he is to be just to existence as a whole! If occupation with the history of past or foreign nations is of any value, it is of most value to the philosopher who wants to arrive at a just verdict on the whole fate of man – not, that is, only on the average fate but above all on the highest fate that can befall individual men or entire nations. But everything contemporary is importunate; it affects and directs the eye even when the philosopher does not want it to; and in the total

---

* Quoted from Goethe's *Faust*, Part I Scene 1.

accounting it will involuntarily be appraised too high. That is why, when he compares his own age with other ages, the philosopher must deliberately under-assess it and, by overcoming the present in himself, also overcome it in the picture he gives of life, that is to say render it unremarkable and as it were paint it over. This is a difficult, indeed hardly achievable task. The verdict of the philosophers of ancient Greece on the value of existence says so much more than a modern verdict does because they had life itself before and around them in luxuriant perfection and because, unlike us, their minds were not confused by the discord between the desire for freedom, beauty, abundance of life on the one hand and on the other the drive to truth, which asks only: what is existence worth as such? It will always be worth knowing what Empedocles, living as he did in the midst of the most vigorous and exuberant vitality of Greek culture, had to say about existence; his verdict possesses great weight, especially as it is not contradicted by a counter-verdict from any other great philosopher of the same great era. He speaks the most clearly, but essentially – that is if we listen carefully – they are all saying the same thing. A modern thinker will, to repeat, always suffer from an unfulfilled desire: he will want first to be shown life again, true, red-blooded, healthy life, so that he may then pronounce his judgment on it. To himself at least he will regard it as necessary that he should be a living human being if he is to believe he can be a just judge. This is the reason it is precisely the more modern philosophers who are among the mightiest promoters of life, of the will to live, and why from out of their own exhausted age they long for a culture, for a transfigured physis. But this longing also constitutes their *danger*: there is a struggle within them between the reformer of life and the philosopher, that is to say the judge of life. Wherever the victory may incline, it is a victory that will involve a loss. And how, then, did Schopenhauer elude this danger too?

If it is commonly accepted that the great man is the genuine child of his age, if he in any event suffers from the deficiencies of his age more acutely than do smaller men, then a struggle by such a great man *against* his age seems to be only a senseless and destructive attack on himself. But only seems so; for he is contending against those aspects of his age that prevent him from being great, which means, in his case, being free and entirely himself. From which it follows that his hostility is at bottom directed against that which, though he finds it in himself, is not truly himself: against the indecent compounding and confusing of things eternally incompatible, against the soldering of time-bound things on to his own untimeliness; and in the end the supposed child of his time proves to be only its stepchild. Thus Schopenhauer strove from his early youth against that false, idle and unworthy mother, his age, and by as it were expelling her from him, he healed and purified his being and rediscovered himself in the health and purity native to him. That is why Schopenhauer's writings can be used as a mirror of his age; and it is certainly not due to a fault in the mirror if everything time-bound in his age appears as a disfiguring illness, as thin and pale, as enervated and hollow eyed, as the recognizable sufferings of his stepchildhood. The longing for a stronger nature, for a healthier and simpler humanity, was in his case a longing for himself; and when he had conquered his age in himself he beheld with astonished eyes the genius in himself. The secret of his being was now revealed to him, the intention of his stepmother age to conceal his genius from him was frustrated, the realm of transfigured *physis* was disclosed. When he now turned his fearless eye upon the question: 'What is life worth as such?' – it was no longer a confused and pallid age and its hypo-critical, uncertain life upon which he had to pass judgment. He knew well that there is something higher and purer to be found and attained on this earth than the life of his own time, and that he who knows existence only in this ugly shape, and assesses it accordingly, does it a grave injustice. No, genius itself is now summoned, so that one may hear whether genius, the highest fruit of life, can perhaps justify life as such; the glorious, creative human being is now to answer the question: 'Do you affirm this existence in the depths of your heart? Is it sufficient for you? Would you be its advocate, its redeemer? For you have only to pronounce a single heartfelt Yes! – and life, though it faces such heavy accusations, shall go free.' – What answer will he give? – The answer of Empedocles.

4

This last remark may be allowed to remain incomprehensible for the moment: for I have now to deal with something extremely com-prehensible, namely to explain how through Schopenhauer we are all *able* to educate ourselves *against* our age – because through him we possess the advantage of really *knowing* this age. Supposing, that is, that it *is* an advantage! In any event, it may no longer be possible a couple of centuries hence. I find it amusing to reflect on the idea that mankind may sometime soon grow tired of reading and that writers will do so too, that the scholar will one day direct in his last will and testament that his corpse shall be buried surrounded by his books and especially by his own writings. And if it is true that the forests are going to get thinner and thinner, may the time not come one day when the libraries should be used for timber, straw and brushwood? Since most books are born out of smoke and vapour of the brain, they ought to return to smoke and vapour. And if they have no fire of their own in them, fire should punish them for it. It is thus possible that a later century will regard our era as a *saeculum obscurum*,* because its productions have been used most abundantly for heating the stoves. How fortunate we are, therefore, that we are still able to know this age. For if concerning oneself with one's own age makes any sense at all, then it is a good thing to concern oneself with it as thoroughly as possible, so as to leave absolutely no doubt as to its nature: and it is precisely this that Schopenhauer enables us to do.

Of course, it would be a hundred times better if this investigation should reveal that nothing so proud and full of hope as our own age has ever before existed. And there are indeed at this moment naive people in this and that corner of the earth, in Germany for instance, who are prepared to believe such a thing, and even go so far as to assert in all seriousness that the world was put to rights a couple of years ago† and that those who persist in harbouring dark misgivings about the nature of existence are refuted by the 'facts'. The chief fact is that the founding of the new German Reich is a decisive and annihilating blow to all 'pessimistic' philosophizing – that is supposed to be firm and certain. – Whoever is seeking to answer the question of what the philosopher as educator can mean in our time has to contest this view, which is very widespread and is propagated especially in our universities; he must declare: it is a downright scandal that such nauseating, idolatrous flattery can be rendered to our time by supposedly thinking and honourable men – a proof that one no longer has the slightest notion how different the seriousness of philosophy is from the seriousness of a newspaper. Such men have lost the last remnant not only of a philosophical but also of a religious mode of thinking, and in their place have acquired not even optimism but journalism, the spirit and spiritlessness of our day and our daily papers. Every philosophy which believes that the problem of existence is touched on, not to say solved, by a political

---

Saeculum obscurum: dark age   †i.e. with the founding of the Reich in 1871.

event is a joke- and pseudo-philosophy. Many states have been founded since the world began; that is an old story. How should a political innovation suffice to turn men once and for all into contented inhabitants of the earth? But if anyone really does believe in this possibility he ought to come forward, for he truly deserves to become a professor of philosophy at a German university, like Harms in Berlin, Jürgen Meyer in Bonn and Carrière in Munich.

Here, however, we are experiencing the consequences of the doctrine, lately preached from all the rooftops, that the state is the highest goal of mankind and that a man has no higher duty than to serve the state: in which doctrine I recognize a relapse not into paganism but into stupidity. It may be that a man who sees his highest duty in serving the state really knows no higher duties; but there are men and duties existing beyond this – and one of the duties that seems, at least to me, to be higher than serving the state demands that one destroys stupidity in every form, and therefore in this form too. That is why I am concerned here with a species of man whose teleology extends somewhat beyond the welfare of a state, with philosophers, and with these only in relation to a world which is again fairly independent of the welfare of a state, that of culture. Of the many rings which, interlocked together, make up the human community, some are of gold and others of pinchbeck.

Now, how does the philosopher view the culture of our time? Very differently, to be sure, from how it is viewed by those professors of philosophy who are so well contented with their new state. When he thinks of the haste and hurry now universal, of the increasing velocity of life, of the cessation of all contemplativeness and simplicity, he almost thinks that what he is seeing are the symptoms of a total extermination and uprooting of culture. The waters of religion are ebbing away and leaving behind swamps or stagnant pools; the nations are again drawing away from one another in the most hostile fashion and long to tear one another to pieces. The sciences, pursued without any restraint and in a spirit of the blindest *laissez faire*, are shattering and dissolving all firmly held belief; the educated classes and states are being swept along by a hugely contemptible money economy. The world has never been more worldly, never poorer in love and goodness. The educated classes are no longer lighthouses or refuges in the midst of this turmoil of secularization; they themselves grow daily more restless, thoughtless and loveless. Everything, contemporary art and science included, serves the coming barbarism. The cultured man has degenerated to the greatest enemy of culture, for he wants lyingly to deny the existence of the universal sickness and thus obstructs the physicians. They become incensed, these poor wretches, whenever one speaks of their weakness and resists their pernicious lying spirit. They would dearly like to make us believe that of all the centuries theirs has borne the prize away, and they shake with artificial merriment. Their way of hypocritically simulating happiness sometimes has something touching about it, because their happiness is something so completely incomprehensible. One does not even feel like asking them what Tannhäuser asked Biterolf: 'What then, poor man, have you enjoyed?'* For ah! we ourselves know better and know otherwise. A winter's day lies upon us, and we dwell in high mountains, dangerously and in poverty. Every joy is brief, and every ray of sunlight is pale that creeps down to us on our white mountain. Music sounds, an old man turns a barrel-organ, the dancers revolve – the wanderer is deeply moved when he sees it: all is so wild, so taciturn, so colourless, so hopeless, and now there sounds within it a note of joy, of sheer, unreflecting joy! But already the mists of early evening are creeping in, the note dies away, the wanderer's step grates on the ground; for as far as he can still see, he sees nothing but the cruel and desolate face of nature.

If it may be one-sided to emphasize only the weakness of the outlines and the dullness of the colours in the picture of modern life, the other side of the picture is in no way more gratifying but only more disturbing. There are certainly forces there, tremendous forces, but savage, primal and wholly merciless. One gazes upon them with a fearful expectation, as though gazing into the cauldron of a witch's kitchen: at any moment sparks and flashes may herald dreadful apparitions. For a century we have been preparing for absolutely fundamental convulsions; and if there have recently been attempts to oppose this deepest of modern inclinations, to collapse or to explode, with the constitutive power of the so-called nation state, the latter too will for a long time serve only to augment the universal insecurity and atmosphere of menace. That individuals behave as though they knew nothing of all these anxieties does not mislead us: their restlessness reveals how well they know of them; they think with a precipitancy and with an exclusive preoccupation with themselves never before encountered in man, they build and plant for their own day alone, and the pursuit of happiness is never greater than when it

---

*In Wagner's *Tannhäuser*, Act II.

has to be caught today or tomorrow: because perhaps by the day after tomorrow there will be no more hunting at all. We live in the age of atoms, of atomistic chaos. In the Middle Ages the hostile forces were held together by the church and, through the strong pressure it exerted, to some extent assimilated with one another. When the bond broke, the pressure relaxed, they rebelled against one another. The Reformation declared many things to be *adiaphora*, domains where religion was not to hold sway; this was the price at which it purchased its existence: just as Christianity had already had to pay a similar price in face of the much more religiously inclined world of antiquity. From there on the division spread wider and wider. Nowadays the crudest and most evil forces, the egoism of the money-makers and the military despots, hold sway over almost everything on earth. In the hands of these despots and money-makers, the state certainly makes an attempt to organize everything anew out of itself and to bind and constrain all those mutually hostile forces: that is to say, it wants men to render it the same idolatry they formerly rendered the church. With what success? We have still to learn; we are, in any case, even now still in the ice-filled stream of the Middle Ages; it has thawed and is rushing on with devastating power. Ice-floe piles on ice-floe, all the banks have been inundated and are in danger of collapse. The revolution is absolutely unavoidable, and it will be the atomistic revolution: but what are the smallest indivisible basic constituents of human society?

It is incontestable that the spirit of humanity is almost in greater danger during the approach of such eras than it is when they and the chaotic turmoil they bring with them have actually arrived: the anxiety of waiting and the greedy exploitation of every minute brings forth all the cowardice and the self-seeking drives of the soul, while the actual emergency, and especially a great universal emergency, usually improves men and makes them more warm-hearted. Who is there then, amid these dangers of our era, to guard and champion *humanity*, the inviolable sacred treasure gradually accumulated by the most various races? Who will set up the *image of man* when all men feel in themselves only the self-seeking snake and currish fear and have thus declined from that image to the level of the animals or even of automata?

There are three images of man which our modern age has set up one after the other and which will no doubt long inspire mortals to a transfiguration of their own lives: they are the man of Rousseau, the man of Goethe and finally the man of Schopenhauer. Of these, the

first image possesses the greatest fire and is sure of producing the
greatest popular effect; the second is intended only for the few, for
contemplative natures in the grand style, and is misunderstood by
the crowd. The third demands contemplation only by the most
active men; only they can regard it without harm to themselves, for it
debilitates the contemplative and frightens away the crowd. From
the first there has proceeded a force which has promoted violent
revolutions and continues to do so; for in every socialist earthquake
and upheaval it has always been the man of Rousseau who, like
Typhon under Etna, is the cause of the commotion. Oppressed and
half crushed by arrogant upper classes and merciless wealth, ruined
by priests and bad education and rendered contemptible to himself
by ludicrous customs, man cries in his distress to 'holy nature' and
suddenly feels that it is as distant from him as any Epicurean god.
His prayers do not reach it, so deeply is he sunk in the chaos of
unnaturalness. Scornfully he throws from him all the gaudy finery
which only a short time before had seemed to him to constitute his
essential humanity, his arts and sciences, the advantages of a refined
life; he beats with his fists against the walls in whose shadow he has so
degenerated, and demands light, sun, forest and mountain. And
when he cries: 'Only nature is good, only the natural is human,' he
despises himself and longs to go beyond himself: a mood in which
the soul is ready for fearful decisions but which also calls up from its
depths what is noblest and rarest in it.

The man of Goethe is no such threatening power, indeed in a certain
sense he is the corrective and sedative for precisely those dangerous
excitations of which the man of Rousseau is the victim. In his youth
Goethe was himself a devotee of the gospel of nature with his whole
loving heart; his Faust was the highest and boldest reproduction of
the man of Rousseau, at any rate so far as concerns his ravenous
hunger for life, his discontent and longing, his traffic with the
demons of the heart. But then see what eventuates from this great
bank of clouds – certainly not lightning! And it is in precisely this that
there is revealed the new image of man, Goethean man. One would
think that Faust would be led through a life everywhere afflicted and
oppressed as an insatiable rebel and liberator, as the power that
denies out of goodness, as the actual religious and demonic genius
of subversion, in contrast to his altogether undemonic companion,
though he cannot get rid of this companion and has to employ and at
the same time despise his sceptical malice and denial – as is the tragic
fate of every rebel and liberator. But one is mistaken if one expects

151

anything of that kind; the man of Goethe here turns away from the man of Rousseau; for he hates all violence, all sudden transition – but that means: all action; and thus the world-liberator becomes as it were only a world-traveller. All the realms of life and nature, all the past, all the arts, mythologies and sciences, see the insatiable spectator fly past them, the deepest desires are aroused and satisfied, even Helen does not detain him for very long – and then there must come the moment for which his mocking companion is lying in wait. At some suitable spot on earth his flight comes to an end, his wings fall off, Mephistopheles is at hand. When the German ceases to be Faust there is no greater danger than that he will become a philistine and go to the Devil – heavenly powers alone can save him from it. The man of Goethe is, as I have said, the contemplative man in the grand style, who can avoid languishing away on earth only by bringing together for his nourishment everything great and memorable that has ever existed or still exists and thus lives, even though his life may be a living from one desire to the next; he is not the man of action: on the contrary, if he does ever become a member of any part of the existing order established by the men of action one can be sure that no good will come of it – Goethe's own enthusiastic participation in the world of the theatre is a case in point – and, above all, that no 'order' will be overthrown. The Goethean man is a preservative and conciliatory power – but with the danger, already mentioned, that he may degenerate to a philistine, just as the man of Rousseau can easily become a Catilinist. If the former had a little more muscle-power and natural wildness, all his virtues would be greater. Goethe seems to have realized where the danger and weakness of his type of man lay, and he indicates it in the words of Jarno to Wilhelm Meister: 'You are vexed and bitter, that is very good; if only you would get really angry for once it would be even better.'*

Thus, to speak frankly: it is necessary for us to get really angry for once in order that things shall get better. And to encourage us to that we have the Schopenhauerean image of man. *The Schopenhauerean man voluntarily takes upon himself the suffering involved in being truthful*, and this suffering serves to destroy his own wilfulness and to prepare that complete overturning and conversion of his being, which it is the real meaning of life to lead up to. This utterance of truth seems to other men a discharge of malice, for they regard the conservation of their inadequacies and humbug as a human duty and think that any-

---

*In *Wilhelm Meisters Lehrjahre* (1795–6), Book 8.

one who disrupts their child's play in this way must be wicked. They are tempted to cry to such a man what Faust said to Mephistopheles: 'So to the eternal active and creative power you oppose the cold hand of the Devil';* and he who would live according to Schopenhauer would probably seem more like a Mephistopheles than a Faust – seem, that is, to purblind modern eyes, which always see in denial the mark of evil. But there is a kind of denying and destroying that is the discharge of that mighty longing for sanctification and salvation and as the first philosophical teacher of which Schopenhauer came among us desanctified and truly secularized men. All that exists that can be denied deserves to be denied; and being truthful means: to believe in an existence that can in no way be denied and which is itself true and without falsehood. That is why the truthful man feels that the meaning of his activity is metaphysical, explicable through the laws of another and higher life, and in the profoundest sense affirmative: however much all that he does may appear to be de-structive of the laws of this life and a crime against them. So it is that all his acts must become an uninterrupted suffering; but he knows what Meister Eckhart also knows: 'The beast that bears you fastest to perfection is suffering.' I would think that anyone who set such a life's course before his soul must feel his heart open and a fierce desire arise within him to be such a Schopenhauerean man: that is to say, strangely composed about himself and his own welfare, in his knowledge full of blazing, consuming fire and far removed from the cold and contemptible neutrality of the so-called scientific man, exalted high above all sullen and ill-humoured reflection, always offering himself as the first sacrifice to perceived truth and per-meated with the awareness of what sufferings must spring from his truthfulness. He will, to be sure, destroy his earthly happiness through his courage; he will have to be an enemy to those he loves and to the institutions which have produced him; he may not spare men or things, even though he suffers when they suffer; he will be misunderstood and for long thought an ally of powers he abhors; however much he may strive after justice he is bound, according to the human limitations of his insight, to be unjust: but he may con-sole himself with the words once employed by his great teacher, Schopenhauer: 'A happy life is impossible: the highest that man can attain to is a *heroic one*. He leads it who, in whatever shape or form, struggles against great difficulties for something that is to the benefit

* In *Faust*, Part I Scene 3.

153

of all and in the end is victorious, but who is ill-rewarded for it or not rewarded at all. Then, when he has done, he is turned to stone, like the prince in Gozzi's *Re corvo*, but stands in a noble posture and with generous gestures. He is remembered and is celebrated as a hero; his will, mortified a whole life long by effort and labour, ill success and the world's ingratitude, is extinguished in Nirvana.'* Such a heroic life, to be sure, together with the mortification accomplished in it, corresponds least of all to the paltry conception of those who make the most noise about it, celebrate festivals to the memory of great men, and believe that great men are great in the same way as they are little, as it were through a gift and for their own satisfaction or by a mechanical operation and in blind obedience to this inner compulsion: so that he who has not received this gift, or does not feel this compulsion, has the same right to be little as the other has to be great. But being gifted or being compelled are contemptible words designed to enable one to ignore an inner admonition, slanders on him who has paid heed to this admonition, that is to say on the great man; he least of all lets himself be given gifts or be compelled – he knows as well as any little man how to take life easily and how soft the bed is on which he could lie down if his attitude towards himself and his fellow men were that of the majority: for the objective of all human arrangements is through distracting one's thoughts to cease *to be aware* of life. Why does he desire the opposite – to be aware precisely of life, that is to say to suffer from life – so strongly? Because he realizes that he is in danger of being cheated out of himself, and that a kind of agreement exists to kidnap him out of his own cave. Then he bestirs himself, pricks up his ears, and resolves: 'I will remain my own!' It is a dreadful resolve; only gradually does he grasp that fact. For now he will have to descend into the depths of existence with a string of curious questions on his lips: why do I live? what lesson have I to learn from life? how have I become what I am and why do I suffer from being what I am? He torments himself, and sees how no one else does as he does, but how the hands of his fellow men are, rather, passionately stretched out to the fantastic events portrayed in the theatre of politics, or how they strut about in a hundred masquerades, as youths, men, greybeards, fathers, citizens, priests, officials, merchants, mindful solely of their comedy and not at all of

---

*From Schopenhauer's *Parerga und Paralipomena*: 'Nachträge zur Lehre von der Bejahung und Verneinung des Willens zum Leben'.

themselves. To the question: 'To what end do you live?' they would all quickly reply with pride: *'To become* a good citizen, or scholar, or statesman' – and yet they *are* something that can never become something else, and why are they precisely this? And not, alas, something better? He who regards his life as no more than a point in the evolution of a race or of a state or of a science, and thus regards himself as belonging wholly to the history of becoming, has not understood the lesson set him by existence and will have to learn it over again. This eternal becoming is a lying puppet-play in beholding which man forgets himself, the actual distraction which disperses the individual to the four winds, the endless stupid game which the great child, time, plays before us and with us. That heroism of truthfulness consists in one day ceasing to be the toy it plays with. In becoming, everything is hollow, deceptive, shallow and worthy of our contempt; the enigma which man is to resolve he can resolve only in being, in being thus and not otherwise, in the imperishable. Now he starts to test how deeply he is entwined with becoming, how deeply with being – a tremendous task rises before his soul: to destroy all that is becoming, to bring to light all that is false in things. He too wants to know everything, but not, in the way the Goethean man does, for the sake of a noble pliability, to preserve himself and to take delight in the multiplicity of things; he himself is his first sacrifice to himself. The heroic human being despises his happiness and his unhappiness, his virtues and vices, and in general the measuring of things by the standard of himself; he hopes for nothing more from himself and in all things he wants to see down to this depth of hopelessness. His strength lies in forgetting himself; and if he does think of himself he measures the distance between himself and his lofty goal and seems to see behind and beneath him only an insignificant heap of dross. The thinkers of old sought happiness and truth with all their might – and what has to be sought shall never be found, says nature's evil principle. But for him who seeks untruth in everything and voluntarily allies himself with unhappiness a miracle of disappointment of a different sort has perhaps been prepared: something inexpressible of which happiness and truth are only idolatrous counterfeits approaches him, the earth loses its gravity, the events and powers of the earth become dreamlike, transfiguration spreads itself about him as on summer evenings. To him who sees these things it is as though he were just beginning to awaken and what is playing about him is only the clouds of a vanishing dream. These too will at some time be wafted away: then it will be day. –

155

5

But I have undertaken to exhibit my experience of Schopenhauer as an *educator*, and it is thus not nearly sufficient for me to paint, and to paint imperfectly, that ideal man who, as his Platonic ideal as it were, holds sway in and around him. The hardest task still remains: to say how a new circle of duties may be derived from this ideal and how one can proceed towards so extravagant a goal through a practical activity – in short, to demonstrate that this ideal *educates*. One might otherwise think it nothing but an intoxicating vision granted us only for moments at a time, and then leaving us all the more painfully in the lurch and prey to an even deeper dissatisfaction. It is also indisputable that that is how we *begin* our association with this ideal – with a sudden contrast of light and darkness, intoxication and nausea – and that this is a repetition of an experience which is as old as ideals themselves. But we ought not to stand long in the doorway, we ought soon to get through the beginning. And so we have seriously to ask the definite question: is it possible to bring that incredibly lofty goal so close to us that it educates us while it draws us aloft? – that Goethe's mighty words may not be fulfilled in us: 'Man is born to a limited situation; he is able to understand simple, accessible, definite goals, and he accustoms himself to employing the means that happen to lie close at hand; but as soon as he oversteps his limits he knows neither what he wants nor what he ought to do, and it is all one whether he is distracted by the multiplicity of the things he encounters or whether his head is turned by their loftiness and dignity. It is always a misfortune when he is induced to strive after something which he cannot proceed towards through a practical activity.'* The Schopenhauerean man appears to be singularly open to this objection: his dignity and loftiness can only turn our heads and thereby exclude us from any participation in the world of action; coherent duties, the even flow of life are gone. One man perhaps at last accustoms himself to living discontentedly according to two different rules of conduct, that is to say in conflict with himself, uncertain of how to act and therefore daily more feeble and unfruitful: while another may even renounce all action on principle and almost cease to pay any attention to the actions of others. The dangers are always great when things are made too difficult for a man and when

*From *Wilhelm Meisters Lehrjahre*, Book 4.

he is incapable of *fulfilling* any duties at all; stronger natures can be destroyed by it, the weaker, more numerous natures decline into a reflective laziness and in the end forfeit through laziness even their ability to reflect.

Now, in face of such objections I am willing to concede that in precisely this respect our work has hardly begun and that from my own experience I am sure of only one thing: that from that ideal image it is possible to fasten upon ourselves a chain of fulfillable duties, and that some of us already feel the weight of this chain. But before I can conscientiously reduce this new circle of duties to a formula I must offer the following preliminary observations.

More profoundly feeling people have at all times felt sympathy for the animals because they suffer from life and yet do not possess the power to turn the goad of life against themselves and understand their existence metaphysically; one is, indeed, profoundly indignant at the sight of senseless suffering. That is why there has arisen in more than one part of the earth the supposition that the bodies of animals contain the guilt-laden souls of men, so that this suffering which at first sight arouses indignation on account of its senselessness acquires meaning and significance as punishment and atonement before the seat of eternal justice. And it is, truly, a harsh punishment thus to live as an animal, beset by hunger and desire yet incapable of any kind of reflection on the nature of this life; and no harder fate can be thought of than that of the beast of prey pursued through the wilderness by the most gnawing torment, rarely satisfied and even then in such a way that satisfaction is purchased only with the pain of lascerating combat with other animals or through inordinate greed and nauseating satiety. To hang on to life madly and blindly, with no higher aim than to hang on to it; not to know that or why one is being so heavily punished but, with the stupidity of a fearful desire, to thirst after precisely this punishment as though after happiness – that is what it means to be an animal; and if all nature presses towards man, it thereby intimates that man is necessary for the redemption of nature from the curse of the life of the animal, and that in him existence at last holds up before itself a mirror in which life appears no longer senseless but in its metaphysical significance. Yet let us reflect: where does the animal cease, where does man begin? – man, who is nature's sole concern! As long as anyone desires life as he desires happiness he has not yet raised his eyes above the horizon of the animal, for he only desires more consciously what the animal seeks through blind impulse. But that is what we all do for the greater part of our lives: usually we fail to emerge out of animality, we ourselves are the animals whose suffering seems to be senseless.

But there are moments *when we realize this*: then the clouds are rent asunder, and we see that, in common with all nature, we are pressing towards man as towards something that stands high above us. In this sudden illumination we gaze around us and behind us with a shudder: we behold the more subtle beasts of prey and there we are in the midst of them. The tremendous coming and going of men on the great wilderness of the earth, their founding of cities and states, their wars, their restless assembling and scattering again, their confused mingling, mutual imitation, mutual outwitting and downtreading, their wailing in distress, their howls of joy in victory – all this is a continuation of animality: as though man was to be deliberately retrogressed and defrauded of his metaphysical disposition, indeed as though nature, after having desired and worked at man for so long, now drew back from him in fear and preferred to return to the unconsciousness of instinct. Nature needs knowledge and it is terrified of the knowledge it has need of; and so the flame flickers restlessly back and forth as though afraid of itself and seizes upon a thousand things before it seizes upon that on account of which nature needs knowledge at all. In individual moments we all know how the most elaborate arrangements of our life are made only so as to flee from the tasks we actually ought to be performing, how we would like to hide our head somewhere as though our hundred-eyed conscience could not find us out there, how we hasten to give our heart to the state, to money-making, to sociability or science merely so as no longer to possess it ourselves, how we labour at our daily work more ardently and thoughtlessly than is necessary to sustain our life because to us it is even more necessary not to have leisure to stop and think. Haste is universal because everyone is in flight from himself; universal too is the shy concealment of this haste because everyone wants to seem content and would like to deceive more sharp-eyed observers as to the wretchedness he feels; and also universal is the need for new tinkling word-bells to hang upon life and so bestow upon it an air of noisy festivity. Everyone is familiar with the strange condition in which unpleasant memories suddenly assert themselves and we then make great efforts, through vehement noise and gestures, to banish them from our minds: but the noise and gestures which are going on everywhere reveal that we are all in such a condition all the time, that we live in fear of memory and of turning inward. But what is it that assails us so frequently, what is the gnat that will not let us sleep? There are spirits all around us, every moment of our life wants to say something to us, but we refuse to listen to these spirit-voices. We are afraid that when we are alone and quiet something will be whispered into our ear, and so we hate quietness and deafen ourselves with sociability.

Now and again, as already said, we realize all this, and are amazed at all this vertiginous fear and haste and at the whole dreamlike condition in which we live, which seems to have a horror of awakening and dreams the more vividly and restlessly the closer it is to this awakening. But we feel at the same time that we are too weak to endure those moments of profoundest contemplation for very long and that we are not the mankind towards which all nature presses for its redemption: it is already much that we should raise our head above the water at all, even if only a little, and observe what stream it is in which we are so deeply immersed. And even this momentary emerging and awakening is not achieved through our own power, we have to be lifted up – and who are they who lift us?

They are those true *men, those who are no longer animal, the philosophers, artists and saints*; nature, which never makes a leap, has made its one leap in creating them, and a leap of joy moreover, for nature then feels that for the first time it has reached its goal – where it realizes it has to unlearn having goals and that it has played the game of life and becoming with too high stakes. This knowledge transfigures nature, and a gentle evening-weariness, that which men call 'beauty', reposes upon its face. That which it now utters with this transfigured countenance is the great *enlightenment* as to the character of existence; and the supreme wish that mortals can wish is lastingly and with open ears to participate in this enlightenment. If we think of how much Schopenhauer for instance must have *heard* during the course of his life, then we might well say to ourselves afterwards: 'Alas, your deaf ears, your dull head, your flickering understanding, your shrivelled heart, all that I call mine, how I despise you! Not to be able to fly, only to flutter! To see what is above you but not to be able to reach it! To know the way that leads to the immeasurable open prospect of the philosopher, and almost to set foot on it, but after a few steps to stagger back! And if that greatest of all wishes were fulfilled for only a day, how gladly one would exchange for it all the rest of life! To climb as high into the pure icy Alpine air as a philosopher ever climbed, up to where all the mist and obscurity cease and where the fundamental constitution of things speaks in a voice rough and rigid but ineluctably comprehensible! Merely to think of this makes the soul infinitely solitary; if its wish were fulfilled, however, if its glance once fell upon things straight and bright as a beam of light, if shame, fear and desire died away – what word could then describe the condition it would be in, that new and enigmatic animation without agitation with which it would, like the soul of Schopenhauer, lie extended over the tremendous hieroglyphics of existence, over the petrified doctrine of becoming, not as the darkness of night but as the glowing light of dawn streaming out over all the world. And what a fate, on the other hand, to sense sufficient of the certainty and happiness of the philosopher to be able to feel the whole uncertainty and unhappiness of the non-philosopher, of him who desires without hope! To know oneself a fruit on the tree which can never become ripe because one is too much in the shadow, and at the same time to see close at hand the sunshine that one lacks!'

There is enough torment here to make a man who is mis-talented in such a way malicious and envious, if he is capable of malice and envy at all; probably, however, he will at last turn his soul in another direction so that it shall not consume itself in vain longing – and now he will *discover* a new circle of duties.

Here I have arrived at an answer to the question whether it is possible to pursue the great ideal of the Schopenhauerean man by means of a practical activity. One thing above all is certain: these new duties are not the duties of a solitary; on the contrary, they set one in the midst of a mighty community held together, not by external forms and regulations, but by a fundamental idea. It is the fundamental idea of *culture*, insofar as it sets for each one of us but one task: *to promote the production of the philosopher, the artist and the saint within us and without us and thereby to work at the perfecting of nature.* For, as nature needs the philosopher, so does it need the artist, for the achievement of a metaphysical goal, that of its own self-enlightenment, so that it may at last behold as a clear and finished picture that which it could see only obscurely in the agitation of its evolution – for the end, that is to say, of self-knowledge. It was Goethe who declared, in an arrogant but profound assertion, that nature's experiments are of value only when the artist finally comes to comprehend its stammerings, goes out to meet it halfway, and gives expression to what all these experiments are really about. 'I have often said', he once exclaimed, 'and I shall often repeat, that the *causa finalis* of the activities of men and the world is dramatic poetry. For the stuff is of absolutely no other use.' And so nature at last needs the saint, in whom the ego is completely

melted away and whose life of suffering is no longer felt as his own
life – or is hardly so felt – but as a profound feeling of oneness and
identity with all living things: the saint in whom there appears that
miracle of transformation which the game of becoming never hits
upon, that final and supreme becoming-human after which all
nature presses and urges for its redemption from itself. It is incontestable that we are all related and allied to the saint, just as we are
related to the philosopher and artist; there are moments and as it
were bright sparks of the fire of love in whose light we cease to
understand the word 'I', there lies something beyond our being
which at these moments moves across into it, and we are thus
possessed of a heartfelt longing for bridges between here and there.
It is true that, as we usually are, we can contribute nothing to the production of the man of redemption: that is why we *hate* ourselves as we
usually are, and it is this hatred which is the root of that pessimism
which Schopenhauer had again to teach our age, though it has existed
for as long as the longing for culture has existed. Its root, not its
flower; its bottom floor, so to speak, not its roof; the commencement
of its course, not its goal: for at some time or other we shall have to
learn to hate something else, something more universal, and cease
to hate our own individuality and its wretched limitations,
changeableness and restlessness: it will be in that elevated condition
in which we shall also love something else, something we are now
unable to love. Only when, in our present or in some future incar-
nation, we ourselves have been taken into that exalted order of
philosophers, artists and saints, shall we also be given a new goal for
our love and hate – in the meantime we have our task and our circle
of duties, our hate and our love. For we know what culture is.
Applied to the Schopenhauerean man, it demands that we prepare
and promote his repeated production by getting to know what is
inimical to it and removing it – in short, that we unwearyingly combat that which would deprive *us* of the supreme fulfilment of our
existence by preventing us from becoming such Schopenhauerean
men ourselves. –

6

Sometimes it is harder to accede to a thing than it is to see its truth;
and that is how most people may feel when they reflect on the proposition: 'Mankind must work continually at the production of
individual great men – that and nothing else is its task.' How much

one would like to apply to society and its goals something that can be learned from observation of any species of the animal or plant world: that its only concern is the individual higher exemplar, the more uncommon, more powerful, more complex, more fruitful – how much one would like to do this if inculcated fancies as to the goal of society did not offer such tough resistance! We ought really to have no difficulty in seeing that, when a species has arrived at its limits and is about to go over into a higher species, the goal of its evolution lies, not in the mass of its exemplars and their wellbeing, let alone in those exemplars who happen to come last in point of time, but rather in those apparently scattered and chance existences which favourable conditions have here and there produced; and it ought to be just as easy to understand the demand that, because it can arrive at a conscious awareness of its goal, mankind ought to seek out and create the favourable conditions under which those great redemptive men can come into existence. But everything resists this conclusion: here the ultimate goal is seen to lie in the happiness of all or of the greatest number, there in the development of great communities; and though one may be ready to sacrifice one's life to a state, for instance, it is another matter if one is asked to sacrifice it on behalf of another individual. It seems to be an absurd demand that one man should exist for the sake of another man; 'for the sake of all others, rather, or at least for as many as possible!' O worthy man! as though it were less absurd to let number decide when value and significance are at issue! For the question is this: how can your life, the individual life, receive the highest value, the deepest significance? How can it be least squandered? Certainly only by your living for the good of the rarest and most valuable exemplars, and not for the good of the majority, that is to say those who, taken individually, are the least valuable exemplars. And the young person should be taught to regard himself as a failed work of nature but at the same time as a witness to the grandiose and marvellous intentions of this artist: nature has done badly, he should say to himself; but I will honour its great intentions by serving it so that one day it may do better.

By coming to this resolve he places himself within the circle of *culture*; for culture is the child of each individual's self-knowledge and dissatisfaction with himself. Anyone who believes in culture is thereby saying: 'I see above me something higher and more human than I am; let everyone help me to attain it, as I will help everyone who knows and suffers as I do: so that at last the man may appear

162

who feels himself perfect and boundless in knowledge and love, perception and power, and who in his completeness is at one with nature, the judge and evaluator of things.' It is hard to create in anyone this condition of intrepid self-knowledge because it is impossible to teach love; for it is love alone that can bestow on the soul, not only a clear, discriminating and self-contemptuous view of itself, but also the desire to look beyond itself and to seek with all its might for a higher self as yet still concealed from it. Thus only he who has attached his heart to some great man is by that act *consecrated to culture*; the sign of that consecration is that one is ashamed of oneself without any accompanying feeling of distress, that one comes to hate one's own narrowness and shrivelled nature, that one has a feeling of sympathy for the genius who again and again drags himself up out of our dryness and apathy and the same feeling in anticipation for all those who are still struggling and evolving, with the profoundest conviction that almost everywhere we encounter nature pressing towards man and again and again failing to achieve him, yet everywhere succeeding in producing the most marvellous beginnings, individual traits and forms: so that the men we live among resemble a field over which is scattered the most precious fragments of sculpture where everything calls to us: come, assist, complete, bring together what belongs together, we have an immeasurable longing to become whole.

This sum of inner states is, I said, the first sign that one is consecrated to culture; now, however, I have to describe the *further* stage of this consecration, and I realize that here my task is more difficult. For now we have to make the transition from the inward event to an assessment of the outward event; the eye has to be directed outwards so as to rediscover in the great world of action that desire for culture it recognized in the experiences of the first stage just described; the individual has to employ his own wrestling and longing as the alphabet by means of which he can now read off the aspirations of mankind as a whole. But he may not halt even here; from this stage he has to climb up to a yet higher one; culture demands of him, not only inward experience, not only an assessment of the outward world that streams all around him, but finally and above all an act, that is to say a struggle on behalf of culture and hostility towards those influences, habits, laws, institutions in which he fails to recognize his goal: which is the production of the genius.

He who is capable of raising himself to this further stage is struck first of all by *how extraordinarily sparse and rare knowledge of this goal is,* how universal, by contrast, cultural endeavour is and what an unspeakable amount of energy is expended in its service. One asks oneself in amazement: is such knowledge perhaps completely unnecessary? Does nature attain its goal even when the majority misunderstand the objective of their endeavours? He who has accustomed himself to thinking highly of the unconscious purposefulness of nature will perhaps experience no difficulty in replying: 'Yes, that is how it is! Men may reflect and argue about their ultimate goal as much as they like, in the obscure impulse in the depths of them they are well aware of the rightful path.' To be able to contradict this, one must have experienced certain things; but he who really is convinced that the goal of culture is to promote the production of true *human beings* and nothing else, and then sees how even now, with all our expenditure and pomp of culture, the production of such human beings is hardly to be distinguished from cruelty to animals protracted into the human world, will think it very necessary finally to replace that 'obscure impulse' with a conscious willing. And he will think so especially for a second reason: that it shall cease to be possible for that drive which does not know its goal, that celebrated obscure impulse, to be employed for quite different objectives and directed on to paths which can never lead to the supreme goal, the production of the genius. For there exists a species of *misemployed and appropriated culture* – you have only to look around you! And precisely those forces at present most actively engaged in promoting culture do so for reasons they reserve to themselves and not out of pure disinterestedness.

Among these forces is, first of all, *the greed of the money-makers*, which requires the assistance of culture and by way of thanks assists culture in return, but at the same time, of course, would like to dictate its standards and objectives. It is from this quarter that there comes that favourite proposition and chain of conclusions which goes something like this: as much knowledge and education as possible, therefore as much demand as possible, therefore as much production as possible, therefore as much happiness and profit as possible – that is the seductive formula. Education would be defined by its adherents as the insight by means of which, through demand and its satisfaction, one becomes time-bound through and through but at the same time best acquires all the ways and means of making money as easily as possible. The goal would then be to create as many current human beings as possible, in the sense in which one speaks of a coin as being current; and, according to this conception,

164

the more of these current human beings it possesses the happier a nation will be. Thus the sole intention behind our modern educational institutions should be to assist everyone to become current to the extent that lies in his nature, to educate everyone in such a way that they can employ the degree of knowledge and learning of which they are capable for the accumulation of the greatest possible amount of happiness and profit. What is demanded here is that the individual must be able, with the aid of this general education, exactly to assess himself with regard to what he has a right to demand of life; and it is asserted, finally, that there exists a natural and necessary connection between 'intelligence and property', between 'wealth and culture', more, that this connection is a *moral* necessity. Here there is a hatred of any kind of education that makes one a solitary, that proposes goals that transcend money and money-making, that takes a long time; such more serious forms of education are usually disparaged as 'refined egoism' and as 'immoral cultural Epicureanism'. Precisely the opposite of this is, of course, held in esteem by the morality that here counts as valid: namely, a speedy education so that one may quickly become a money-earning being, yet at the same time an education sufficiently thorough to enable one to earn a very great deal of money. A man is allowed only as much culture as it is in the interest of general money-making and world commerce he should possess, but this amount is likewise demanded of him. In short: 'Man has a claim to earthly happiness and for that reason he needs education, but only for that reason!'

Secondly, there is *the greed of the state*, which likewise desires the greatest possible dissemination and universalization of culture and has in its hands the most effective instruments for satisfying this desire. Presupposing it knows itself sufficiently strong to be able, not only to unchain energies, but at the right time also to yoke them, presupposing its foundations are sufficiently broad and secure to sustain the whole educational structure, then the dissemination of education among its citizens can only be to its advantage in its competition with other states. Whenever one now speaks of the 'cultural state', one sees it as facing the task of releasing the spiritual energies of a generation to the extent that will serve the interests of existing institutions: but only to this extent; as a forest river is partially diverted with dams and breakwaters so as to operate a mill with the diminished driving-power thus produced – while the river's full driving-power would rather endanger the mill than operate it. This releasing of energies is at the same time, and much more, an enchaining of them. One has only to recall what Christianity has gradually become through the greed of the state. Christianity is certainly one of the purest revelations of the impulse to culture and especially of the impulse to the ever-renewed production of the saint; but since it has been employed in a hundred ways to propel the mills of state power it has gradually become sick to the very marrow, hypocritical and untruthful, and degenerated into a contradiction of its original goal. Even the most recent event in its history, the German Reformation, would have been no more than a sudden and quickly extinguished flare-up if it had not stolen fresh fuel from the fires of conflict between the states.

Thirdly, culture is promoted by all those who are conscious of possessing an *ugly or boring content* and want to conceal the fact with so-called '*beautiful form*'. Under the presupposition that what is inside is usually judged by what is outside, the observer is to be constrained to a false assessment of the content through externalities, through words, gestures, decoration, display, ceremoniousness. It sometimes seems to me that modern men bore one another to a boundless extent and that they finally feel the need to make themselves interesting with the aid of all the arts. They have themselves served up by their artists as sharp and pungent repasts; they soak themselves in all the spices of the Orient and the Occident, and to be sure! they now smell very interesting, smelling as they do of all the Orient and the Occident. Now they are suitably prepared for satisfying every taste; and everyone shall have something, whether his inclination be for the fresh-smelling or foul-smelling, for the sublimated or for peasant coarseness, for the Greek or the Chinese, for tragedies or for dramatized lewdness. The most celebrated chefs for these modern men who want to be interesting and interested at any cost are, as is well known, to be found among the French, the worst among the Germans. At bottom this fact is more consoling to the latter than to the former, and let us not hold it against the French in the least if they mock at us precisely because we are uninteresting and lack elegance and if, when individual Germans desire to be suave and elegant, it reminds them of the Indian who wanted a ring through his nose and demanded to be tattooed.

– And here I shall make a digression. Since the late war with France there have been many changes in Germany and it is clear that the return to peace has also brought with it certain new demands in regard to German culture. The war was for many their first visit to the more elegant half of the world; how unprejudiced the victor now appears when he does not disdain to acquire a little culture from the vanquished! Handicrafts especially are repeatedly invited to compete with the more cultivated neighbour, the fitting-out of the German house is to be made similar to that of the French, even the German language is, through the foundation of an academy after the French model, to acquire 'sound taste' and rid itself of the questionable influence supposedly exerted upon it by Goethe – a view expressed quite recently by the Berlin academician Dubois-Reymond. Our theatres have for long been quietly and with due decorum aspiring towards the same goal, even the elegant German scholar has already been invented: so that we can expect that everything that has up to now refused to conform to the law of elegance – German music, tragedy and philosophy – will henceforth be set aside as un-German. – But truly, German culture would not be worth lifting a finger for if the German understood by the culture he still lacks and is to aspire to, nothing but arts and artifices for prettifying life, including all the ingenuities of the dancing-master and the wallpaper-hanger, if in the matter of language too he was concerned only with academically approved rules and a certain general polish. The late war and self-comparison with the French seem, however, hardly to have evoked any higher pretentions than these; on the contrary, I am often assailed by the suspicion that the German now wants violently to cast off those ancient obligations which his wonderful talentedness and the profound seriousness of his nature imposed upon him. He prefers to play monkey-tricks and to learn the arts and manners that make life entertaining. But there can be no more grievous slander against the German spirit than to treat it as though it were wax to be moulded in any way one pleases and thus also into a semblance of elegance. And if it is unfortunately true that a good proportion of the German nation is only too willing to be moulded and kneaded into shape in this fashion, then one has to reiterate until the words are heeded: it no longer dwells in you, that ancient German nature which, though hard, austere and full of resistance, is so as the most precious of materials, upon which only the greatest of sculptors are permitted to work because they alone are worthy of it. What you have in you, on the contrary, is soft, pulpy matter; make with it what you will, form it into elegant dolls and interesting idols – here too the words of Richard Wagner will hold true: 'The German is angular and clumsy when he affects polish and politeness; but he is sublime and superior to everyone when he catches fire.' And the elegant have every reason to beware of this German fire, or one day it may con-

167

sume them together with all their dolls and idols of wax. – One could, to be sure, derive that inclination for 'beautiful form' now getting the upper hand in Germany from other and deeper sources: from the prevailing haste, from the breathless grasping at every moment, from the precipitation that plucks all things from the bough too soon, from the race and pursuit that nowadays carves furrows in men's faces and as it were covers all they do with tattoos. As though a potion that prevents them from catching their breath were working within them, they storm ahead with indecent anxiety as the harassed slaves of the moment, opinion and fashion: so that the lack of dignity and decorum is indeed all too painfully evident and a deceitful elegance required to mask the sickness of this undignified haste. For that is how the fashionable greed for beautiful form is connected with the ugly content of contemporary man: the former is intended to conceal, the latter to be concealed. To be cultivated means: to hide from oneself how wretched and base one is, how rapacious in going for what one wants, how insatiable in heaping it up, how shameless and selfish in enjoying it. When I have in the past pointed out to someone that a German culture does not exist, more than once I have received the reply: 'But that is quite natural, for hitherto the Germans have been too poor and modest. Just let our compatriots become rich and self-confident, and then they will possess a culture too!' Though belief may make blessed, *this* kind of belief has the opposite effect on me, because I feel that the German culture which is here believed to possess a future – a culture of wealth, polish and feigned gentility – is the most hostile antithesis of the German culture in which I believe. Certainly, he who has to live among Germans suffers greatly from the notorious greyness of their life and thought, from their formlessness, their stupidity and dull-mindedness, their coarseness in more delicate affairs, even more from their envy and a certain secretiveness and uncleanliness in their character; he is pained and offended by their rooted joy in what is false and ungenuine, in bad imitations, in the translation of good foreign things into bad native ones: now, however, that one has in addition, and as the most painful experience of all, their feverish restlessness, their search for success and profit, their overestimation of the moment, one is limitlessly indignant to think that all these maladies and weaknesses are on principle never to be cured but only painted over – with a 'culture of interesting form'! And this in the case of a nation which produced *Schopenhauer* and *Wagner*! And ought to do so often again! Or are we desperately deceiving ourselves? Do those named perhaps no longer offer any guarantee whatever that such energies as theirs still exist in the German mind and spirit? Are they themselves exceptions, as it were the last tendrils of qualities formerly regarded as German? I admit I am here nonplussed, and thus I return to the path of more general reflection from which my anxious doubts often seek to divert me. I have not yet numbered all those powers which, though they demand culture, do so without recognizing the goal of culture, the production of the genius; three have been named: the greed of the money-makers, the greed of the state, and the greed of all those who have reason to disguise themselves behind form. I name fourthly *the greed of the sciences* and the characteristic qualities of their servants, the *men of learning*.

Science is related to wisdom as virtuousness is related to holiness; it is cold and dry, it has not love and knows nothing of self-dissatisfaction and longing. It is as useful to itself as it is harmful to its servants, insofar as it transfers its own character to them and thereby ossifies their humanity. As long as what is meant by culture is essentially the promotion of science, culture will pass the great suffering human being by with pitiless coldness, because science sees everywhere only problems of knowledge and because within the world of the sciences suffering is really something improper and incomprehensible, thus at best only one more problem.

But if one accustoms oneself to translating every experience into a dialectical question-and-answer game and into an affair purely of the head, it is astonishing in how short a time such an occupation will wither a man up, how soon he becomes almost nothing but bones. Everyone knows and perceives this fact: so how is it nonetheless possible for young men not to start back at the sight of such skeletons, but on the contrary again and again blindly to give themselves over to the sciences without restraint or selectivity? It can hardly originate in any supposed 'desire for truth': for how could there exist any desire at all for cold, pure, inconsequential knowledge! What it really is that impels the servants of science is only too obvious to the unprejudiced eye: and it is very advisable to prove and dissect the men of learning themselves for once, since they for their part are quite accustomed to laying bold hands on everything in the world, even the most venerable things, and taking them to pieces. If I am to speak out, I would say this: the man of learning consists of a confused network of very various impulses and stimuli, he is an altogether impure metal. First of all there is a strong and ever more intense curiosity, the search for adventures in the domain of knowledge, the constant stimulation exercised by the new and rare in contrast to the old and tedious. Then there is a certain drive to dialectical investigation, the huntsman's joy in following the sly fox's path in the realm of thought, so that it is not really truth that is sought but the seeking itself, and the main pleasure consists in the cunning tracking, encircling, and correct killing. Now add to this the impulse to contradiction, the personality wanting to be aware of itself and to make itself felt in opposition to all others; the struggle becomes a pleasure and the goal is personal victory, the struggle for truth being only a pretext. Then, the man of learning is to a great extent also motivated to the discovery of *certain* 'truths', motivated that is by his subjection to certain ruling persons, castes, opinions, churches, governments: he feels it is to his advantage to bring 'truth' over to their side. The following qualities are also prominently displayed in the man of learning, less regularly than the previous ones yet frequently enough. Firstly, probity and a sense for simplicity, very worthy things provided they are something more than clumsiness and lack of practice in dissimulation, for which, after all, a certain amount of wit is needed. Indeed, wherever wit and dexterity are strikingly in evidence, one should be a little on one's guard and reserve one's judgment as to the uprightness of character of the person possessing them. On the other hand, this probity is for the most part of little worth and seldom fruitful even in the cause of science, since it is wholly tied to convention and usually tells the truth only in simple things or in *adiaphoris*; for in these cases laziness finds it easier to tell the truth than to keep silent about it. And because everything new makes it necessary to relearn, this probity will always, in case of need, revere the old opinion and reproach the innovator with a lack of *sensus recti*.* It certainly resisted the teachings of Copernicus because in this case it had appearance and convention on its side. The hatred of philosophy not at all uncommon among men of learning is above all hatred of the long chains of conclusions and the artificiality of the proofs. At bottom, indeed, every generation of men of learning has an unconscious canon of *permitted* sagacity; whatever goes beyond it is called into question and all but employed to cast suspicion on the probity of its propounder. – Secondly, sharpsightedness for things close up, combined with great myopia for distant things and for what is universal. His field of vision is usually very small and he has to hold his eyes close to the object. If the man of learning wants to go

---

*sensus recti: sense of what is right

from one point he has just subjected to scrutiny to another, he has to move his whole seeing-apparatus to this new point. He dissects a picture into little patches, like one who employs opera-glasses to view the stage and then has a sight now of a head, now of a piece of clothing, but never of anything whole. He never gets to see these patches joined together, his perception of how they are connected is only the result of a conclusion, and thus he has no very strong conception of anything universal. Because he is incapable of viewing a piece of writing as a whole, for example, he judges it by a few passages or sentences or errors; he would be tempted to assert that an oil-painting is a disorderly heap of blots. – Thirdly, the sobriety and conventionality of his nature in its likes and dislikes. This quality leads him to take an especial pleasure in history, insofar as he can trace the motives of men of the past in accordance with the motives he himself knows of. A mole-tunnel is the right place for a mole. He is secure against any artificial or extravagant hypotheses; if he sticks at it, he will dig out all the commonplace motives that inform the past, because he feels himself to be of the same commonplace species. For precisely that reason, of course, he is usually incapable of understanding or appreciating what is rare, great and uncommon, that is to say what is essential and vital, in the past. – Fourthly, poverty of feeling and aridity. It makes him capable even of vivisection. He has no inkling of the suffering which knowledge often brings with it, and therefore has no fear of venturing into regions where the hearts of others fail them. He is cold and may therefore easily seem cruel. He is also considered daring, but he is no more daring that the mule, which is immune from vertigo. – Fifthly, low self-esteem, amounting to modesty. Though confined to a wretched little corner, they feel no sense of being sacrificed or wasted, they often seem to realize in the depths of them that they are not flying but creeping creatures. There is even something touching about this quality. – Sixth, loyalty towards their teachers and leaders. They sincerely want to help them, and they are well aware that they can best help them through discovery of truth. For their feeling towards them is one of gratitude, for it is only through them that they have gained entry to the worthy halls of science, which they would never have been able to do on their own. He who nowadays knows how to open up a new field within which even the weakest heads can labour with some degree of success becomes famous in a very short time: so great is the crowd that at once presses in. Every one of these loyal and grateful people is at the same time a misfortune for the master, to be

sure, since they all imitate him and his defects then seem dispro-
portionately great and exaggerated because they appear in such tiny
individuals, while it is the opposite with his virtues, which are pro-
portionately diminished when these same individuals display them.
– Seventh, routine continuation along the path on to which the
scholar has been pushed, a conception of truth determined by
unthinking subjection to an acquired habit. Such natures are collec-
tors, explainers, compilers of indices and herbariums; they study
and prowl around a single domain simply because it never occurs to
them that other domains exist. Their industriousness possesses
something of the tremendous stupidity of the force of gravity: which
is why they often achieve a great deal. – Eighth, flight from boredom.
While the genuine thinker longs for nothing more than he longs for
leisure, the ordinary scholar flees from it because he does not know
what to do with it. His consolation lies in books: that is to say, he listens
to what someone else thinks, and in this way he lets himself be enter-
tained throughout the long day. He chooses especially books which
in some way or other excite his personal sympathies, which permit
him, through the arousal of like or dislike, to feel some emotion: that
is to say, books in which he himself, or his class, his political or
aesthetic or even merely grammatical dogmas, are the subject of discussion; and if there is a field of study in which he specializes he
never lacks means of entertainment or fly-swatters against boredom.
– Ninth, the motive of breadwinning, that is to say at bottom the
celebrated 'borborygm of an empty stomach'. Truth is served when
it is in a position directly to procure salaries and advancement, or at
least to win the favour of those who have bread and honours to dis-
tribute. But it is only *this* truth which is served: which is why a frontier
can be drawn between the profitable truths served by many and the
unprofitable truths: only a very few – those who do not act on the
principle *ingenii largitor venter** – are devotees of the latter. – Tenth,
recognition of fellow scholars, fear of lacking their recognition; a
rarer and higher motive than the previous one, yet still very common.
All the members of the guild keep a very jealous watch on one
another, so that the truth upon which so much – bread, office, honours
– depends shall be baptized with the name of its real discoverer. One
gives punctual recognition to the discoverer of a truth, so that one
can demand it in return if one should happen to discover a truth
oneself. Untruth, error, is resoundingly exploded, so that the number

---

**ingenii largitor venter*: the stomach is the squanderer of talent of fellow candidates shall not grow too big; yet now and then the actual truth is exploded too, so as to make room, at least for a time, for obstinate and impudent errors; since here as elsewhere there is no lack of 'moral idiocies', otherwise called roguish pranks. – Eleventh, the scholar from vanity, a rarer variety. He wants if possible to have a domain all to himself and to that end selects strange and curious studies, especially if they necessitate an unusually high expenditure, travelling, excavations, numerous connections in various countries. He is usually content to be gazed at in astonishment as something strange and curious himself and has no thought of earning his bread by means of his scholarly studies. – Twelfth, the scholar for fun. The amusement consists in looking for tangles in the sciences and unravelling them, while at the same time taking care not to lose the feeling of playing through trying too hard. This scholar, it goes without saying, never penetrates into the depths of a problem, yet he will often notice things that the professional, with his laborious poring over it, never does. – If, finally, I designate as the thirteenth motive for scholarship the impulse to justice, one could object that this noble impulse, which is indeed likely to be regarded as virtually a metaphysical one, is altogether too hard to distinguish from the other impulses and fundamentally vague and ungraspable to the human eye; which is why I append this last number with the pious hope that this impulse is more common and influential among scholars than it appears to be. For a spark from the fire of justice fallen into a scholar's soul suffices to enkindle and purify his life and strivings, so that he no longer knows any rest and is for ever expelled from the lukewarm or frosty mood in which scholars usually accomplish their daily work.

If one now imagines all these elements, or some of them, vigorously mingled and shaken together, one has the coming-into-being of the servant of truth. It is very strange how here, for the benefit of an affair basically extra- and suprahuman, pure, inconsequential and thus impulseless knowledge, a host of little, very human impulses should be poured together to produce a chemical compound, and how the product, the man of learning, should appear so transfigured in the light of that supraterrestrial, exalted and altogether pure affair that one quite forgets the mixing and mingling that was needed for his production. Yet there are times when one is obliged to think of and remember precisely this: those times when the scholar's significance for culture is in question. For he who knows how to must observe that the scholar is by nature

173

unfruitful – a consequence of how he comes into existence! – and that he harbours a certain natural hatred for the fruitful man; which is why geniuses and scholars have at all times been at odds with one another. For the latter want to kill, dissect and understand nature, while the former want to augment nature with new living nature; and so there exists a conflict of activities and intentions. Wholly fortunate ages did not need the scholar and did not know him, wholly morbid and listless ages have valued him as the highest and most venerable of men and accorded him the highest rank.

How it stands with our own age in regard to health and sickness – who is sufficient of a physician to know that! Certainly the scholar is in very many ways still too highly valued, which has a harmful effect especially in all that concerns the evolving genius. The scholar has no heart for the latter's distress; he speaks past him in a sharp, cold voice, and all too soon he shrugs his shoulders as though over something queer and strange for which he has neither time nor inclination. Knowledge of the goal of culture cannot be found in him either. –

But what have we gained at all from these reflections? The knowledge that where today culture seems to be most vigorously pursued nothing is known of this goal. However loudly the state may proclaim its service to culture, it furthers culture in order to further itself and cannot conceive of a goal higher than its own welfare and continued existence. What the money-makers really want when they ceaselessly demand instruction and education is in the last resort precisely money. When those who require form ascribe to themselves the actual labour on behalf of culture and opine, for instance, that all art belongs to them and must stand in the service of their requirements, what is quite clear is that by affirming culture they are merely affirming themselves: that they too are therefore still involved in a misunderstanding. Enough has been said of the scholarly man of learning. And so we see that, however zealous all four powers together may be in promoting their *own* interests with the aid of culture, they are dull and without inspiration when these interests are not involved. And that is why the conditions for the production of the genius have *not improved* in modern times, and why antipathy for original men has increased to such an extent that Socrates could not have lived among us and would in any event not have attained seventy.

Now I recall the theme I developed in the third section: that our whole modern world has so little the appearance of permanence and solidity that one cannot prophesy an eternity even for its conception of culture. One has even to consider it probable that the next thousand years will hit on a couple of new ideas which might make the hair of our contemporaries stand on end. *The belief in a metaphysical significance of culture* would in the end not be as alarming as all that: but perhaps some of the inferences one might draw from it in respect of education and schooling might be.

It demands, to be sure, a quite exceptional reflective capacity to be able to see beyond the educational institutions of the present to those altogether strange and different institutions which may perhaps be required only two or three generations hence. For while the efforts of our present-day higher educators serve to produce either the scholar or the civil servant or the money-maker or the cultural philistine or, finally and more usually, a compound of them all, those institutions still to be invented would have a more difficult task – though not one more difficult as such, since it would be in any event a more natural and to that extent also easier task; and can anything be more difficult than, for example, to train a young man to be a scholar, a thing contrary to nature by the methods at present employed? The difficulty, however, lies for mankind in relearning and envisaging a new goal; and it will cost an unspeakable amount of effort to exchange the fundamental idea behind our present system of education, which has its roots in the Middle Ages and the ideal of which is actually the production of the medieval scholar, for a new fundamental idea. It is already time we took a clear view of these antitheses, for some generation has to commence the struggle if another is to win it. The individual who has grasped this new fundamental idea of culture already finds himself at the crossroads; if he takes one path he will be welcome to his own age, it will not fail to offer him laurels and rewards, powerful parties will bear him along, behind him there will be as many likeminded men as there will be before him, and when the man in the front line gives the word of command it will re-echo through all the ranks. Here the first duty is 'to fight in rank and file', the second to treat as enemies all who refuse to fall in. The other path will offer him companions more seldom, it will be more difficult, more tortuous, steeper; those who have taken the first path will mock at him because his path is more wearisome and more often dangerous, and will try to entice him over to themselves. If the two paths happen to cross he will be mishandled, thrown aside or isolated by being cautiously walked around. Now, what does a cultural institution mean to these dissimilar wanderers on differing paths? The tremendous crowd that presses towards its goal along the first path understands by it the rules and arrangements by means of which it itself is brought to order and marches forward and through which all the solitary and recalcitrant, all who are looking for higher and more remote goals, are excommunicated. For the smaller band on the other path an institution would have a quite different purpose to fulfil; it wants the protection of a firm organization so as to prevent itself from being washed away and dispersed by that tremendous crowd, and so that the individuals that comprise it shall not die from premature exhaustion or even become alienated from their great task. These individuals have to complete their work – that is the sense of their staying together; and all who participate in the institution have, through continual purification and mutual support, to help to prepare within themselves and around them for the birth of the genius and the ripening of his work. Not a few, including some from the ranks of the second- and third-rate talents, are destined for the task of rendering this assistance and only in subjection to such a destiny do they come to feel they have a duty and that their lives possess significance and a goal. Nowadays, however, it is precisely these talents who are diverted from their path and estranged from their instincts by the seductive voices of that modish 'culture'; the temptation is directed at their self-seeking impulses, at their weaknesses and vanities; it is to them precisely that the *Zeitgeist* whispers insinuatingly: 'Follow me and do not go there! For there you are only servants, assistants, instruments, outshone by higher natures, never happy in being what you really are, pulled along in bonds, laid in chains, as slaves, indeed as automata; here with me you shall, as masters, enjoy your free personality, your talents may glitter by their own light, you yourselves shall stand in the foremost rank, a tremendous following will throng around you, and the public acclamation will surely please you better than a noble assent bestowed from the cold ethereal heights of genius.' Even the best can succumb to such enticements: and what is decisive here is hardly the rarity and strength of the talent but rather the influence of a certain heroic basic disposition and the degree of profound kinship and involvement with the genius. For there *do* exist men who feel it as their *own* distress when they see the genius involved in toilsome struggle, or in danger of destroying himself, or when the shortsighted greed of the state, the superficiality of the money-makers, the arid self-satisfaction of the scholars treat his work with indifference: and so I also hope there are some who understand what I am trying to say with this exhibition of Schopenhauer's destiny and to what end, according to my notion, Schopenhauer as educator is actually *to educate*. –

7

But leaving aside all thoughts of the distant future and a possible revolution in education: what would one have to desire and, if necessary, procure for an evolving philosopher *at present* to enable him to enjoy any leisure at all and, in the most favourable case, achieve the kind of existence demonstrated by Schopenhauer – not an easy one, to be sure, but certainly not possible? What would have also to be devised to make it more probable that he would produce some effect on his contemporaries? And what obstacles would have to be removed so that above all his example should produce its full effect, so that the philosopher should again educate philosophers? Here our reflections turn to practicalities and hard realities.

Nature wants always to be of universal utility, but it does not know how to find the best and most suitable means and instruments for this end: that is what it suffers from most, that is why nature is melancholy. That nature has wanted to make existence explicable and significant to man through the production of the philosopher and the artist is, given nature's own desire for redemption, certain; yet how uncertain, how dull and feeble is the effect it generally achieves with the philosophers and artists! How rarely does it achieve any effect at all! In the case of the philosopher especially it experiences great difficulty in employing him in a universally useful way; the means it employs seem to be only probing experiments and ideas it has chanced upon, so that countless times it fails to achieve its objective and most philosophers fail to become universally useful. Nature seems to be bent on squandering; but it is squandering, not through a wanton luxuriousness, but through inexperience; it can be assumed that if nature were human it would never cease to be annoyed at itself and its ineptitude. Nature propels the philosopher into mankind like an arrow; it takes no aim but hopes the arrow will stick somewhere. But countless times it misses and is depressed at the fact. Nature is just as extravagant in the domain of culture as it is in that of planting and sowing. It achieves its aims in a broad and ponderous manner: and in doing so it sacrifices much too much energy. The artist is related to the lovers of his art as a heavy cannon is to a flock of sparrows. It is an act of simplicity to start an avalanche so as to sweep away a little snow, to strike a man dead so as to kill a fly on his nose. The artist and the philosopher are evidence against the purposiveness of nature as regards the means it employs, though they are also first-rate evidence as to the wisdom of its purpose. They strike home at only a few, while they ought to strike home at everybody – and even these few are not struck with the force with which philosopher and artist launch their shot. It is sad to have to arrive at an assessment of art as cause so different from our assessment of art as effect: how tremendous it is as cause, how paralysed and hollow as effect! The artist creates his work according to the will of nature for the good of other men: that is indisputable; nonetheless he knows that none of these other men will ever love and understand his work as he loves and understands it. Thus this greater degree of love and understanding is, given the ineptitude of nature, required for the production of a smaller degree; the greater and nobler is employed as a means of producing the lesser and ignoble. Nature is a bad economist: its expenditure is much larger than the income it procures; all its wealth notwithstanding, it is bound sooner or later to ruin itself. It would have ordered its affairs more rationally if its house-rule were: small expenses and hundredfold profit; if, for example, there were only a few artists, and these of weaker powers, but on the other hand numerous recipients of art of a stronger and more mighty species than the species of the artist: so that the effect of the work of art in relation to its cause would be a hundredfold magnification. Or ought one not at least to expect that cause and effect would be of equal force? – but how little nature comes up to this expectation! It often seems as though an artist and especially a philosopher only *chances* to exist in his age, as a hermit or a wanderer who has lost his way and been left behind. Just think of the true greatness of Schopenhauer – and then of how absurdly small his effect has been! No honourable man of our age can fail to feel ashamed when he sees how Schopenhauer seems to belong to it only by accident and what forces and impotencies are to blame for the fact that his influence has been so minimal. First, for a long time, and to the everlasting shame of our era of literature, he had against him his lack of readers; then, when he acquired them, he had against him the inadequacy of his earliest advocates: even more, it seems to me, he had against him the obtuseness on the part of all modern men with regard to books, which they are altogether unwilling to take seriously; a new danger has gradually appeared in addition, deriving from the manifold attempts that have been made to adapt

Schopenhauer to this feeble age or even to employ him as an exotic and stimulating spice, as it were a kind of metaphysical pepper. So it is that, though he has gradually become famous and his name is, I think, already known to more people than Hegel's, he is nonetheless still a hermit and has still produced no effect! The honour of this achievement belongs least of all to his actual literary opponents and denigrators, firstly because there are few who can endure to read them, secondly because they lead those who can endure to do so directly to Schopenhauer; for who would let a donkey-driver dissuade him from mounting a handsome horse, no matter how extravagantly he extolled his donkey at the horse's expense?

He who has recognized the unreason in the nature of this age, then, will have to think of means of rendering it a little assistance; his task, however, will be to make the free spirits and those who suffer profoundly from our age acquainted with Schopenhauer, assemble them together and through them to engender a current capable of overcoming the ineptitude with which nature employs the philosopher. Such men will come to realize that the forces which blunt the effect of a great philosophy are the same as those which stand in the way of the production of a philosopher; which is why they are entitled to regard it as their goal to prepare the way for the reproduction of Schopenhauer, that is to say of the philosophical genius. That which opposed the effect and propagation of his teaching from the first, however, that which in the end wants to vitiate any rebirth of the philosopher with every means in its power, is, to speak bluntly, the perversity of contemporary human nature: which is why all great human beings have to squander an incredible amount of energy in the course of their development merely to fight their way through this perversity in themselves. The world they now enter is shrouded in humbug; it does not have to be religious dogma, it can also be such bogus concepts as 'progress', 'universal education', 'national', 'modern state', 'cultural struggle'; one can say, indeed, that all generalizing words now wear artificial and unnatural finery, so that a more enlightened posterity will reproach our age with being to an unheard-of degree distorted and degenerate, however much we may boast of our 'health'. The beauty of antique vessels, says Schopenhauer, arises from the fact that they express in so naive a way what they are intended to be and to perform; and the same applies to all the other articles of the ancients: on beholding them one feels that, if nature produced vases, amphorae, lamps, tables, chairs, helmets, shields, armour and so forth, this is how they would look. Conversely: whoever observes general modern attitudes to art, state, religion, education – not to speak, for good reasons, of our 'vessels' – discovers in mankind a certain barbaric capriciousness and intemperance of expression, and the genius is hampered most of all in his development by the prevalence in his time of such strange concepts and fanciful requirements: these are the leaden pressures which, invisible and inexplicable, so often weigh down his hand when he sets it to the plough – so that, because even his supreme works have had to force their way up violently, they too to some extent bear the traces of this violence.

If I now seek out the conditions with the assistance of which a born philosopher can in the most favourable case at least avoid being crushed by the perversity of our times just described, I notice something singular: they are in part precisely the conditions under which Schopenhauer himself on the whole grew up. There is no lack of contrary conditions, to be sure: the perversity of the age came fearfully close to him, for example, in the person of his vain and culturally pretentious mother. But the proud, free, republican character of his father as it were saved him from his mother and bestowed upon him the first thing a philosopher needs: inflexible and rugged manliness. This father of his was neither an official nor a scholar: he travelled a great deal with the boy in foreign countries – all of these things so many encouragements for one who was to study not books but men, and revere not governments but truth. He learned in good time to be indifferent to national narrownesses or extremely critical of them; he lived in England, France and Italy as he did in his own country and felt not a little affinity with the spirit of Spain. On the whole he did not regard it as an honour to have been born among Germans; and I do not know that he would have felt differently under the new political dispensation. As is well known, he considered the purpose of the state to be to provide protection against forces from without, protection against forces from within, and protection against the protectors, and that if any purpose was invented for it other than the provision of protection its true purpose could easily be imperilled –: that is why, to the horror of all so-called liberals, he left his property to the survivors among the Prussian troops whose comrades had fallen fighting for the preservation of order in 1848. It will probably be increasingly the sign of spiritual superiority from now on if a man takes the state and his duties

towards it lightly; for he who has the *furor philosophicus** within him
will already no longer have time for the *furor politicus*† and will wisely
refrain from reading the newspapers every day, let alone working for
a political party: though he will not hesitate for a moment to be at his
place when his fatherland experiences a real emergency. Every state
in which anyone other than the statesman has to concern himself
with politics is ill organized and deserves to perish by all these
politicians.

Another great advantage Schopenhauer enjoyed was the fact that
he was not brought up destined from the first to be a scholar, but
actually worked for a time, if with reluctance, in a merchant's office
and in any event breathed throughout his entire youth the freer air of
a great mercantile house. A scholar can never become a philosopher;
for even Kant was unable to do so but, the inborn pressure of his
genius notwithstanding, remained to the end as it were in a chrysalis
stage. He who thinks that in saying this I am doing Kant an injustice
does not know what a philosopher is, namely not merely a great thinker
but also a real human being; and when did a scholar ever become a
real human being? He who lets concepts, opinions, past events,
books, step between himself and things – he, that is to say, who is in
the broadest sense born for history – will never have an immediate
perception of things and will never be an immediately perceived
thing himself; but both these conditions belong together in the
philosopher, because most of the instruction he receives he has to
acquire out of himself and because he serves himself as a reflection
and brief abstract of the whole world. If a man perceives himself by
means of the opinions of others, it is no wonder if he sees in himself
nothing but the opinions of others! And that is how scholars are, live
and see. Schopenhauer, on the other hand, had the indescribable
good fortune to be able to see genius from close up not only in himself, but also outside himself in Goethe: through this twofold reflection he was aware of and wise to all scholarly goals and cultures from
the ground up. By virtue of this experience he knew what the strong
and free human being for which every artistic culture longs must be
like; given this insight, how could he have had much desire left to
involve himself with so-called 'art' in the scholarly or hypocritical

furor philosophicus: philosophical passion
†*furor politicus*: political passion

manner of modern man? For he had seen something higher: a dreadful scene in a supraterrestrial court in which all life, even the highest and most perfect, had been weighed and found wanting: he had seen the saint as judge of existence. We cannot determine at all closely how early in his life Schopenhauer must have perceived this picture of life in all its details and as he sought to reproduce it in all his subsequent writings; we can demonstrate that he saw this tremendous vision as a young man, and can well believe he had already seen it as a child. Everything he subsequently appropriated to himself from life and books, from the whole wealth of the sciences, was to him hardly more than colouring and means of expression; he employed even the Kantian philosophy above all as an extraordinary rhetorical instrument through which he believed he could speak of that picture more clearly: just as he occasionally made use of Buddhist and Christian mythology to the same end. For him there was only one task and a hundred-thousand means of encompassing it: one meaning and countless hieroglyphics with which to express it.

Among the most glorious conditions of his existence was the fact that he was able, in accordance with his motto *vitam impendere vero*,* really to live for such a task and that he was oppressed by none of the petty necessities of life: – how generously he attributed this circumstance to the efforts of his father is well known; whereas in Germany the theoretical man usually pursues his scholarly destiny at the expense of the purity of his character, as a 'thinking ragamuffin', greedy for posts and honours, cautious and pliable, ingratiating towards those with influence and position. Of all the offence Schopenhauer has given to numerous scholars, nothing has offended them more than the unfortunate fact that he does not resemble them.

8

These, then, are some of the conditions under which the philosophical genius can at any rate come into existence in our time despite the forces working against it: free manliness of character, early knowledge of mankind, no scholarly education, no narrow patriotism, no necessity for bread-winning, no ties with the state – in short, freedom and again freedom: that wonderful and perilous element in which the Greek philosophers were able to grow up.

*vitam impendere vero: devote one's life to the truth

Whoever wants to reproach him, as Niebuhr reproached Plato, with being a bad citizen, let him do so and be a good citizen himself: thus he will be in the right and so will Plato. Another will see this great freedom as a piece of presumption: he too is right, for he himself would do nothing with it and it would be very presumptuous in him to claim it for himself. That freedom is in fact a heavy debt which can be discharged only by means of great deeds. In truth, every ordinary son of earth has the right to regard with resentment a man favoured in this way: only may some god guard him from being thus favoured himself, that is from becoming so fearfully indebted. For he would at once perish of his freedom and solitude, and become a fool, and a malicious fool at that, out of boredom. –

From what we have discussed perhaps some father or other may be able to learn something and apply it in some way to the private education of his son; though it is truly not to be expected that fathers will want only philosophers for sons. It is probable that fathers in every age have put up the most determined resistance to their sons' being philosophers, as though it were extremely perverse; as is well known, Socrates fell victim to the wrath of the fathers over his 'seduction of youth', and Plato for that reason considered it necessary to institute a whole new state if the existence of the philosopher was not to be imperilled by the unreason of the fathers. It almost looks now as though Plato really did achieve something. For the modern state regards the promotion of philosophy as among *its* tasks and seeks at all times to bless a number of men with that 'freedom' which we understand as the most essential condition for the genesis of the philosopher. But historically speaking Plato has been singularly unfortunate: as soon as a structure has appeared which has essentially corresponded to his proposals, it has always turned out on close examination to be a changeling, an ugly elf-child; such as the medieval priestly state was by comparison with the rule of the 'sons of god' he had dreamed of. The last thing the modern state wants to do, of course, is to install philosophers as rulers – God be praised! every Christian will add –: but even promotion of philosophy as the state understands it will one day have to be inspected to see whether the state understands it *Platonically*, which is to say as seriously and honestly as though its highest objective were to produce new Platos. If the philosopher as a rule appears in his age by chance – does the state now really set itself the task of consciously translating this fortuitousness into necessity and here too rendering assistance to nature?

183

Experience unfortunately teaches us better – or rather, worse: it tells us that nothing stands so much in the way of the production and propagation of the great philosopher by nature as does the bad philosopher who works for the state. A painful fact, is it not? – recognizably the same as that to which Schopenhauer first directed attention in his celebrated treatise on university philosophy. I shall return to it later: for one has to compel men to take it seriously, that is to say to let it inspire them to action, and I consider every word behind which there does not stand such a challenge to action to have been written in vain; and it is in any event a good thing again to demonstrate the truth of Schopenhauer's always valid propositions, and to do so by direct reference to our closest contemporaries, since a well-disposed man might think that since he launched his accusations everything has taken a turn for the better in Germany. Even on this point, minor though it is, his work is not yet done.

Considered more closely, that 'freedom' with which, as I have said, the state now blesses some men for the good of philosophy is no freedom at all but an office of profit. The promotion of philosophy nowadays consists, it seems, only in the state's enabling a number of men to *live* from their philosophy by making of it a means of livelihood: whereas the sages of ancient Greece were not paid by the state but at most were, like Zeno, honoured with a gold crown and a monument in the Ceramicus. Whether truth is served when one is shown a way of living off it I cannot say in general, because here it all depends on the quality of the individual who is shown it. I could well envisage a degree of pride and self-esteem which would lead a man to say to his fellow-men: look after me, for I have something better to do, namely to look after you. In the case of Plato or Schopenhauer, such grandeur of disposition and expression would not alienate one; which is why precisely they could even be university philosophers, as Plato was for a time a court philosopher, without demeaning the dignity of philosophy. But even Kant was, as we scholars are accustomed to be, cautious, subservient and, in his attitude towards the state, without greatness: so that, if university philosophy should ever be called to account, he at any rate could not justify it. And if there are natures capable of justifying it – such natures as those of Schopenhauer and Plato – I fear they will never have occasion for doing so, since no state would ever dare to favour such men and install them in university posts. Why is that so? Because every state fears them and will favour only philosophers it does not fear. For it does happen that the state is afraid of philosophy as such, and when this is the case it will try all the more to draw to it philosophers who will give it the appearance of having philosophy on its side – because it has on its side those men who bear the name of philosopher and yet are patently nothing to inspire fear. If, however, a man should arise who really gave the impression of intending to apply the scalpel of truth to all things, including the body of the state, then the state would, since it affirms its own existence before all else, be justified in expelling such a man and treating him as an enemy: just as it expels and treats as an enemy a religion which sets itself above the state and desires to be its judge. So if anyone is to tolerate being a philosopher in the employ of the state, he will also have to tolerate being regarded as having abandoned any attempt to pursue truth into all its hideouts. At the very least he is obliged, so long as he is the recipient of favours and offices, to recognize something as being higher than truth, namely the state. And not merely the state but at the same time everything the state considers necessary for its wellbeing: a certain form of religion, for example, or of social order, or of army regulations – a *noli me tangere** is inscribed upon everything of this sort. Can a university philosopher ever have realized to the full the whole gamut of duties and limitations imposed upon him? I do not know; if he has done so and has nonetheless remained an official of the state he has been a bad friend of truth; if he has never done so – well, I would say he would still be no friend of truth.

This is the most general objection: to people as they are now, however, it is of course the weakest objection and the one to which they are most indifferent. Most will be content to shrug their shoulders and say: 'as though anything great and pure has ever been able to maintain itself on this earth without making concessions to human baseness! Would you prefer it if the state persecuted the philosopher rather than paid him and took him into service?' Without immediately replying to this question, I shall only observe that these concessions to the state on the part of philosophy go very far at the present time. Firstly: it is the state which selects its philosophical servants, and which selects just the number it needs to supply its institutions; it therefore takes on the appearance of being able to distinguish between good philosophers and bad ones and, even worse, it presupposes that there must always be a sufficiency of *good* philosophers to fill all its academic chairs. It is now the authority, not only with regard to the quality of philosophers, but also in

noli me tangere: do not touch me

185

regard to how many good philosophers are needed. Secondly: it compels those it has chosen to reside in a certain place, to live among certain people, to undertake a certain activity; they are obliged to instruct every academic youth who desires instruction, and to do so daily at certain fixed hours. Question: can a philosopher really undertake with a good conscience to have something to teach every day? And to teach it to anyone who cares to listen? Will he not be obliged to give the impression of knowing more than he does know? Will he not be obliged to speak before an audience of strangers of things which he can safely speak of only among his nearest friends? And speaking generally: is he not robbing himself of his freedom to follow his genius whenever and wherever it calls him? – through being obligated to think in public about predetermined subjects at predetermined hours? And to do so before youths! Is such thinking not as it were emasculated from the first! Supposing one day he said to himself: I can't think of anything today, at least not of anything worthwhile – he would still have to present himself and pretend to think!

But, you will object, he is not supposed to be a thinker at all, but at most a learned presenter of what others have thought: and as to that, he will always have something to say his pupils do not already know. – But precisely this – to undertake to appear first and foremost as scholarliness – is the third perilous concession which philosophy makes to the state. Above all when it appears as knowledge of the history of philosophy: for to the genius, who gazes upon things as a poet does, with pure and loving eyes, and cannot immerse himself too deeply in them, grubbing around in countless strange and perverse opinions is the most repugnant and inappropriate occupation imaginable. The learned history of the past has never been the business of a true philosopher, neither in India nor in Greece; and if a professor of philosophy involves himself in such work he must at best be content to have it said of him: he is a fine classical scholar, antiquary, linguist, historian – but never: he is a philosopher. And that, as remarked, is only at best: for most of the learned work done by university philosophers seems to a classicist to be done badly, without scientific rigour and mostly with a detestable tediousness. Who, for example, can clear the history of the Greek philosophers of the soporific miasma spread over it by the learned, though not particularly scientific and unfortunately all too tedious, labours of Ritter, Brandis and Zeller? I for one prefer reading Laertius Diogenes to Zeller, because the former at least breathes the spirit of the philosophers of antiquity, while the latter breathes neither that nor any other spirit. And finally, what in the world have our young men to do with the history of philosophy? Is the confusion of opinions supposed to discourage them from having opinions of their own? Are they supposed to learn how to join in the rejoicing at how wonderfully far we ourselves have come? Are they supposed even to learn to hate philosophy or to despise it? One might almost think so when one knows how students have to torment themselves for the sake of their philosophical examinations so as to cram into their poor brain the maddest and most caustic notions of the human spirit together with the greatest and hardest to grasp. The only critique of a philosophy that is possible and that proves something, namely trying to see whether one can live in accordance with it, has never been taught at universities: all that has ever been taught is a critique of words by means of other words. And now imagine a youthful head, not very experienced in living, in which fifty systems in the form of words and fifty critiques of them are preserved side-by-side and intermingled – what a desert, what a return to barbarism, what a mockery of an education in philosophy! But of course it is admittedly no such thing; it is a training in passing philosophical examinations, the usual outcome of which is well known to be that the youth to be tested – tested all too severely, alas! – admits to himself with a sigh of relief: 'Thank God I am no philosopher, but a Christian and a citizen of my country!'

What if this sigh of relief were the state's actual objective and 'education in philosophy' only a means of deterring from philosophy? Let one ask oneself this question. – If it really is so, however, there is only one thing to be feared: that youth may one day finally come to realize to what end philosophy is here being misused. The supreme objective, the production of the philosophical genius, nothing but a pretext? The goal perhaps the prevention of his production? The meaning of it all reversed into its opposite? In that case – woe to the whole complex of state and professorial policy! –

And is something of the sort not supposed to have transpired already? I do not know; but I do know that university philosophy is now the object of universal disrespect and scepticism. This is in part due to the fact that a feebler race now holds sway over the lecture-room; and if Schopenhauer had to write his treatise on university philosophy now, he would no longer have need of the club but would conquer with a reed. They are the heirs and progeny of those pseudo-thinkers whose much-turned heads he battered: their appearance is sufficiently infantile and dwarfish for us to be reminded of the Indian saying: 'Men are born, in accordance with their deeds, stupid, dumb, deaf, misshapen.' Their fathers deserved such a progeny by virtue of their 'deeds', as the saying has it. That is why it is quite indisputable that academic youth will very soon be able to manage without the philosophy taught at their universities, and that unacademic men are already able to manage without it. One has only to recall one's own student days; in my case, for example, academic philosophers were men towards whom I was perfectly indifferent: I counted them as people who raked together something for themselves out of the results of the other sciences and employed their leisure time in reading newspapers and going to concerts, and for the rest were treated by their own academic comrades with a politely masked contempt. They were credited with knowing little and with never being at a loss for some obscure expression with which to conceal this lack of knowledge. They thus preferred to dwell in gloomy places where the clear-eyed cannot endure to be for long. One of them urged it against the natural sciences: none of them can completely explain to me the simplest process of becoming, so what have any of them to do with me? Another said of history: to him who has ideas it has nothing new to say – in short, they always discovered reasons why it was more philosophical to know nothing than to learn something. If they did engage in learning, their secret motive in doing so was to elude science and to found a dark domain in one or other of its lacunae. Thus they went on ahead of the sciences only in the sense that the deer is ahead of the huntsmen who are after it. Lately they have been content to assert that they are really no more than the frontier guards and spies of the sciences; to which end they are especially served by the teachings of Kant, out of which they are intent upon fashioning an idle scepticism that will soon be of no interest to anybody. Only now and then does one of them still hoist himself up to a little system of metaphysics, with the consequences that usually follow, namely dizziness, headache and nosebleed. After having so often enjoyed no success on this trip into the mist and clouds, after some rude, hard-headed disciple of the real sciences has again and again seized them by the pigtail and pulled them back down, their face habitually assumes an expression of primness and of having been found out. They have lost their confidence, so that none of them lives even a moment for the sake of his philosophy. Formerly some of them believed themselves capable of inventing new religions or of replacing old ones with their philosophical systems; nowadays they have lost all this old arrogance and are as a rule pious, timid and uncertain folk, never brave like Lucretius or wrathful at human oppression. Neither can one any longer learn from them how to think logically and, with a correct estimation of their powers, they have ceased the formal disputations they used to practise. It is indisputable that the individual sciences are now pursued more logically, cautiously, modestly, inventively, in short more philosophically, than is the case with so-called philosophers: so that everyone will agree with the impartial Englishman Bagehot when he says of our contemporary system-builders: 'Who is not almost sure beforehand that they will contain a strange mixture of truth and error, and therefore that it will not be worthwhile to spend life in reasoning over their consequences? The mass of a system attracts the young and impresses the unwary; but cultivated people are very dubious about it. They are ready to receive hints and suggestions and the smallest real truth is ever welcome. But a large book of deductive philosophy is much to be suspected. Unproved abstract principles without number have been eagerly caught up by sanguine men and then carefully spun out into books and theories which were to explain the whole world. The world goes totally against these abstractions, and it must do so since they require it to go in antagonistic directions.'* If formerly philosophers, especially in Germany, used to be sunk in such profound reflection that they were in constant danger of hitting their head on a beam, they are now supplied with a whole regiment of flappers, such as Swift describes in the Voyage to Laputa, to give them a gentle blow now and then on the eyes or elsewhere. Sometimes these blows may be a little too heavy, on which occasions the enraptured thinker can easily forget himself and hit back – something that always results in his discomfiture. Can't you see the beam, you sleepy-head! the flapper then says – and often the philosopher really does see the beam and becomes tractable again. These flappers are history and the natural sciences; they have gradually come so to overawe the German dream- and thought-business which was for long confused with philosophy that these thought-mongers would be only too glad to abandon any attempt at an independent existence; if however they should happen to impede the former or try to fasten leading-strings on to them, the flappers at once start to flap as violently as they can – as though they

---

*Quoted from Bagehot's *Physics and Politics*. The order of the sentences in the original passage is inverted in Nietzsche's quotation of it, but this appears not to affect the meaning.

wanted to say: 'For a thought-monger like this to profane our history or natural sciences would be the last straw! Away with him!' Then they totter back into their own uncertainty and perplexity: they really do want to get a little natural science into their possession, perhaps like the Herbartians in the shape of empirical psychology, they really do want a little history as well – then they can act, at least in public, as though they were engaged in scientific undertakings, even though in private they would like to consign all philosophy and science to the devil.

But granted that this troop of bad philosophers is ludicrous – and who will not grant it? – to what extent are they also *harmful?* The answer, in brief, is: *to the extent that they make philosophy itself ludicrous*. As long as this officially recognized guild of pseudo-thinkers continues to exist, any effectiveness of a true philosophy will be brought to naught or at least obstructed, and it will suffer this fate through nothing other than the curse of the ludicrous which the representatives of that philosophy have called down upon themselves but which also strikes at philosophy itself. That is why I say it is a demand of culture that philosophy should be deprived of any kind of official or academic recognition and that state and academy be relieved of the task, which they cannot encompass, of distinguishing between real and apparent philosophy. Let the philosophers grow untended, deny them all prospect of place and position within the bourgeois professions, cease to entice them with salaries, more, persecute them, show them disfavour – you will behold miracles! The poor seeming philosophers will flee apart and seek a roof wherever they can find it; one will become a parson, another a schoolmaster, a third will creep into the shelter of an editorial job on a newspaper, a fourth will write instruction manuals for girls' high schools, the most sensible of them will take up the plough and the vainest will go to court. Suddenly it will all be empty, everyone will have flown the nest: for it is easy to get rid of bad philosophers, one only has to cease rewarding them. And that is in any event more advisable than for the state publicly to patronize any philosophy, *whichever it may be.*

The state never has any use for truth as such, but only for truth which is useful to it, more precisely for anything whatever useful to it whether it be truth, half-truth or error. A union of state and philosophy can therefore make sense only if philosophy can promise to be unconditionally useful to the state, that is to say, to set usefulness to the state higher than truth. It would of course be splendid for the state if it also had truth in its pay and service; but the state itself well knows that it is part of the *essence* of truth that it never accepts pay or stands in anyone's service. Thus what the state has is only false 'truth', a person in a mask; and unfortunately this cannot do for it what it so much desires genuine truth to do: validate and sanctify it. It is true that if a medieval prince wanted to be crowned by the Pope but the Pope refused to do it, he nominated an anti-Pope who then performed for him this service. This might have worked then to some extent; but for a modern state to nominate an anti-philosophy to legitimatize it will not work: for it will still have philosophy against it as before, and now more than before. I believe in all seriousness that it is more useful to the state to have nothing at all to do with philosophy, to desire nothing from it and for as long as possible to regard it as something to which it is completely indifferent. If this condition of indifference does not endure, if it becomes dangerous and hostile to the state, then let the state persecute it. – Since the state can have no interest in the university other than seeing it raise useful and devoted citizens of the state, it should hesitate to place this usefulness and devotion in jeopardy by demanding that these young men should sit an examination in philosophy: it could well be, of course, that the dull and incompetent would be frightened off university study altogether by this spectre of a philosophy examination; but this gain could not compensate for the harm done to rash and restless youth by this enforced drudgery; they get to know books forbidden them, begin to criticize their teachers and finally even become aware of the objective of university philosophy and its examinations – not to speak of the misgivings which this circumstance can excite in young theologians and as a result of which they are beginning to die out in Germany, as the ibex is in the Tyrol. – I understand well enough the objections the state could have raised against this whole way of looking at things so long as the fair green shoots of Hegelianism were sprouting up in every field: but now that this harvest has come to nothing, all the expectations built upon it have proved vain and all the barns remained empty – one prefers no longer to raise objections but to turn away from philosophy altogether. One now possesses power: formerly, in Hegel's time, one wanted to possess it – that is a vast distinction. Philosophy has become superfluous to the state because the state no longer needs its sanction. If the state no longer maintains its professors or, as I foresee in the near future, appears to maintain them but in fact neglects them, it derives advantage from doing so – yet it appears to me of more importance that the universities should see

191

that it is to their benefit too. At least I would think that an institution for the real sciences must see it is good for it no longer to have to keep company with a semi-science. The universities enjoy so little regard, moreover, they must on principle desire the exclusion of disciplines which academics themselves hold in low esteem. For non-academics have good reason for a certain general disrespect for universities; they reproach them with being cowardly, since the small ones fear the big ones and the big ones fear public opinion; with failing to take the lead in questions of higher culture but limping slowly and tardily in the rear, with ceasing to maintain the respected sciences on their true course. Linguistic studies, for example, are pursued more zealously than ever, but no one considers it necessary to educate himself in correct writing and speaking. Indian antiquity is opening its gates, yet the relationship of those who study it to the imperishable works of the Indians, to their philosophies, hardly differs from that of an animal to a lyre: even though Schopenhauer considered its acquaintance with Indian philosophy the greatest advantage our century possessed over all others. Classical antiquity has become a take-it-or-leave-it antiquity and has ceased to produce a classic and exemplary effect; a fact demonstrated by its disciples, who are truly not exemplary. Whither has the spirit of Friedrich August Wolf departed, of which Franz Passow could say it appeared a genuinely patriotic, genuinely human spirit which, if it needed to, possessed the force to set a continent on fire and in ferment – where has this spirit gone? On the other hand, the spirit of the journalist is penetrating the universities more and more, and not seldom under the name of philosophy; a smooth, highly coloured mode of address, Faust and Nathan the Wise constantly invoked, the language and views of our nauseating literary journals, lately even chattering about our sacred German music and the demand for chairs for the study of Goethe and Schiller – all signs that the spirit of the university is beginning to confuse itself with the *Zeitgeist*. It thus seems to me of the first importance that there should be created outside the universities a higher tribunal whose function would be to supervise and judge these institutions in regard to the education they are promoting; and as soon as philosophy departs from the universities, and therewith purifies itself of all unworthy considerations and prejudices, it must constitute precisely such a tribunal: devoid of official authority, without salaries or honours, it will know how to perform its duty free of the *Zeitgeist* and free from fear of it – in short, as Schopenhauer lived, as the judge of the so-called culture around him. In this way the philosopher, if instead of amalgamating with it he supervises it from a dignified distance, is able to be of use to the university.

Finally, however – of what concern to us is the existence of the state, the promotion of universities, when what matters above all is the existence of philosophy on earth! or – to leave absolutely no doubt as to what I think – if it is so unspeakably more vital that a philosopher should appear on earth than that a state or a university should continue to exist. The dignity of philosophy can increase in the measure that servitude to public opinion and the danger to freedom increases; it was at its greatest during the earthquake attending the fall of the Roman republic and during the imperial era, when its name and that of history became *ingrata principibus nomina.** Brutus demonstrates more for its dignity than does Plato; he belonged to an age in which ethics ceased to be platitudinous. If philosophy is little regarded at present, one ought only to ask why it is that no great general or statesman at present has anything to do with it – the answer is simply that at the time he sought it he encountered a feeble phantom bearing the name of philosophy, a scholarly lecture-hall wisdom and lecture-hall cautiousness; in short, it is because in his early years philosophy became to him something ludicrous. What it ought to be to him, however, is something fearsome, and men called to the search for power ought to know what a source of the heroic wells within it. Let an American tell them what a great thinker who arrives on this earth signifies as a new centre of tremendous forces. 'Beware', says Emerson, 'when the great God lets loose a thinker on this planet. Then all things are at risk. It is as when a conflagration has broken out in a great city, and no man knows what is safe, or where it will end. There is not a piece of science but its flank may be turned tomorrow; there is not any literary reputation, not the so-called eternal names of fame, that may not be revised and condemned; the things which are dear to men at this hour are so on account of the ideas which have emerged on their mental horizon, and which cause the present order of things, as a tree bears its apples. *A new degree of culture would instantly revolutionize the entire system of human pursuits.†* Now, if such thinkers are dangerous, it is of course clear why our academic thinkers are not dangerous; for their thoughts grow as peacefully out of tradition as

ingrata principibus nomina: names displeasing to princes

†Quoted from Emerson's essay entitled 'Circles'.

any tree ever bore its apples: they cause no alarm, they remove nothing from its hinges; and of all their art and aims there could be said what Diogenes said when someone praised a philosopher in his presence: 'How can he be considered great, since he has been a philosopher for so long and has never yet *disturbed* anybody?' That, indeed, ought to be the epitaph of university philosophy: 'it disturbed nobody'. But this, of course, is praise of an old woman rather than of the goddess of truth, and it is not to be wondered at if those who know that goddess only as an old woman are themselves very unmanly and thus, as might be expected, completely ignored by the men of power.

But if this is how things stand in our time, then the dignity of philosophy is trampled into the dust; it has even become something ludicrous, it would seem, or a matter of complete indifference to anyone: so that it is the duty of all its true friends to bear witness against this confusion, and at the least to show that it is only its false and unworthy servants who are ludicrous or a matter of indifference. It would be better still if they demonstrated by their deeds that love of truth is something fearsome and mighty.

Schopenhauer demonstrated both these things – and will demonstrate them more and more as day succeeds day.

4
Richard Wagner
in Bayreuth

1

For an event to possess greatness two things must come together: greatness of spirit in those who accomplish it and greatness of spirit in those who experience it. No event possesses greatness in itself, though it involve the disappearance of whole constellations, the destruction of entire peoples, the foundation of vast states or the prosecution of wars involving tremendous forces and tremendous losses: the breath of history has blown away many things of that kind as though they were flakes of snow. It can also happen that a man of force accomplishes a deed which strikes a reef and sinks from sight having produced no impression; a brief, sharp echo, and all is over. History has virtually nothing to report about such as it were truncated and neutralized events. And so whenever we see an event approaching we are overcome with the fear that those who will experience it will be unworthy of it. Whenever one acts, in small things as in great, one always has in view this correspondence between deed and receptivity; and he who gives must see to it that he finds recipients adequate to the meaning of his gift. This is why even the individual deed of a man great in himself lacks greatness if it is brief and without resonance or effect; for at the moment he performed it he must have been in error as to its necessity at precisely that time: he failed to take correct aim and chance became master over him – whereas to be great and to possess a clear grasp of necessity have always belonged strictly together.

We can therefore happily leave any dubiety as to whether that which is now taking place in Bayreuth is necessary and taking place at the right time to those who doubt Wagner's grasp of necessity itself. To us with greater faith it must seem that he believes in the greatness of his deed just as he does in the greatness of those who are to experience it. All to whom this belief is accorded should feel proud of the fact, whether they be few or many – for that it is not accorded to everyone, neither to the whole of our age nor even to the German people as it stands at present, he told us himself in his dedicatory address of 22 May 1872; and though to contradict him in this would be a consolation to him, none of us dares do it. 'When I sought those who would sympathize with my plans,' he said then, 'I had only you, the friends of my particular art, my most personal work and creation, to turn to: it was only from you that I could expect assistance in presenting this work in pure and undisfigured form to those who had demonstrated a serious interest in my art even though it had hitherto been presented to them only in impure and disfigured form.'*

In Bayreuth the spectator too is worth seeing, there is no doubt about that. A wise observer who moved from one century to another to compare noteworthy cultural movements would have much to see there; he would feel as though he had suddenly entered warmer water, like one swimming in a lake who approaches a current from a hot spring: this water must be coming from other, deeper sources, he says to himself, the water around it, which has in any case a shallower origin, does not account for it. Thus all those who attend the Bayreuth Festival will be felt to be untimely men: their home is not in this age but elsewhere, and it is elsewhere too that their explanation and justification is to be found. It has grown ever clearer to me that the 'cultivated person', insofar as he is wholly the product of this present age, can approach all that Wagner does and thinks only when it is presented to him in the shape of parody – as everything Wagner does and thinks has indeed been parodied – and that he will let the event at Bayreuth too be illumined for him only by the very unmagical lantern of our facetious newspaper journalists. And we shall be lucky if it stops at parody! For there is in it a spirit of alienation and hostility that could seek quite different ways of discharging itself, and has on occasion done so. Such an uncommon degree of sharpness and tension between opposites would likewise attract the attention of this cultural observer. That a single individual could, in the course of an average human lifespan, produce something altogether new may well excite the indignation of those who cleave to the gradualness of all evolution as though to a kind of moral law: they themselves are slow and demand slowness in others – and here they see someone moving very fast, do not know how he does it, and are angry with him. For such an undertaking as that at Bayreuth there were no warning signs, no transitional events, nothing intermediate; the long path to the goal, and the goal itself, none knew but Wagner. It is the first circumnavigation of the world in the domain of

---

*Spoken at the ceremony attending the laying of the foundation stone of the Festival Theatre at Bayreuth.

art: as a result of which, as it seems, there has been discovered not only a new art but art itself. All the arts of modern times have, as isolated and stunted or as luxury arts, been almost disvalued; and the uncertain, ill coordinated recollections of a true art which we moderns have derived from the Greeks may now also rest in peace, except insofar as they are now able to shine of themselves in the light of a new understanding. For many things the time has come to die out; this new art is a prophet which sees the end approaching for other things than the arts. Its admonishing hand must make a very disquieting impression upon our entire contemporary culture as soon as the laughter provoked by parodies of it has subsided: let the merriment go on for a little while yet!

We, on the other hand, we disciples of art resurrected, will have the time and the will for profound, serious reflection! The noise and chatter which has hitherto gone on about art we are bound to find shamelessly importunate from now on; everything imposes upon us silence, the five-year silence of the Pythagoreans. Who of us has not dirtied his hands and heart in the service of the idols of modern culture? Who is not in need of the water of purification, who does not hear the voice that admonished him: be silent and be cleansed! be silent and be cleansed! Only as those who listen to this voice are we also granted the *mighty insight* with which we have to view the event at Bayreuth, and only in this insight does there lie the *mighty future* of that event.

When on that day in the May of 1872 the foundation stone was laid on the hill at Bayreuth amid pouring rain and under a darkened sky, Wagner drove with some of us back to the town; he was silent and he seemed to be gazing into himself with a look not to be described in words. It was the first day of his sixtieth year: everything that had gone before was a preparation for this moment. We know that at times of exceptional danger, or in general at any decisive turning-point of their lives, men compress together all they have experienced in an infinitely accelerated inner panorama, and behold distant events as sharply as they do the most recent ones. What may Alexander the Great not have seen in the moment he caused Asia and Europe to be drunk out of the same cup? What Wagner beheld within him on that day, however – how he became what he is and what he will be – we who are closest to him can to a certain extent also see: and it is only from this Wagnerian inner view that we shall be able to understand his great deed itself – *and with this understanding guarantee its fruitfulness*.

2

It would be strange if that which a man can do best and most likes to do failed to become a visible presence within the total formation of his life; and in the case of men of exceptional abilities their life must become not only a reflection of their character, as is the case with everyone, but first and foremost a reflection of their intellect and of the capacities most personal to them. The life of the epic poet will have something of the epic about it – as is the case with Goethe, by the way, whom the Germans insist, quite wrongly, in seeing as principally a lyric poet – and the life of the dramatist will take a dramatic course.

The dramatic element in Wagner's *development* is quite unmistakable from the moment when his ruling passion became aware of itself and took his whole nature in its charge: from that time on there was an end to fumbling, straying, to the proliferation of secondary shoots, and within the most convoluted courses and often daring trajectories assumed by his artistic plans there rules a single inner law, a will, by which they can be explained, however strange this explanation will often sound. But there was also a pre-dramatic era in Wagner's life, that of his childhood and youth, and one cannot pass this era in review without encountering riddles. He *himself* does not yet seem to be present at all and that which, with hindsight, one might perhaps interpret as a sign of his presence appears at first as the simultaneous existence of qualities which must excite misgivings rather than hopeful anticipation: a spirit of restlessness, of irritability, a nervous hastiness in seizing hold upon a hundred different things, a passionate delight in experiencing moods of almost pathological intensity, an abrupt transition from the most soulful quietude to noise and violence. He was held in check by no traditional family involvement in any particular art: he might as easily have adopted painting, poetry, acting, music as academic scholarship or an academic future; and a superficial view of him might suggest that he was a born dilettante. The little world under whose spell he grew up was not such as one could have congratulated an artist on having for a homeland. He was very close to enjoying the perilous pleasure in the superficial tasting of one thing after another in the intellectual realm, as he was to the self-conceit engendered by much superficial knowledge which is commonplace in cities of scholars; his sensibilities were easily aroused and as easily satisfied; wherever the eyes of the boy rested he saw himself surrounded by a strangely precocious yet animated existence to which the gaudy world of the theatre stood in a ludicrous, and the soul-compelling sound of music in an incomprehensible, contrast. Now, it is in general remarkable that, when a modern man is gifted with a great talent, he seldom possesses in his youth and childhood the quality of naivety, of simply being himself; and that when, in such rare cases as Goethe and Wagner, he does attain to naivety, he does so in adulthood. The artist especially, in whom the power of imitation is particularly strong, must fall prey to the feeble manysidedness of modern life as to a serious childhood illness; in his youth and childhood he will look more like an adult than his real self. The marvellously accurate archetypal youth who is the Siegfried of the *Ring des Nibelungen** could have been produced only by a man, and by a man moreover who had found his own youth late in life. And as Wagner's youth came late, so did his full maturity; so that in this respect at least he is the opposite of an anticipatory nature.

As soon as his spiritual and moral maturity arrives, the drama of his life also begins. And how different he looks now! His nature appears in a fearful way simplified, torn apart into two drives or spheres. Below there rages the precipitate current of a vehement will which as it were strives to reach up to the light through every runway, cave and crevice, and desires power. Only a force wholly pure and free could direct this will on to the pathway to the good and benevolent; had it been united with a narrow spirit, such an unbridled tyrannical will could have become a fatality; and a way out into the open, into air and sunlight, was in any event bound to be found soon. A mighty striving conscious of repeated failure makes one bad; inadequacy can sometimes be inherent in circumstances,

---

* *The Nibelung's Ring*, the tetralogy for the performance of which Wagner designed and erected the Festival Theatre at Bayreuth, in Bavaria, and the first performance of which inaugurated the Bayreuth Festival. Wagner designated the *Ring* a 'Stage Festival Drama for Three Days and a Fore-Evening'. The 'Fore-Evening' is *Das Rheingold* (The Rhine-Gold), a music-drama in a single act (four scenes); the first 'day' is *Die Walküre* (The Valkyrie), a music-drama in three acts; the second 'day' is *Siegfried*, also in three acts; and the third 'day' is *Götterdämmerung* (Twilight of the Gods), in three acts and a prologue. The whole work takes between 15 and 16 hours to perform, depending on the tempo of performance, and is the longest musical composition in existence (*The Rhine-Gold*, which runs for about two-and-a-half hours, is the longest uninterrupted musical movement). The present essay was published in July 1876 to coincide with the inauguration of the festival, which took place on 13, 14, 16 and 17 August with the first public performance of the *Ring*.

in the unalterability of fate, and not in lack of force; but he who cannot cease from striving in spite of this insufficiency becomes as it were embittered and thus irritable and unjust. Perhaps he seeks the cause of his lack of success in others; he can, indeed, with a passionate hatred treat all the world as being to blame for it; perhaps he goes off defiantly along sidepaths and into subterfuges, or takes to violence: thus it happens that benevolent natures turn savage on their way to a laudable goal. Even among those whose objective is only their own moral purification, among hermits and monks, there are to be found such savage and morbid men, hollowed out and consumed by failure. It was a spirit full of love, with voice overflowing with goodness and sweetness, with a hatred of violence and self-destruction, which desires to see no one in chains – it was such a spirit that spoke to Wagner. It descended upon him, covered him with its wings, and showed him the path. We are now taking a look into the other sphere of Wagner's nature: but how are we to describe it?

The figures which an artist creates are not he himself, but a succession of figures upon whom he has patently bestowed his love does tell us at any rate something about the artist himself. Now call to mind Rienzi, the Flying Dutchman and Senta, Tannhäuser and Elizabeth, Lohengrin and Elsa, Tristan and Marke, Hans Sachs, Wotan and Brünnhilde: there passes through all of them a subterranean current of moral ennoblement and enlargement which unites them, a current which flows ever more clear and pure – and here, if with shy reserve, we stand before a development in the innermost recesses of Wagner's own soul. In what artist can we perceive anything similar at a similar peak of greatness? Schiller's figures, from the Robbers to Wallenstein and Tell, go through such a course of ennoblement and likewise express something of the development of their creator, but Wagner's standard is higher and the course is longer. Everything participates in this purification and expresses it, not only the myth but also the music; in the *Ring des Nibelungen* I discover the most moral music I know, for example when Brünnhilde is awoken by Siegfried; here he attains to an elevation and sanctity of mood that makes us think of the glowing ice- and snow-covered peaks of the Alps, so pure, solitary, inaccessible, chaste and bathed in the light of love does nature appear here; clouds and storms, even the sublime itself, are beneath it. Looking back from this vantage point upon Tannhäuser and the Dutchman, we feel how Wagner evolved: how he started darkly and restlessly, how he stormily

202

sought relief, strove for power and intoxication, often flew back in disgust, how he wanted to throw off his burden, longed to forget, to deny, to renounce – the entire stream plunged now into this valley, now into that, and bored its way into the darkest ravines: – in the night of this half-subterranean turmoil a star appeared high above him shining with a sad light, and he named it for what he recognized it to be: *loyalty, selfless loyalty*! Why did it seem to him to shine more brightly and purely than any other? what secret does the word loyalty hold for his whole being? For the image and problem of loyalty is impressed upon everything he thought and created; there exists in his works a virtually complete series of all possible kinds of loyalty, the most glorious and rarest among them: loyalty of brother to sister, of friend to friend, of servant to master, Elizabeth to Tannhäuser, Senta to the Dutchman, Elsa to Lohengrin, Isolde, Kurwenal and Marke to Tristan, Brünnhilde to Wotan's innermost desire – to make only a start on the series. It is the most personal primal event that Wagner experiences within himself and reveres like a religious mystery: he expresses it in the word loyalty and he never wearies of displaying it in a hundred shapes and, in the abundance of his gratitude, of bestowing upon it the finest things he possesses and the finest he can do – that marvellous experience and recognition that one sphere of his being remains loyal to the other, shows loyalty out of free and most selfless love, the creative, innocent, more illuminated sphere to the dark, intractable and tyrannical.

3

It was in the relationship of these two profound forces with one another, in the surrender of the one to the other, that there lay the great necessity which had to be fulfilled if he was to be whole and wholly himself: at the same time it was the only act that did not lie in his own power, which he could only watch and endure, while the possibility of seduction to disloyalty, and the frightful danger it represented to him, was always present. In the uncertainty that thus arose there lay an abundant source of suffering. Each of his drives strove without limit, each of his talents, joyful in its existence, wanted to tear itself free from the others and satisfy itself individually; the greater their abundance, the greater was the tumult and the greater the hostility when they crossed one another. In addition there was the impulse, deriving from chance and from life itself, to acquire power, fame, pleasure, and he was tormented even more frequently by the inexorable need to earn a living: traps and fetters lay everywhere. How is it possible to stay loyal, to remain whole, under these conditions? – This doubt often overcame him, and then, as would happen with an artist, found expression in the figures of his art: Elizabeth can only suffer, pray and die for Tannhäuser, she saves the restless and immoderate man through her loyalty, but not for this life. Danger and despair lie in wait for every true artist thrown into the modern world. He can acquire honours and power in many forms, he is frequently offered peace and contentment, but always only in the shape in which they are known to modern man and in which to the honest artist they must become choking foul air. It is in the temptation to this, and likewise in resistance to this temptation, that his danger lies; in disgust with the modern manner of acquiring pleasure and reputation, in rage at all self-seeking contentment in the manner of modern man. Think of him occupying an official position, as Wagner had to fill the office of conductor at town and court theatres; we can see how the most serious artist will try forcibly to impose seriousness on the institution of which he is part, an institution which has, however, been constructed frivolously and demands frivolity almost as a matter of principle; how he partially succeeds but in the end always fails; how he begins to feel disgust and wants to flee; how he fails to find anywhere to flee to, and is again and again obliged to return to the gypsies and outcasts of our culture as one of them. If he frees himself from one situation he rarely finds a better, and sometimes he is plunged into the direst need. Thus Wagner moves from town to town, companion to companion, country to country, and one hardly knows what it was in each of them that kept him there for as long as it did. A heavy atmosphere lies over the greater part of his life hitherto; he seems to have abandoned any general hopes and to have lived from day to day: and thus he eluded despair, but at the price of abandoning belief. He must often have felt like a wanderer in the night, heavily burdened and profoundly exhausted, who is yet each night revitalized; sudden death then appeared to his eyes, not as something to fear, but as an alluring spectre. Burden, pathway and night, all gone in a trice! – that was a seductive idea. A hundred times he threw himself back into life with short-breathed hope and put all spectres behind him. But he almost always did so with an immoderation which revealed that he placed no great faith in this hope but was only intoxicating himself with it. The contrast between his desires and his incapacity to fulfil them was a goad tormenting him; exasperated by continual deprivation, his judgment gave way to excess whenever his poverty was for once suddenly eased. His life became ever more complicated; but the expedients by means of which he handled it became ever bolder and more inventive, though they were in fact merely the emergency actions of the dramatist, designed to deceive only for a moment. As soon as he needs them he has them, and they are used up just as quickly. Seen from close to and without love, Wagner's life has, to recall an idea of Schopenhauer's, much of the comedy about it, and markedly grotesque comedy at that. How the feeling and recognition that whole stretches of his life are marked by a grotesque lack of dignity must affect an artist who, more than any other, can breathe freely only in the sublime and more than sublime – that is something for the thinker to reflect on.

In the midst of all this activity, of which only a detailed account can evoke the degree of pity, horror and admiration it deserves, there was unfolded a *talent for learning* quite extraordinary even among Germans, the nation most gifted in learning; and in this talent there again appeared a danger even greater than that attending a life apparently unstable and rootless and confusedly directed by restless illusion. From an experimenting novice Wagner grew into an omniscient master of music and of the stage and in all technical matters an innovator and developer. No one will any longer contest that he has provided the supreme model for all art in the grand manner. But he became even more, and to become it he was spared as little as anyone else would be the task of appropriating to himself all that is highest in culture. And how he did it! It is a joy to see; he acquired and absorbed it from all sides, and the bigger and heavier the structure became, the firmer grew the arch of thought that was to order and control it. And yet it has rarely been made so hard for anyone to discover the way into the sciences and skills, and often he had to improvise these ways in for himself. The rejuvenator of the simple drama, the discoverer of the place of the arts in a true human society, the poetic elucidator of past philosophies of life, the philosopher, the historian, the aesthetician and critic, the master of language, the mythologist and mytho-poet who for the first time enclosed the whole glorious, primeval structure within a ring and carved upon it the runes of his spirit – what an abundance of knowledge Wagner had to assemble and encompass to be able to become all that! And yet the weight of it as a whole did not stifle his will to action, nor did the attractions of its individual aspects entice him aside. To judge how uncommon such a posture is, one should compare it with that of its great counter-example, Goethe, who, as a learner and man of knowledge, appears like a many-branched river system which fails to sustain its full force as far as the sea but loses and scatters at least as much on its windings and meanderings as it bears on to its estuary. It is true that such a nature as Goethe's has and gives more enjoyment, something mild and nobly prodigal hovers about it, whereas the violence of Wagner's current may terrify and scare one away. But let him who will be afraid: we others shall take courage from the sight of a hero who, even in regard to modern culture, 'has not learned fear'.*

Just as little has he learned to let himself be placated by history and philosophy, to allow their softening and quietist effects to operate upon him. Neither the creative nor the embattled artist was deflected from his course by the force of what he had learned or the act of learning itself. As soon as his creative power takes hold on him history becomes malleable clay in his hands; his relationship towards it suddenly becomes quite different from that of any scholar, it becomes similar to that of the Greek towards his myths, that is to say towards something which offers material for plastic and poetic invention, performed with love and a certain shy devotion, to be sure, but nonetheless also with the magisterial right of the creator. And precisely because it is to him even more flexible and changeable than any dream, he can transform a single event into something that typifies whole ages and thus achieve a truth of representation such as the historian can never attain to. Where else has the courtly Middle Ages been transformed into a flesh-and-blood figure as it has in Lohengrin? And will the *Meistersinger* not speak of the German nature to all future ages – more, will it not constitute one of the ripest fruits of that nature, which always seeks reformation not revolution, and though broadly content with itself has not forgotten that noblest expression of discontent, the innovative deed?

And it was to precisely this kind of discontent that Wagner was compelled again and again by his involvement with history and philosophy: he discovered here, not only weapons and armour, but also and above all the inspiring afflatus that wafts from the tombs of all great warriors, of all great sufferers and thinkers. One cannot stand out more clearly from the whole contemporary age than through the way one employs history and philosophy. The former,

*A phrase from *Siegfried*.

as it is commonly understood, now seems to have been assigned the task of letting modern man catch his breath as he runs panting and sweating towards his goal, so that for a moment he can feel as it were unharnessed. What the individual Montaigne signifies within the agitation of the spirit of the Reformation, a coming to rest within oneself, a peaceful being for oneself and relaxation – and that was certainly how his best reader, Shakespeare, experienced him – is what history is for the modern spirit. If the Germans have for a century been especially devoted to the study of history, this shows that within the agitation of the contemporary world they represent the retarding, delaying, pacifying power: which some might perhaps turn into a commendation of them. On the whole, however, it is a dangerous sign when the spiritual struggles of a people are concerned principally with the past, a mark of debility, of regression and feebleness: so that it is exposed in the most dangerous fashion to every rampant fever going, the political fever for instance. In the history of the modern spirit our scholars represent such a condition of weakness, in antithesis to all revolutionary and reform movements; the task they have set themselves is not the proudest, but they have secured for themselves a kind of peaceable happiness. Every freer, more manly step goes past them, to be sure – though by no means past history itself! The latter has quite different forces within it, a fact realized by precisely such natures as Wagner: only it has to be written in a much more serious, much stricter manner, out of a mighty soul and in general no longer optimistically, as it always has been hitherto; differently, that is to say, from how German scholars have written it up to now. There is something palliative, obsequious and contented about all their work, and they approve of the way things are. It is a great deal if one of them lets it be seen that he is contented only because things could have been worse: most of them involuntarily believe that the way things have turned out is very good. If history were not still a disguised Christian theodicy, if it were written with more justice and warmth of feeling, it would truly be of no use whatever for the purpose to which it is now put: to serve as an opiate for everything revolutionary and innovative. Philosophy is in a similar situation: all most people want to learn from it is a rough – very rough! – understanding of the world, so as then to accommodate themselves to the world. And even its noblest representatives emphasize so strongly its power to soothe and console that the indolent and those who long for rest must think they are seeking the same thing philosophy is seeking. To me, on the other hand, the most vital of questions for philosophy appears to be to what extent the character of the world is unalterable: so as, once this question has been answered, to set about *improving that part of it recognized as alterable* with the most ruthless courage. True philosophers themselves teach this lesson, through the fact that they have worked to improve the very much alterable judgments of mankind and have not kept their wisdom to themselves; it is also taught by those true disciples of true philosophers who, like Wagner, know how to imbibe from them an enhanced resolution and inflexibility but no soporific juices. Wagner is most a philosopher when he is most energetic and heroic. And it was precisely as a philosopher that he passed through not only the fire of various philosophical systems without feeling fear, but also through the smoke of scholarly knowledge, and remained loyal to his higher self, which demanded of him *deeds in which his many-faceted nature participated as a whole* and bade him suffer and learn so as to be capable of these deeds.

4

The history of the evolution of culture since the Greeks is short enough, if one takes into account the actual distance covered and ignores the halts, regressions, hesitations and lingerings. The Hellenization of the world and, to make this possible, the orientalization of the Hellenic – the twofold task of the great Alexander – is still the last great event; the old question whether a culture can be transplanted to a foreign soil at all is still the problem over which the moderns weary themselves. The rhythmic play against one another of these two factors is what has especially determined the course of history hitherto. Here Christianity, for example, appears as a piece of oriental antiquity, thought and worked through by men with excessive thoroughness. As its influence has waned, the power of the Hellenic cultural world has again increased; we experience phenomena which are so peculiar they would hang in the air incomprehensible to us if we could not look back over a tremendous space of time and connect them with their Greek counterparts. Thus there are between Kant and the Eleatics,* Schopenhauer and Empedocles, Aeschylus and Richard Wagner such approximations and affinities

---

*The Eleatics: the followers of the pre-Socratic philosopher Parmenides (born about 510 BC), the first European metaphysician any of whose writings have survived.

that one is reminded almost palpably of the very relative nature of all concepts of time: it almost seems as though many things belong together and time is only a cloud which makes it hard for our eyes to perceive the fact. The history of the exact sciences especially evokes the impression that we even now stand in the closest proximity to the Alexandrian–Hellenic world and that the pendulum of history has swung back to the point from which it started its swing into enigmatic distant and lost horizons. The picture presented by our contemporary world is certainly not a novel one: to him who knows history it must seem more and more as though he were recognizing the old familiar features of a face. The spirit of Hellenic culture lies endlessly dispersed over our present-day world: while forces of all kinds crowd forward and the fruits of the modern sciences and accomplishments are bartered, the pale features of the Hellenic appear ghostlike in the distance. The earth, which has now been sufficiently orientalized, longs again for the Hellenic; he who wants to assist here has need of speed and a winged foot, to be sure, if he is to bring together all the manifold disseminated points of knowledge, the remotest continents of talent, to run through and command the whole tremendous region. Thus it is that we now have need of a series of *counter-Alexanders* possessing the mighty capacity to draw together and unite, to reach the remotest threads and to preserve the web from being blown away. Not to cut the Gordian knot, as Alexander did, so that its ends fluttered to all the corners of the earth, but *to tie it again* – that is now the task. I recognize in Wagner such a counter-Alexander: he unites what was separate, feeble and inactive; if a medicinal expression is permitted, he possesses an *astringent* power: to this extent he is one of the truly great cultural masters. He is master of the arts, the religions, the histories of the various nations, yet he is the opposite of a polyhistor, a spirit who only brings together and arranges: for he is one who unites what he has brought together into a living structure, a *simplifier of the world*. One will not misunderstand such an idea if one compares this most general task set for him by his genius with the much narrower one which the name of Wagner usually calls to mind. What is expected of him is a reform of the theatre: supposing he achieved it, what would thereby have been accomplished for that higher and remoter task?

Certainly modern man would have been altered and reformed: everything in our modern world is so dependent on everything else that to remove a single nail is to make the whole building tremble and collapse. This may seem an exaggerated thing to say of the

Wagnerian reform, yet any real reform could be expected to lead to a similar result. It is quite impossible to produce the highest and purest effect of which the art of the theatre is capable without at the same time effecting innovations everywhere, in morality and politics, in education and society. Love and justice grown mighty in one domain, in this instance that of art, must in accordance with the law of their inner compulsion extend themselves into other domains and cannot return to the inert condition of their former chrysalis stage. Even to grasp the extent to which the relationship of our arts to life is a symbol of the degeneration of this life, the extent to which our theatre is a disgrace to those who maintain and frequent it, one has to adopt a completely new viewpoint and be able for once to regard the commonplace and everyday as something very uncommon and complex. Strangely clouded judgment, ill-dissembled thirst for amusement, for distraction at any cost, scholarly considerations, pomposity and affectation on the part of the performers, brutal greed for money on that of the proprietors, vacuity and thoughtlessness on that of a society which thinks of the people only insofar as it is employable or dangerous to it and attends concerts and the theatre without any notion of possessing a duty towards them – all this together constitutes the musty corrupted air of our world of art today: but if one is as accustomed to it as our cultivated people are, one no doubt believes it necessary for one's health and feels ill if deprived of it for any length of time. There is really only one short way of convincing oneself of how vulgar, how peculiarly and oddly vulgar, our theatrical institutions are, and that is to compare them with the former reality of the Greek theatre. If we knew nothing of the Greeks, then the conditions that now obtain would perhaps be unavoidable and the kind of objections first raised in the grand manner by Wagner would be regarded as the dreams of dwellers in the land of nowhere. The way people are, it might perhaps be said, the kind of art we have is satisfactory and suited to them – and they have never been any different! – But they most certainly have been different, and even now there are people who are not satisfied with our present institutions – as the fact of Bayreuth itself demonstrates. Here you will discover spectators prepared and dedicated, people with the feeling of being at the summit of their happiness and that their whole nature is being pulled together for yet higher and wider endeavours; here you will discover the most devoted self-sacrifice on the part of the artists and, the spectacle of all spectacles, the victorious creator of a work which is itself the epitome of an abundance of victorious artistic deeds. Must it not seem almost like magic to encounter such a phenomenon in the world of today? Must not those who are permitted to participate in it not be transformed and renewed, so as henceforth to transform and renew in other domains of life? Has a harbour not been reached after the desert expanse of the sea, does a stillness not lie over the water here? – When he who has experienced the profound and solitary mood which reigns here returns to the shallows and lowlands of life, must he not ask with Isolde: 'How could I have endured it? How do I endure it now?'* And if he cannot endure to keep his happiness and unhappiness selfishly to himself, he will henceforth seize every opportunity to bear witness through his actions. Where are those who suffer on account of the institutions of the present? he will ask. Where are our natural allies, together with whom we can fight against the rampant aggression of contemporary bogus culture? For at present – at present! – we have only one enemy, those 'cultivated people' for whom the word 'Bayreuth' signifies one of their most shattering defeats – they rendered no assistance, they raged against it, or they exhibited that even more effective hardness-of-hearing which has now become a customary weapon of refined opposition. But the fact that their enmity and malice was incapable of destroying Wagner or of hindering his work teaches us one more thing: it betrays that they are weak and that the resistance of the former rulers will no longer be able to withstand many more attacks. The time has come for those who want conquest and victory, the greatest domains lie open, and wherever there are possessions a question-mark is set against the name of the possessor. Thus the structure of education, for example, has been recognized as rotten, and everywhere there are those who have already silently quitted it. If only those who are already in fact profoundly disaffected could be incited to a public declaration and to public indignation! If only they could be roused out of their despairing despondency! I know that if one were to deduct what these natures contribute to the proceeds of our whole system of culture, the latter would be subjected to the most enfeebling blood-letting imaginable. Of the scholars, for example, only those infected with the political mania and the literary scribblers of all kinds would be left behind under the old regime. The repellent structure which now derives its strength from the spheres of power and injustice, from the state and society, and sees its advantage in rendering the latter ever

*From *Tristan und Isolde*.

more evil and ruthless, would without it be something feeble and weary: at the first sign of open contempt it would collapse. He who fights for love and justice between men has least to fear from it: for it is only when he has come to the end of the struggle he is now waging against their advanced guard, the culture of today, that he will encounter his real enemies.

To us, Bayreuth signifies the morning consecration on the day of battle. We could not be done a greater injustice than if it were assumed we were concerned only with art: as though it were a kind of cure and intoxicant with the aid of which one could rid oneself of every other sickness. What we see depicted in the tragic art-work of Bayreuth is the struggle of the individual against everything that opposes him as apparently invincible necessity, with power, law, tradition, compact and the whole prevailing order of things. The individual cannot live more fairly than in being prepared to die in the struggle for love and justice and in sacrificing himself to it. The glance with which the mysterious eye of tragedy gazes upon us is no sorcery that prostrates us and paralyses our limbs. Even though it demands that we be quiet so long as it is gazing upon us – for art does not exist for the struggle itself, but for the intervals of quiet before and in the midst of it, for those moments when, glancing behind and looking ahead, we comprehend the symbolic, when feelings of tiredness which overcome us are attended by a refreshing dream. Day and the battle dawn together, the sacred shadows disperse and art is again far distant from us; but its morning consolation lies upon us still. For the individual discovers everywhere else nothing but what is personally dissatisfying and impervious to him: how could he fight with any kind of courage if he had not first been consecrated to something higher than his own person! The greatest causes of suffering there are for the individual – that men do not share all knowledge in common, that ultimate insight can never be certain, that abilities are divided unequally – all this puts him in need of art. We cannot be happy so long as everything around us suffers and creates suffering; we cannot be moral so long as the course of human affairs is determined by force, deception and injustice; we cannot even be wise so long as the whole of mankind has not struggled in competition for wisdom and conducted the individual into life and knowledge in the way dictated by wisdom. How could we endure to live in the feeling of this threefold incapacity if we were unable to recognize in our struggles, striving and failures something sublime and significant and did not learn from tragedy to take delight in the rhythm of grand passion and in its victim. Art is, to be sure, no instructor or educator in direct action; the artist is never an educator or counsellor in this sense; the objectives for which the tragic hero strives are not without further ado the things worth striving for *per se.* Our evaluation of things so long as we are firmly under the spell of art is different, as it is in a dream: that which, while the spell lasts, we consider so much worth striving for that we ally ourselves with the hero when he prefers to die rather than renounce it – in real life this is seldom of the same value or worthy of the same degree of effort: that is precisely why art is the activity of man in repose. The struggles it depicts are simplifications of the real struggles of life; its problems are abbreviations of the endlessly complex calculus of human action and desire. But the greatness and indispensability of art lie precisely in its being able to produce the *appearance* of a simpler world, a shorter solution of the riddle of life. No one who suffers from life can do without this appearance, just as no one can do without sleep. The harder it becomes to know the laws of life, the more ardently do we long for this appearance of simplification, even if only for moments, the greater grows the tension between general knowledge of things and the individual's spiritual–moral capacities. Art exists *so that the bow shall not break.*

The individual must be consecrated to something higher than himself – that is the meaning of tragedy; he must be free of the terrible anxiety which death and time evoke in the individual: for at any moment, in the briefest atom of his life's course, he may encounter something holy that endlessly outweighs all his struggle and all his distress – this is what it means to have a *sense for the tragic;* all the ennoblement of mankind is enclosed in this supreme task; the definite rejection of this task would be the saddest picture imaginable to a friend of man. That is my view of things! There is only one hope and one guarantee for the future of humanity: it consists in his *retention of the sense for the tragic.* An unheard-of cry of distress would resound across the earth if mankind should ever lose it completely; and, conversely, there is no more rapturous joy than to know what we know – that the tragic idea has again been born into the world. For this joy is altogether universal and suprapersonal, the rejoicing of mankind at the guarantee of the unity and continuance of the human as such.

5

Wagner subjected the life of the present and the past to the illumination of an insight strong enough to penetrate to uncommonly remote regions: that is why he can be called a simplifier of the world, for simplification of the world consists in being able to view and thus master the tremendous abundance of an apparently chaotic wilderness and to bring together in unity that which was formerly thought to be set irreconcilably asunder. Wagner did this by discovering a relationship between two things which appeared to be completely alien to one another as though they dwelt in different spheres: between *music and life*, and likewise between *music and drama*. He did not invent or create these relationships: they are there, lying in everybody's path, just as every great problem is like the precious stone which thousands walk over before one finally picks it up. What does it signify, Wagner asked himself, that precisely such an art as music should have arisen with such incomparable force in the life of modern man? It is not at all necessary to have a low opinion of this life in order to perceive a problem here; no, when one considers all the great forces pertaining to this life and pictures to oneself an existence striving mightily upwards and struggling for *conscious freedom* and *independence of thought* – only then does music appear truly an enigma in this world. Must one not say that music *could* not arise out of this age! But what then is the meaning of its existence? Is it a chance event? A single great artist might be a chance event, certainly; but the appearance of a series of great artists such as the history of modern music discloses – a series equalled only once before, in the age of the Greeks – makes one think it is not chance but necessity that rules here. This necessity is precisely the problem to which Wagner furnishes an answer.

First of all he recognized a state of distress extending as far as civilization now unites nations: everywhere *language* is sick, and the oppression of this tremendous sickness weighs on the whole of human development. Inasmuch as language has had continually to climb up to the highest rung of achievement possible to it so as to encompass the realm of thought – a realm diametrically opposed to that for the expression of which it was originally supremely adapted, namely the realm of strong feelings – it has during the brief period of contemporary civilization become exhausted through this excessive effort: so that now it is no longer capable of performing that function for the sake of which alone it exists: to enable suffering mankind to come to an understanding with one another over the simplest needs of life. Man can no longer express his needs and distress by means of language, thus he can no longer really communicate at all: and under these dimly perceived conditions language has everywhere become a power in its own right which now embraces mankind with ghostly arms and impels it to where it does not really want to go. As soon as men seek to come to an understanding with one another, and to unite for a common work, they are seized by the madness of universal concepts, indeed even by the mere sounds of words, and, as a consequence of this incapacity to communicate, everything they do together bears the mark of this lack of mutual understanding, inasmuch as it does not correspond to their real needs but only to the hollowness of those tyrannical words and concepts: thus to all its other sufferings mankind adds suffering from *convention*, that is to say from a mutual agreement as to words and actions without a mutual agreement as to feelings. Just as when every art goes into decline a point is reached at which its morbidly luxuriant forms and techniques gain a tyrannical domination over the souls of youthful artists and make them their slaves, so with the decline of language we are the slaves of words; under this constraint no one is any longer capable of revealing himself, of speaking naively, and few are capable of preserving their individuality at all in the face of an education which believes it demonstrates its success, not in going out to meet clear needs and feelings in an educative sense, but in entangling the individual in the net of 'clear concepts' and teaching him to think correctly: as if there were any sense whatever in making of a man a being who thinks and concludes correctly if one has not first succeeded in making of him one who feels rightly. Now when the music of our German masters resounds in the ears of mankind injured to this extent, what is it really that here becomes audible? Precisely this *right feeling*, the enemy of all convention, all artificial alienation and incomprehension between man and man: this music is a return to nature, while being at the same time the purification and transformation of nature; for the pressing need for that return to nature arose in the souls of men filled with love, and *in their art there sounds nature transformed into love*.

Let us take this to be one of Wagner's answers to the question as to what music signifies in our time: he also has a second. The relationship between music and life is not only that of one kind of language to another kind of language, it is also the relationship between the perfect world of sound and the totality of the world of sight. Regarded as a phenomenon for the eyes, however, and compared with the phenomena of life of earlier times, the existence of modern men exhibits an unspeakable poverty and exhaustion, despite the unspeakable gaudiness which can give pleasure only to the most superficial glance. If one looks a little more closely and analyses the impression made by this vigorously agitated play of colours, does the whole not appear as the glitter and sparkle of countless little stones and fragments borrowed from earlier cultures? Is everything here not inappropriate pomp, imitated activity, presumptuous superficiality? A suit of gaudy patches for the naked and freezing? A dance of seeming joy exacted from sufferers? An air of haughty pride worn by one wounded to the depths? And amid it all, concealed and dissembled only by the rapidity of the movement and confusion – hoary impotence, nagging discontent, industrious boredom, dishonourable wretchedness! The phenomenon of modern man has become wholly appearance; he is not visible in what he represents but rather concealed by it; and the remnant of artistic inventiveness retained by a nation, by the French and Italians for instance, is employed in this art of concealment. Wherever 'form' is nowadays demanded, in society and in conversation, in literary expression, in traffic between states, what is involuntarily understood by it is a pleasing appearance, the antithesis of the true concept of form as shape necessitated by content, which has nothing to do with 'pleasing' or 'displeasing' precisely because it is necessary and not arbitrary. But even in civilized nations where this form is not expressly demanded, that necessary shape which is true form is just as little in evidence: it is only that the striving after a pleasing appearance has been less successful, even though pursued with at least as much zeal. For *how pleasing* the appearance is, in the one case or the other, and why it must be agreeable to everyone that modern man at least makes an effort at an appearance, each will decide to the degree to which he himself is a modern man. 'Only galley-slaves understand one another', says Tasso, 'but we politely *misunderstand* others so that they shall misunderstand us in return.'*

In this world of forms and desired misunderstanding there now appear souls filled with music – to what purpose? In noble honesty, in a passion that is suprapersonal, they move to a grand, free rhythm, they glow with the mighty tranquil fire of the music that wells up out of inexhaustible depths within them – all this to what purpose?

Through these souls music reaches out to its corresponding necessary shape in the world of the visible, that is to say to *gymnastics*:

*In Goethe's *Torquato Tasso*, Act 5 Scene 5 (the italicizing of 'misunderstand' is Nietzsche's).

in its search for this it becomes judge over the whole visible world of the present. This is Wagner's second answer to the question as to what significance music can have in this age. Help me, he cries to all who can hear, help me to discover that culture whose existence my music, as the rediscovered language of true feeling, prophesies; reflect that the soul of music now wants to create for itself a body, that it seeks its path through all of you to visibility in movement, deed, structure and morality! There are men who comprehend this call, and there will be more and more of them; and they have also for the first time grasped anew what it means to found the state upon music, something the ancient Hellenes not only grasped but also demanded of themselves: whereas they would condemn the contemporary state as unconditionally as most men now condemn the church. The path to so new yet not wholly unheard-of a goal leads to an admission to ourselves that the most shameful shortcoming of our education and the actual ground of its inability to emerge from barbarism is its lack of the enlivening and formative soul of music, and that its demands and institutions are products of a time when the music from which we expect so much had not yet been born. Our education is the most backward structure of the present day, and it is backward precisely in regard to the only new educative force which contemporary mankind has that previous centuries did not have – or which they could have if they would cease their mindless scurrying forward under the lash of the moment! Because they have up to now not let the soul of music lodge within them, they have as yet no inkling of gymnastics in the Greek and Wagnerian sense of the word; and this is again the reason their plastic artists are condemned to hopelessness so long as they continue to desire to dispense with music to conduct them into a new visible world: it does not matter how much talent they have, it will come either too late or too soon and in any case at the wrong time, for it is superfluous and ineffective, since the perfect and highest products of former ages, the pattern for our contemporary artists, are themselves superfluous and almost ineffective and hardly capable now of setting one stone upon another. If they behold within themselves no new figures before them but only the old figures behind them, then they may serve history but they cannot serve life, and they are dead while they are still breathing: he who feels true, fruitful life within him, however – and at present that means music – could he be misled for a moment into expecting anything further from something that exhausts itself in figures, forms and styles? He has gone beyond all vanities of this sort; and he thinks of discovering artistic wonders outside his ideal world of sound as little as he expects great writers still to emerge from our exhausted and colourless languages. Rather than giving ear to any kind of vain consolation, he can endure to direct his profoundly dissatisfied gaze upon our modern world: let him become full of bitterness and hatred if his heart is not warm enough for pity! Even malice and mockery is better than that he should, in the manner of our 'friends of art', give himself over to fraudulent self-contentment and quiet dipsomania! But even if he can do more than deny and mock, if he can love, pity and assist, he *must* nonetheless at first deny, so as to create a pathway for his helpful soul. If music is one day to move many men to piety for music and to acquaint them with its highest objectives, an end must first be made to all pleasure-seeking traffic with so sacred an art; the foundation upon which our artistic entertainments, theatre, museums, concert societies rest, namely the aforesaid 'friend of art', must be placed under an interdict; the public judgment which lays such peculiar stress on cultivating this species of friendship for art must be beaten from the field by a better judgment. In the meantime we must count even the *declared enemy of art* as a real and useful ally, since that of which he has declared himself an enemy is precisely art as the 'friend of art' understands it: for he knows no other! Let him by all means call the friend of art to account for the senseless squandering of money on the construction of his theatres and public monuments, the engagement of his 'celebrated' singers and actors, the maintenance of his wholly unproductive art-schools and picture-galleries: not to speak of all the effort, time and money thrown away in every household on instruction in supposed 'artistic pursuits'. Here there is no hunger and no satiety, but only an insipid pretence of both designed to mislead the judgment of others; or, even worse, if art is taken relatively seriously one demands of it the engendering of hunger and desire and discovers its task to lie precisely in this artificially engendered excitement. As though one feared perishing through one's own self-disgust and dullness, one calls up every evil demon so as to be driven like a deer by these hunters: one thirsts for suffering, anger, passion, sudden terror, breathless tension, and calls upon the artist as the one who can conjure up this spectral chase. Within the spiritual household of our cultivated people art is now a wholly spurious or a shameful, ignominious need, either nothing or something malign. The better and rarer kind of artist is as though caught up in a bewildering dream so as not to see all this, and he hesitantly repeats

218

in an uncertain tone ghostly words he thinks he hears coming from far away but cannot quite grasp; the artist of the modern stamp, on the other hand, is full of contempt for the dreamy groping of his nobler colleague and leads the whole brawling crowd of passions and abominations after him on a string so as to let them loose on modern men when required: for the latter would rather be hunted, injured and torn to pieces than have to live quietly alone with themselves. Alone with themselves! – the idea of this makes modern souls quake, it is *their* kind of terror and fear of ghosts.

When in populous cities I watch the thousands pass by and behold their gloomy or harried expressions, I tell myself repeatedly that they must be feeling unwell. But for all these people art exists merely so that they shall feel even more unwell, even gloomier and more senseless, or even more harried and greedy. For they are unremittingly ridden and drilled by *false feeling*, which in this way prevents them from admitting to themselves how wretched they are; if they want to speak, convention whispers something into their ear which makes them forget what it was they really wanted to say; if they want to come to an understanding with one another, their own understanding is paralysed as though by a spell, so that what they call happiness is really their misfortune and they wilfully collaborate together to advance their own adversity. Thus they are wholly transformed and reduced to the helpless slaves of false feeling.

6

Here are two examples to demonstrate how perverse the sensibilities of our age have become and how the age has no perception of this perversity. In former times one looked down with honest nobility on people who dealt in money as a business, even though one had need of them; one admitted to oneself that every society had to have intestines. Now, as the most covetous of its regions, they are the ruling power in the soul of modern humanity. In former times there was nothing one was warned against more than against taking the day, the moment, too seriously; one was urged *nil admirari* and to be concerned with matters of eternity; now only one kind of seriousness still remains in the modern soul, that directed towards the news brought by the newspapers or the telegraph. To employ the moment and, so as to profit from it, to assess its value as quickly as possible! – one might believe that modern man has retained only one of the virtues, that of presence of mind. Unhappily, it is in truth more like the omnipresence of a dirty, insatiable greed and a prying curiosity. Whether *mind* is now *present* at all – we shall leave that question to the judges of the future who will one day put modern man through their sieve. But that this age is vulgar can be seen already, for it holds in honour that which former noble ages despised; and if it has appropriated to itself all that is valuable in the art and wisdom of the past and promenades around in this most opulent of all raiment, it shows an uncanny awareness of its vulgarity in that it employs this cloak not to keep itself warm, but only to disguise itself. The need to dissemble and to conceal itself seems more pressing than the need not to be cold. Thus our contemporary scholars and philosophers do not employ the wisdom of the Indians and the Greeks so as to grow wise and calm within themselves: the sole purpose of their work is to create for the present day an illusory reputation for wisdom. Students of animal behaviour exert themselves to represent the bestial outbreaks of violence and cunning and revengefulness in the mutual relations between contemporary states and men as unalterable laws of nature. Historians are engaged with anxious assiduity in proving the proposition that every age possesses rights of its own and its own conditions of existence – this by way of preparing the basis of the defence to be presented at the court proceedings which will be visited upon our age. Theories of the state, of the nation, of the economy, trade, justice – they all now have the character of a *preparatory apologia*; it seems, indeed, as though the only task of all active spirit not used up in propelling the great economy- and power-machine is the defence and exculpation of the present.

Before what accuser? one asks in perplexity.

Before its own bad conscience.

And the task of modern art, too, suddenly becomes clear: stupefaction or delirium! To put to sleep or to intoxicate! To silence the conscience, by one means or the other! To help the modern soul to forget its feeling of guilt, not to help it to return to innocence! And this at least for moments at a time! To defend man against himself by compelling him to silence and to an inability to hear! – the few who have felt what this most shameful of tasks, this dreadful degradation of art, really means will find their souls filling to the brim with regret and pity: but also with a new mighty longing. He who desired to liberate art, to restore its desecrated sanctity, would first have to have liberated himself from the modern soul; only when innocent himself could he discover the innocence of art, and he thus has two tremendous acts of purification and consecration to accomplish. If he were victorious, if he spoke to men out of his liberated soul in the language of his liberated art, only then would he encounter his greatest danger and his most tremendous battle; men would rather tear him and his art to pieces than admit they must perish for shame in the face of them. It is possible that the redemption of art, the only gleam of light to be hoped for in the modern age, will be an event reserved to only a couple of solitary souls, while the many continue to gaze into the flickering and smoky fire of their art: for they do not *want* light, they want bedazzlement; they *hate* light – when it is thrown upon themselves.

Thus they avoid the new bringer of light; but, constrained by the love out of which he was born, he pursues them and wants to constrain them. 'You *shall* pass through my mysteries', he cries to them, 'you need their purifications and convulsions. Risk it for the sake of your salvation and desert for once the dimly lit piece of nature and life which is all you seem to know; I lead you into a realm that is just as real, you yourselves shall say when you emerge out of my cave into your daylight which life is more real, which is really daylight and which cave. Nature is in its depths much richer, mightier, happier, more dreadful; in the way you usually live you do not know it: learn to become nature again yourselves and then with and in nature let yourselves be transformed by the magic of my love and fire.'

It is the voice of *Wagner's art* which speaks thus to mankind. That we children of a wretched age were permitted to be the first to hear it shows how worthy of pity precisely our age must be, and shows in general that true music is a piece of fate and primal law; for it is impossible to derive its appearance at precisely this time from an empty, meaningless act of chance; a Wagner who appeared by chance would have been crushed by the superior force of the opposing element into which he was thrown. But there lies over the evolution of the real Wagner a transfiguring and justifying necessity. To behold his art coming into existence is to behold a glorious spectacle, notwithstanding the suffering that attended it, for reason, law, purpose are evident everywhere. In his joy at this spectacle, the beholder will laud this suffering itself and reflect with delight on how primordially determined nature and giftedness must turn everything to prosperity and gain no matter how hard the school it has to pass through; how every kind of peril makes it bolder and every victory more thoughtful; how it feeds on poison and misfortune and grows strong and healthy in the process. Mockery and contradiction by the world around it are a goad and a stimulus; if it wanders into error, it returns home with the most marvellous booty; if it sleeps, 'its sleep only gives it new strength'.* It even steals the body and makes it more robust; it does not consume life however long it lives; it rules over man like a winged passion and at the moment his foot has grown weary in the sand or is hurt against a stone it lifts him into the air. It can do nothing other than communicate, everyone is to collaborate in its work, it is not niggardly with its gifts. If it is repulsed, it gives more abundantly; if the recipient misuses it, it adds to its gifts the most precious jewel it possesses – and the oldest and most recent experience teaches that the recipients have never been quite worthy of the gift. Primordially determined nature through which music speaks to the world of appearance is thus the most enigmatic thing under the sun, an abyss in which force and goodness dwell together, a bridge between the self and the non-self. Who can clearly name the purpose for which it exists at all, even though it may be apparent that purposiveness exists in the way it came into being? But the happiest presentiment may permit us to ask: should the greater exist for the sake of the less, the greatest giftedness for the good of the smallest, the highest virtue and holiness for the sake of frailty? Did true music not resound because mankind *deserved it least but needed it most?* If we let ourselves ponder the boundless miracle of this possibility and then, out of this reflection, look back on life, we shall see all flooded in light, however dark and misty it may have seemed before.

7

Nothing else is possible: he before whom there stands such a nature as Wagner's is from time to time compelled to reflect upon himself, upon his own pettiness and frailty, and to ask himself: what would this nature have with you? to what end do *you* really exist? – Probably he will be unable to find an answer, and will then stand perplexed at his own being. Let him then be satisfied to have experienced even this; let him hear in the fact that he *feels alienated from his own being* the answer to his question. For it is with precisely this feeling that he participates in Wagner's mightiest accomplishment, the central point of his power, the demonic *transmissibility* and self-relinquishment of his nature, with which others are able to communicate just as readily as it communicates with other natures, and whose greatness consists in

---

*From Hans Sachs's monologue in Act III of *Meistersinger*.

its capacity both to surrender and to receive. By apparently succumbing to Wagner's overflowing nature, he who reflects upon it has in fact participated in its energy and has thus as it were *through him* acquired power *against him*; and whoever examines himself closely knows that even mere contemplation involves a secret antagonism, the antagonism involved in comparison. If his art allows us to experience all that a soul encounters when it goes on a journey – participation in other souls and their destiny, acquisition of the ability to look at the world through many eyes – we are then, through knowledge of such strange and remote things, also made capable of seeing him himself after having experienced him himself. Then we feel certain that in Wagner all that is visible in the world wants to become more profound and more intense by becoming audible, that it seeks here its lost soul; and that all that is audible in the world likewise wants to emerge into the light and also become a phenomenon for the eye; that it wants as it were to acquire corporality. His art always conducts him along this twofold path, from a world as an audible spectacle into a world as a visible spectacle enigmatically related to it, and the reverse; he is continually compelled – and the beholder is compelled with him – to translate visible movement back into soul and primordial life, and conversely to see the most deeply concealed inner activity as visible phenomenon and to clothe it with the appearance of a body. All this constitutes the essence of the *dithyrambic dramatist*, this concept extended to embrace at once the actor, poet and composer: as it must be, since it is necessarily derived from the only perfect exemplar of the dithyrambic dramatist before Wagner, from Aeschylus and his fellow Greek artists. If one has tried to see the evolution of the greatest artists as deriving from inner constraints or lacunae; if, for example, poetry was for Goethe a kind of substitute for a failed calling as a painter; if one can speak of Schiller's plays as being vulgar eloquence redirected; if Wagner himself seeks to interpret the promotion of music by the Germans by supposing among other things that, denied the seductive stimulus of a naturally melodious voice, they were compelled to take the art of music with something of the same degree of seriousness as their religious reformers took Christianity –: so, if one wanted in a similar way to associate Wagner's evolution with such an inner constraint, one might assume the existence in him of an original histrionic talent which had to deny itself satisfaction by the most obvious and trivial route and which found its expedient and deliverance in drawing together all the arts into a great histrionic manifestation. But then one would also have to be allowed to say that the mightiest musical natures, in despair at having to speak to the semi- or non-musical, violently forced entry to the other arts so as finally to communicate themselves with hundredfold clarity and compel the people to understand them. But, however one may picture the evolution of the potential dramatist, in his perfect maturity he is a figure without any kind of constraint or lacunae: the actually free artist who can do nothing other than think in all the arts at once, the mediator between and reconciler of spheres apparently divided from one another, the restorer of a unity and totality to the artistic faculty which can in no way be divined or arrived at by reasoning, but only demonstrated through a practical deed. He before whom this deed is suddenly performed, however, will be overpowered by it as by the uncanniest, most magnetic magic: all at once he stands before a power which makes all resistance senseless, which indeed seems to rob all one's previous life of sense and comprehensibility: in an ecstasy, we swim in an enigmatic, fiery element, we no longer know ourself, no longer recognize the most familiar things; we no longer possess any standard of measurement, everything fixed and rigid begins to grow fluid, everything shines in novel colours, speaks to us in new signs and symbols: – now, involved in this mixture of joy and fear, one would have to be Plato to be able to resolve as he did and to say to the dramatist: 'if a man who, by virtue of his wisdom could become all possible things and imitate all things, should enter our community, let us revere him as something miraculous and holy, anoint his head with oil and set a wreath upon it, but then try to persuade him to go away to another community'. It may be that one living in the Platonic community can and must persuade himself to such a thing: all we others, who live in no such community but in communities constituted quite differently, desire and demand that the sorcerer should come to us, even though we may fear him – in order that our community and the false reason and power whose embodiment it is should for once be denied. A condition of mankind, of its communities, moralities, societies, institutions as a whole, which could do without the imitative artist is perhaps not a complete impossibility, but this 'perhaps' is one of the boldest there is and amounts to the same thing as a 'very improbably'; only he should be permitted to speak of it who could anticipate and realize in his mind the supreme moment of all time yet to come and then, like Faust, had to grow blind – had to and had a right to, for *we* have no right even to this blindness, whereas Plato for example, after having cast a single glance into the Hellenic ideal, had the right to be blind to Hellenic reality. We others, on the contrary, need art precisely because we have evolved *looking into the face of reality*; and we need precisely the universal dramatist so that he may, for a few hours at least, redeem us from the fearful tension which the seeing man now feels between himself and the tasks imposed upon him. With him we ascend to the topmost rung of sensibility and only there do we fancy we have returned to free nature and the realm of freedom; from this height we behold, as though in immense air-drawn reflections, our struggles, victories and defeats as something sublime and significant; we have delight in the rhythm of passion and in its victim, with every mighty step the hero takes we hear the dull echo of death and in its proximity we sense the supreme stimulus to life: – thus transformed into tragic men we return to life in a strangely consoled mood, with a new feeling of security, as though out of supreme dangers, excesses, ecstasies, we had found our way back to the limited and familiar: back to where we are now abundantly benevolent and in any event nobler than we were before; for everything that here appears serious and distressful, as progress towards a goal, is now, by comparison with the path we ourselves have traversed, even if only in a dream, more like strangely isolated fragments of that total experience of which we have a terrified recollection; indeed, we shall run into danger, and be tempted to take life too easily, precisely because we have taken art so uncommonly seriously – to allude to an expression with which Wagner characterized the course of his own life. For if we, who can only experience this art of the dithyrambic dramatist, not create it, find the dream almost more real than waking actuality, how must the creator of it evaluate this antithesis! There he stands in the midst of all the noisy summonses and importunities of the day, of the necessities of life, of society, of the state – as what? Perhaps as though he were the only one awake, the only one aware of the real and true, among confused and tormented sleepers, among sufferers deluded by fancy; sometimes no doubt he even feels as though a victim of a protracted sleeplessness, as though condemned to pass a clear and conscious life in the company of sleepwalkers and creatures of a spectral earnestness: so that all that seems everyday to others to him appears uncanny, and he feels tempted to counter the impression produced by this phenomenon with exuberant mockery. But this sensation is crossed, and in a manner quite personal to him, when to the brightness of this exuberance there is joined a quite different impulse, the

225

longing to descend from the heights into the depths, the living desire for the earth, for the joy of communion – then, when he recalls all he is deprived of as a solitary creator, the longing at once to take all that is weak, human and lost and, like a god come to earth, 'raise it to Heaven in fiery arms', so as at last to find love and no longer only worship, and in love to relinquish himself utterly! The crossing of sensations assumed here is, however, the actual miracle in the soul of the dithyrambic dramatist; and if his nature can be conceptualized anywhere, it must be here. For the creative moments in his art are produced by the tension occasioned by this crossing, when the uncanny and exuberant sensation of surprise and amazement at the world is coupled with the ardent longing to approach this same world as a lover. Whatever glances he may then cast upon earth and life, they are always beams of sunlight which 'suck up moisture', congregate mist, spread thunderclouds. His glance falls *at once clear-sighted and lovingly selfless*: and everything he now illuminates with the twofold light of this glance is at once compelled by nature to discharge all its forces with fearful rapidity in a revelation of its most deeply hidden secrets: and it does so out of *shame*. It is more than a figure of speech to say that with this glance he has surprised nature, that he has seen her naked: so that now she seeks to conceal her shame by fleeing into her antitheses. What has hitherto been invisible and inward escapes into the sphere of the visible and becomes appearance; what was hitherto only visible flees into the dark ocean of the audible: *thus, by seeking to hide herself, nature reveals the character of her antitheses*. In an impetuously rhythmic yet hovering dance, in ecstatic gestures, the primordial dramatist speaks of what is now coming to pass within him and within nature: the dithyramb of his dance is as much dread understanding and exuberant insight as it is a loving approach and joyful self-renunciation. Intoxicated, the word follows in the train of this rhythm; coupled with the word there sounds the melody; and melody in turn showers its fire into the realm of images and concepts. A dream apparition, like and unlike the image of nature and her wooer, floats by, it condenses into more human forms, it expands as the expression of a wholly heroic exuberant will, of an ecstatic going-under and cessation of will: – thus does tragedy come into being, thus there is bestowed upon life its most glorious form of wisdom, that of the tragic idea, thus there is at last evolved the greatest sorcerer and benefactor of mortals, the dithyrambic dramatist. –

8

Wagner's actual life, that is to say the gradual revelation of the dithyrambic dramatist, was at the same time an unceasing struggle with himself insofar as he was not only a dithyrambic dramatist: his struggle with the world which resisted him was so furious and uncanny because he heard this 'world', this bewitching enemy, speaking out of his own being and because he harboured within himself a mighty demon of resistance. When the *ruling idea* of his life – the idea that an incomparable amount of influence, the greatest influence of all the arts, could be exercised through the theatre – seized hold on him, it threw his being into the most violent ferment. It did not produce an immediate clear decision as to his future actions and objective; this idea appeared at first almost as a temptation, as an expression of his obscure personal will, which longed insatiably for *power and fame*. Influence, incomparable influence – how? over whom? – that was from now on the question and quest that ceaselessly occupied his head and heart. He wanted to conquer and rule as no artist had done before, and if possible to attain with a single blow that tyrannical omnipotence for which his instincts obscurely craved. With a jealous, deeply probing glance he scanned everything that enjoyed success, he observed even more those upon whom influence had to be exerted. Through the magical eye of the dramatist, who can read souls as easily as he can the most familiar writing, he saw to the bottom of the spectators and listeners, and though he was often disturbed by what he learned he nonetheless reached at once for the means of mastering it. These means were always available to him; what produced a strong effect upon him he was able himself to produce; of his models he understood at every stage just as much as he was himself able to create, and he never doubted that he could do whatever he wanted to. In this he is perhaps an even more 'presumptuous' nature than Goethe, who said of himself: 'I always believed I had everything; they could have set a crown upon my head and I would have thought it quite in order.' Wagner's ability and his 'taste' and likewise his objective – these have at all times corresponded as closely to one another as a key does to a lock: – together they *became* great and free – but they were not so at first. What to him were the feeble, noble yet selfishly solitary sensations experienced far from the great crowd by this or that friend of art educated in literature and aesthetically refined? But those violent storms of the soul produced by the great crowd when dramatic song rises in intensity, that sudden explosive intoxication of spirit, honest through and through and selfless – that was the echo of his own feeling and experience, and when he heard it he was permeated with a glowing anticipation of supreme power and influence! Thus it was he came to understand that *grand opera* was the means through which he could give expression to his ruling idea; his desire drew him towards it, his eyes turned in the direction of its home. A long period of his life, together with the daring changes and alterations his plans, studies, places of residence, acquaintanceships underwent, are explicable only by reference to this desire and to the external resistance the needy, restless, passionately naive German artist was bound to encounter. Another artist understood better how to become master in this domain; and now it has gradually become known with what an intricate web of influences of every kind Meyerbeer prepared and achieved each of his great victories, and with what scrupulous care he weighed the succession of 'effects' in the opera itself, it is also possible to understand how shamed and incensed Wagner felt when his eyes were opened to the kind of 'artifices' the artist was virtually obliged to employ if he was to wrest a success from the public. I doubt whether there has been another great artist in all history who started out so greatly in error and who engaged in the most revolting form of his art with such goodwill and naivety: and yet the way in which he did it had greatness in it and was therefore extraordinarily fruitful. For out of the despair he felt when he came to recognize his error he also came to comprehend the nature of modern success, of the modern public and of the whole of modern artistic falsity. By becoming a critic of 'effect' he produced in himself the first trembling awareness of how he himself might be purified. It was as though from then on the spirit of music spoke to him with a wholly novel psychical magic. As if he were returning to life after a long illness, he hardly trusted his eyes or his hands, he crept along groping; and thus it appeared to him a miraculous discovery when he found he was still a musician, still an artist, indeed that it was only now that he had become a musician and artist at all.

Every further stage in Wagner's evolution is characterized by a closer and closer union between his two fundamental drives: their wariness of one another diminishes, and hereafter his higher self no longer condescends to serve its violent, more earthly brother, it *loves* it and cannot but serve it. Finally, when the goal of this evolution has been reached, the most tender and pure elements are contained within the most powerful, the impetuous drive goes its way as before but along a different path to where the higher self is at home; and conversely, the latter descends to earth and in everything earthly recognizes its own image. If it were possible to speak in this fashion of the ultimate goal and issue of this evolution and still remain intelligible, then it would also be possible to discover the metaphysical expression which would describe a lengthy, intermediate stage in this evolution; but I doubt if the former can be done, and I shall therefore not attempt the latter either. This intermediate stage can be distinguished historically from the earlier and later stages with two phrases: Wagner becomes a *social revolutionary*, Wagner recognizes that the only artist there has been hitherto is the *poetizing folk*.* He was led to both by the ruling idea which, after that period of great despair and atonement, appeared before him in a new shape and more powerfully than ever. Influence, incomparable influence by means of the theatre! – but over whom? He shuddered when he recalled those whom he had hitherto sought to influence. From his own experience he knew the whole shameful situation in which art and artists find themselves: how a soulless or soul-hardened society, which calls itself good but is in fact evil, counts art and artists as among its retinue of slaves whose task it is to satisfy its *imaginary needs*. Modern art is luxury: he grasped that fact, as he did the fact that it must stand or fall with the society to which it belongs. Just as it has employed its power over the powerless, over the folk, in the most hardhearted and cunning fashion so as to render them ever more serviceable, base and less natural, and to create out of them the modern 'worker', so it has deprived the folk of the greatest and purest things its profoundest needs moved it to produce and in which, as the true and only artist, it tenderly expressed its soul – its mythology, its song, its dance, its linguistic inventiveness – in order to distil from them a lascivious antidote to the exhaustion and boredom of its existence, the arts of today. How this society came into being, how it knew how to imbibe new strength from apparently antagonistic spheres of power, how for example Christianity degenerated to hypocrisy and superficiality and allowed itself to be used as a shield against the folk, as a fortress for this society and its property, and how science and scholarship offered themselves only too pliably to

---

*Paraphrasing Wagner, here and elsewhere in this essay, Nietzsche uses the word *Volk* in the sense in which Wagner used it, i.e. the 'people' or the 'nation' as a cultural, as opposed to political, entity. This sense of *Volk* has an English analogue in the phrases 'folk-story' and 'folk-music'; and, although the word by itself is now archaic in English, there seems to be no alternative to using it here.

this forced service – all this Wagner pursued through the ages, only to spring up in rage and disgust when he had finished: he had become a revolutionary out of pity for the folk. From then on he loved the folk and yearned for them as he yearned after his art, for ah! it was only in them, only in the folk, though it was now artificially suppressed so that it could hardly any longer be imagined, that he now saw the only spectator and listener who might be worthy of and equal to the power of his art-work as he dreamed of it. Thus his reflections collected around the question: how does the folk come into being? how can it be resurrected?

He found only one answer: – if a multiplicity of people suffered the same need as he suffered, that would be the folk, he said to himself. And where the same need led to the same impulse and desire, the same kind of satisfaction must necessarily be sought and the same happiness discovered in this satisfaction. When he then cast around for that which cheered and consoled him the most in his need, which came to meet it most warmly and profoundly, he was aware with inspiriting certainty that it could only be the myth and music – the myth which he recognized as the product and language of the folk's need, music having a similar though even more enigmatic origin. In these two elements he bathed and healed his soul, they were what he desired most ardently: – from this condition he could infer how closely related his need was to that experienced by the folk when it came into being, and in what manner the folk would have to be resurrected if there were to be *many Wagners*. How, then, did myth and music fare in our modern society, insofar as they had not fallen victim to it? They had both suffered a similar fate, a witness to their mysterious affinity: myth had been deeply debased and disfigured, transformed into the 'fairy tale', the plaything of the women and children of the degenerate folk and quite divested of its miraculous and serious manly nature; music had maintained itself among the poor and simple, among the solitary, the German musician had failed to establish himself in the luxury trade in the arts and had himself become a fairy tale full of monsters and touching sounds and signs, an asker of the wrong questions, something quite enchanted and in need of redemption. Here the artist heard clearly the command directed at him alone – to restore to the myth its manliness, and to take the spell from music and bring it to speech: all at once he felt his strength for *drama* unfettered, his right to rule over an as yet undiscovered middle realm between myth and music established. He now set before mankind his new art-work, within which he had enclosed all he knew of power, effectiveness and joy, with the great, painfully incisive *question*: 'Where are you who suffer and desire as I do? Where are the many which I long to see become a folk? The sign by which I shall know you is that you shall have the same happiness and the same comfort in common with me: your suffering shall be revealed to me through your joy!' Thus he questioned in *Tannhäuser* and *Lohengrin*, thus he looked about him for his own kind; the solitary thirsted for the many.

Yet what happened? No one answered, no one understood the question. Not that there was utter silence; on the contrary, there were answers to a thousand questions he had never asked at all, there were twitterings about the new art-works as though they had been created for the express purpose of being talked to pieces. The whole lust for aesthetic chattering and scribbling erupted among the Germans like a fever, the art-works and the person of the artist were assessed and fingered with that shamelessness which characterizes German scholars no less than it does German journalists. Wagner tried to assist an understanding of his question through prose writings: fresh confusion, fresh buzzing – a musician who writes and thinks was to all the world in those days a monstrosity; then they cried: he is a theorist who wants to transform art according to intellectual concepts, stone him! – Wagner was as though stunned; his question had not been understood, his need not comprehended, his art-works were like communications to the deaf and blind, his folk was like a phantom; he reeled and faltered. The possibility of a total upheaval of all things rose before his eyes, and he no longer shrank from this possibility: perhaps a new hope could be erected on the other side of revolution and destruction, perhaps not – and in any event nothingness is better than something repulsive. Before long he was a political refugee and penniless.

Yet it was only now, when his outward and inner destiny had taken so fearful a turn, that the great man entered upon the period of his life over which the light of supreme mastery lies like the glitter of liquid gold! Only now did the genius of the dithyrambic drama throw off his last concealment! He is utterly alone, time seems nothing to him, he has abandoned hope: thus his universal glance again descends into the depths, and this time to the very bottom: there he sees that suffering pertains to the essence of things and from then on, grown as it were more impersonal, he accepts his own share of suffering more calmly. The desire for supreme power, the inheritance of earlier years, is wholly translated into artistic creativity; now he speaks through his art only to himself and no longer to a 'public' or folk, and struggles to bestow upon it the greatest clarity and capacity to conduct such a mighty colloquy. His works too had been different during the preceding period: in them too he had, if nobly and tenderly, sought to produce an immediate effect: for these works were meant as a question designed to evoke an instant answer; and how often Wagner desired to make himself more easily understood by those to whom he put it – so that he went out to meet them and their inexperience in being questioned and conformed to older forms and means of expression; where he had to fear that he would fail to convince and be understood in his own language, he had tried to put his question in a tongue half foreign to him, though familiar to his listeners. Now there was no longer anything to constrain him to such consideration; now he wanted only one thing: to come to terms with himself, to think of the nature of the world in the form of actions, to philosophize in sound; what was left in him of *intentionality* was bent upon the expression of his final *insights*. He who is worthy to know what took place in him then, what he was accustomed to discuss with himself in the darkest sanctuary of his soul – not many are worthy of it – let him hear, behold and experience *Tristan und Isolde*, the actual *opus metaphysicum* of all art, a work upon which there lies the broken glance of a dying man with his insatiable sweet longing for the mysteries of night and death, far distant from life, which, as evil, deception and separation, shines with an uncanny ghostly morning brightness and distinctness: and with this a drama of the most austere strictness of form, overwhelming in its simple grandeur, and only thus adequate to the mystery of which it speaks, the mystery of death in life, of unity in duality. And yet there is something even more miraculous than this work: the artist himself, who after producing it could soon afterwards create a world of a completely different colouring, the *Meistersinger von Nürnberg*, and who was indeed, in these two works, only as it were resting and refreshing himself so as then to complete with measured pace the four-part giant structure he had already sketched out and begun, the object of his reflection and invention over twenty years, his Bayreuth art-work, the *Ring des Nibelungen*! Whoever can feel perplexed at the proximity of *Tristan* and the *Meistersinger* has failed to understand the life and nature of all truly great Germans on an important point: he does not know upon what basis alone that uniquely *German cheerfulness* exhibited by Luther, Beethoven and Wagner can grow, a kind of cheerfulness which other nations completely fail to understand and which contemporary Germans themselves appear to have lost – that golden, thoroughly fermented mixture of simplicity, the penetrating glance of love, reflective mind and roguishness such as Wagner has dispensed as the most delicious of draughts to all who have suffered profoundly from life and return to it as it were with the smile of convalescents. And, as he himself looked upon the world with more reconciled eyes, was seized less often with rage and disgust, renounced power more in sorrow and love than with a shudder, as he thus quietly pushed forward his greatest work and laid score beside score, something happened which made him stop and listen: *friends* were coming to tell him of a subterranean movement of many souls – it was far from being the 'folk' that was here in motion and announcing itself, but perhaps the germ and first source of life of a truly human community to be perfected in the distant future; for the present no more than a guarantee that his great work could one day be placed in the hands and care of faithful men charged with and worthy of guarding this most glorious of legacies in the years to come; in the love of friends the days of his life began to shine in warmer colours; his noblest care and concern, as it were to reach the goal of his work before evening and to find for it a shelter, was no longer his care and concern alone. And then there occurred an event which he could understand only symbolically and which signified for him a new comfort, a sign of good fortune. A great German war made him look up, a war of those same Germans whom he knew to have degenerated and fallen so far from the German highmindedness which he had come to know from his observation of himself and of the other great Germans of history – he saw that, in a quite tremendous situation, these Germans had exhibited two genuine virtues, simple bravery and presence of mind, and he began to think that perhaps he was not the last German and that one day his work would secure the protection of a more formidable power than that of his self-sacrificing but few friends, which would preserve it for that future destined to it as the art-work of the future. Perhaps, when he sought to advance this belief to a hope of immediate realization, it was not always possible to shield it from doubt: it is enough that it gave to him a tremendous incitement to remember a lofty *duty* as yet unfulfilled.

His work would not have been finished, not brought to a conclusion, if he had entrusted it to posterity only as a mute score; he had publicly to demonstrate and give instruction in what could not be guessed, in what he alone knew, of the new style needed for its performance and representation, so as to provide a model no other could provide and thus found a *stylistic tradition* inscribed, not in signs on paper, but in effects upon the souls of men. This had become all the more serious a duty inasmuch as his other works had meanwhile suffered the most intolerable and absurd fate precisely in regard to the style of their performance: they were famous, admired and – mishandled without anyone's apparently being indignant over the fact. For, strange though it may sound, as in clearsighted knowledge of what his contemporaries were like he abandoned ever more earnestly the desire for success with them and renounced the idea of power, 'success' and 'power' came to him; at least all the world told him so. It was no good for him to expose repeatedly and emphatically how such 'successes' were complete misunderstandings and, to him, humiliations; people were so unused to seeing an artist distinguish between the differing effects produced by his works that even his most solemn protests were never really taken seriously. After he had realized the connection between our theatrical world and theatrical success and the character of contemporary man, his soul ceased to have anything to do with this theatre; he was no longer concerned with aesthetic enthusiasms or the jubilation of excited masses, indeed he was filled with wrath to see his art fed so indiscriminately into the gaping maw of insatiable boredom and thirst for distraction. Just how superficial and thoughtless every effect produced here must be, how here it was a matter rather of cramming a stomach never satisfied than of feeding a hungry one, he concluded especially from one regularly recurring phenomenon: everywhere, even on the part of the performers and producers, his art was taken to be precisely the same kind of thing as any other music for the stage and subjected to the rules of the repulsive recipe-book of ordinary opera production; indeed, the cultivated conductors cut and hacked at his works until they really were operas which, now they had had the soul taken out of them, the singers felt capable of encompassing; and when attempts were made to perform them properly, Wagner's directions were followed with the sort of ineptitude and prudish anxiety that would, for instance, represent the nocturnal riot in the streets of Nuremberg prescribed for the second act of the *Meistersinger* with a troop of posturing ballet dancers – and in all this everyone appeared to be acting in good faith and without any malicious intent. Wagner's self-sacrificing attempts to indicate by deed and example at any rate simple correctness and completeness in the performance of his works, and to introduce individual singers to his

234

quite novel style of execution, were repeatedly swept away by the sludge of prevailing thoughtlessness and habit; and these effects, moreover, always involved him in mixing with a theatre whose whole being had become for him an object of disgust. Did not Goethe himself lose the desire to attend performances of his own *Iphigenie*: 'I suffer dreadfully', he said in explanation, 'when I have to associate with these phantoms, who never appear as they ought to do.' Meanwhile his 'success' at this theatre grown repulsive to him continued to increase; finally the point was reached at which the great theatres lived for the most part on the fat takings brought them by the Wagnerian art-works disguised as operas. The confusion involved in this growing passion on the part of the opera public even seized hold on many of Wagner's friends: though he had suffered much in patience, he now had to suffer the worst and see his friends intoxicated by 'successes' and 'victories' precisely where his uniquely lofty idea was denied and derided. It almost seemed as though a people in many respects serious and ponderous was refusing to be deprived of a systematic levity in regard to its most serious artist, as though this were why everything vulgar, thoughtless, inept and malicious in the German character had to be discharged at him. – When, therefore, during the German War a more expansive and freer current of feeling seemed to come uppermost, Wagner remembered the duty imposed upon him by his loyalty to rescue at any rate his greatest work from the success born of misunderstanding and the abuse to which his other words had been subjected, and to present it at its own unique tempo as an example for all future time: thus he conceived the *idea of Bayreuth*. In the wake of that current of feeling he believed he saw an enhanced feeling of duty also awaken in those to whom he wished to entrust his most precious possession – and it was out of this feeling of mutual duty that there grew the event which lies like strange sunlight upon recent and immediately coming years; designed for the benefit of a distant future, a future which though possible may in fact never happen, to the present and to men knowing only the present not much more than an enigma or an abomination, to those few permitted to assist in its creation a foretaste and foreexperience of the highest kind through which they know themselves blessed, blessing and fruitful beyond their span of time, to Wagner himself a darkness of toil, care, reflection, wrath, a renewed raging of the hostile elements, but above all the light of the star of *selfless loyalty* and in this light transformed into an unspeakable happiness!

One hardly needs to say that the breath of the tragic lies over this life. And everyone who can sense something of it from out of his own soul, everyone to whom the constraint of a tragic deception as to the goal of life, the bending and breaking of intentions, renunciation and purification through love are things not wholly unknown, must feel in that which Wagner now exhibits as an art-work a dreamlike recollection of the great man's own heroic existence. From some far distance we shall believe we hear Siegfried telling of his deeds: into the touching happiness of recollection there is weaved the profound sadness of late summer, and all nature lies still in a yellow evening light. –

9

To reflect on *what Wagner the artist* is, and to meditate on the spectacle of a truly liberated artistic capacity and autocracy, is something that everyone who has thought about and suffered from *how Wagner the man evolved* will have need of as a means of recovery and refreshment. If art in general is only the ability to communicate to others what one has experienced, if every art-work contradicts itself if it cannot make itself understood, then Wagner's greatness as an artist must consist in precisely that demonic *communicability* of his nature, which as it were speaks of itself in every language and makes known its inner, most personal experience with the extremest clarity; his appearance in the history of the arts is like a volcanic eruption of the total undivided artistic capacity of nature itself after humanity had accustomed itself to seeing the arts isolated from one another as though this were an eternal rule. One can thus be undecided which name to accord him, whether he should be called a poet or a sculptor or a musician, each word taken in an extraordinarily wide sense, or whether a new word has to be created to describe him.

The *poetic element* in Wagner is disclosed by the fact that he thinks in visible and palpable events, not in concepts; that is to say, he thinks mythically, as the folk has always thought. The myth is not founded on a thought, as the children of an artificial culture believe, it is itself a mode of thinking; it communicates an idea of the world, but as a succession of events, actions and sufferings. *Der Ring des Nibelungen* is a tremendous system of thought without the conceptual form of thought. Perhaps a philosopher could set beside it something exactly corresponding to it but lacking all image or action and speaking to us merely in concepts: one would then have presented the same thing in two disparate spheres, once for the folk and once for the antithesis of the folk, the theoretical man. Thus Wagner does not address himself to the latter; for the theoretical man understands of the poetical, of the myth, precisely as much as a deaf man does of music, that is to say both behold a movement which seems to them meaningless. From within one of these disparate spheres one cannot see into the other: so long as one is under the spell of the poet one thinks with him, as though one were a being who only feels, sees and hears; the conclusions one draws are the linking together of the events one sees, that is to say factual causalities, not logical ones.

Now, if the gods and heroes of such mythological dramas as Wagner writes are to communicate also in words, there is no greater danger than that this *spoken language* will awaken the theoretical man in us and thereby heave us over into the other, non-mythical sphere: so that in the end we should not through the employment of words have understood more clearly what is taking place before us but, on the contrary, have failed to understand it at all. That is why Wagner has forced language back to a primordial state in which it hardly yet thinks in concepts and in which it is itself still poetry, image and feeling; the fearlessness with which Wagner set about this quite frightful task shows how forcibly he was led by the spirit of poetry, as one who has to follow wherever his ghostly guide may lead him. Every word of these dramas had to be able to be sung, and it had to be appropriate to gods and heroes: that was the tremendous demand Wagner presented to his linguistic imagination. Anyone else would surely have despaired of succeeding; for our language seems almost too old and too devastated for one to be able to demand of it what Wagner demanded: and yet the blow he struck against the rock called forth an abundant spring. Because he had loved this language more and demanded more of it than other Germans, Wagner had also suffered more from its degeneration and enfeeblement, from the manifold losses and mutilation it had sustained, from its clumsy sentence structure, from its unsingable auxiliary verbs – all things which have entered into the language through sin and depravity. On the other hand, he sensed with profound pride the natural originality and inexhaustibility still existing in this language, the resonant strength of its roots in which he suspected, in contrast to the highly derivative and artificially rhetorical languages of the Roman family, a wonderful inclination to and preparation for music, for true music. A joy in German permeates Wagner's poetry, a cordiality and ingenuousness in dealing with it that is to be encountered in no other German except Goethe. Individuality of expression, bold compression, forcefulness and rhythmic versatility, a remarkable richness in strong and significant words, simplification of sentence construction, an almost unique inventiveness in the language of surging feeling and presentiment, occasionally a quite pure bubbling up of popular colloquialisms and proverbiality – these are among the qualities that would have to be listed, and yet the mightiest and most admirable would still have been forgotten. Whoever reads, one after the other, two such poems as *Tristan* and the *Meistersinger* will feel a sense of amazement and perplexity in respect of the verbal language similar to that which he feels in respect of the music: namely, how it could have been possible to create two worlds as disparate in form, colour and articulation as they are in soul. This is the mightiest of Wagner's gifts, something that only a great master can succeed in: the ability to mint for every work a language of its own and to bestow upon a new subjectivity also a new body and a new sound. Where this rarest of powers expresses itself, censure of individual excesses and singularities, or of the more frequent obscurities of expression and thought, will always be no more than petty and unfruitful. Moreover, those who have hitherto censured most loudly have at bottom found not so much the language as the soul, the whole way of feeling and suffering, repellent and unheard-of. Let us wait until they themselves have acquired a new soul, then they themselves will also speak a new language: and then, it seems to me, the German language as a whole will be in better shape than it is now.

Before all, however, no one who reflects on Wagner as poet and sculptor of language should forget that none of the Wagnerian dramas is intended to be read, and thus they must not be importuned with the demands presented to the spoken drama. The latter wants to influence the feelings solely through concepts and words; this objective brings it beneath the sway of rhetoric. But in life passion is rarely loquacious: in the spoken drama it has to be if it is to communicate itself at all. When the language of a people is already in a state of decay and detrition, however, the poet of the spoken drama is tempted to give his thoughts and language unusual colours and to invent neologisms; he wants to elevate language so that it can again express exalted feelings and he thereby incurs the danger of not being understood at all. He likewise seeks to communicate something of nobility to the passions through witty aphorisms and conceits and thereby falls into another kind of danger: he appears false and artificial. For real passion does not speak in maxims, and the poetic easily arouses distrust of its honesty if it differs essentially from this reality. Wagner, on the other hand, as the first to recognize the inner deficiencies of the spoken drama, presents every dramatic event in a threefold rendering, through words, gestures and music: the music transmits the fundamental impulses in the depths of the persons represented in the drama directly to the soul of the listeners, who now perceive in these same persons' gestures the first visible form of those inner events, and in the words a second, paler manifestation of them translated into a more conscious act of will. All these effects take place simultaneously without in the least interfering with one another, and compel him before whom such a drama is presented to a quite novel understanding and empathy, just as though his senses had all at once grown more spiritual and his spirit more sensual, and as though everything that longs to know is now in a free and blissful transport of knowing. Because every event in a Wagnerian drama, illumined from within as it is by music, communicates itself to the spectator with the utmost clarity, its author was able to dispense with all those means of which the poet of the spoken drama has need if he is to give the events of his play warmth and luminosity. The whole economy of the drama could be made simpler, the architect's rhythmic sense could again venture to reveal itself in the great overall proportions of the building; for there was now no motive whatever for that deliberate complexity and confusing multiplicity through which the poet of the spoken drama seeks to arouse interest and tension and then enhance them to a feeling of happy astonishment. The impression of idealized remoteness and nobility could now be achieved without artifice. Language retreated from rhetorical expansiveness to the economy and force of a speech of feeling: and although the performer talked about his deeds and feelings far less than before, the inward events which the poet of the spoken drama had hitherto kept off the stage on account of their supposedly undramatic nature now compelled the listener to a passionate empathy with them, while the gestures which attended them needed to be only of the gentlest. Now, passion sung takes somewhat longer than passion spoken; music stretches feeling, as it were: from which it follows that in general the performer who is also a singer has to overcome that agitation of movement from which the spoken drama suffers. He finds himself drawn towards an ennoblement of his gestures, and he does so all the more in that the music has plunged his feelings into the bath of a purer aether and has thus involuntarily made them more beautiful.

The extraordinary tasks Wagner has set his actors and singers will for generations to come incite them to competition with one another, so as at last to achieve a perfect visible and palpable representation of the image of the Wagnerian hero which already lies perfectly realized in the music of the drama. Following this lead, the eye of the plastic artist will at last behold the miracle of a new visible world such as only the creator of such works as the *Ring des Nibelungen* has seen before him: as a *sculptor* of the highest kind who, like Aeschylus, points the way to an art of the future. Indeed, must not the jealousy aroused when the plastic artist compares the effect of his art with that of such music as Wagner's not in itself inspire great talents: a music in which there reposes the purest sunlit happiness; so that to him who hears this music it is as though almost all earlier music had spoken in a superficial and constricted language, as though it were a game played before those unworthy of seriousness or a means of instruction and demonstration for those unworthy even of play. That earlier music inspires in us only for brief hours that happiness which we feel in Wagnerian music all the time: rare moments of forgetfulness when it speaks to itself alone and, like Raphael's Cecilia, directs its glance away from its listeners, who demand of it only distraction, merriment or scholarliness.

Of Wagner the *musician* it can be said in general that he has bestowed a language upon everything in nature which has hitherto not wanted to *speak*: he does not believe that anything is obliged to be dumb. He plunges into daybreaks, woods, mist, ravines, mountain heights, the dread of night, moonlight, and remarks in them a secret desire: they want to resound. If the philosopher says it is *one* will which in animate and inanimate nature thirsts for existence, the musician adds: and this will wants at every stage an existence in sound.

Before Wagner, music was as a whole narrowly bounded; it applied to the steady, permanent states of mankind, to that which the Greeks called ethos, and it was only with Beethoven that it began to discover the language of pathos, of passionate desire, of the dramatic events which take place in the depths of man. Formerly the objective was to give expression in sound to a mood, a state of determination or cheerfulness or reverence or penitence; by means of a certain striking uniformity of form, and through protracting this uniformity for some time, one wanted to compel the listener to interpret the mood of the music and in the end to be transported into it himself. Different forms were needed for each of these images of different moods and states; other forms were determined by con-

240

vention. The question of length was a matter for the judgment of the composer, who, while wanting to transport the listener into a certain mood, did not want to bore him by going on for too long. A further step was taken when images of antithetical moods were placed one after the other and the charm of contrast was discovered, and a further step still when a single musical movement took into itself an antithetical ethos, for example by allowing a masculine theme to come into conflict with a feminine theme. All these are still rude and primitive stages of music. The first law originated in fear of passion, the second in fear of boredom; all deepening and excess of feeling was felt to be 'unethical'. But when the art of ethos had presented the same customary states and moods in hundredfold repetition it finally succumbed to exhaustion, notwithstanding the marvellous inventiveness of its masters. Beethoven was the first to let music speak a new language, the hitherto forbidden language of passion: but because his art had grown out of the laws and conventions of the art of ethos, and had as it were to try to justify itself before them, his artistic development was peculiarly difficult and beset with con- fusions. An inner dramatic event – for every passion takes a dramatic course – wanted to break through to a new form, but the traditional scheme of the music of moods set itself in opposition and spoke against it almost as morality speaks against the rise of immorality. It sometimes seems as though Beethoven had set himself the con- tradictory task of expressing pathos through the forms of ethos. This idea is, however, inadequate to his last and greatest works. To re- produce the great vaulting arch of a passion he really did discover a new means: he removed individual portions of its flightpath and illuminated these with the greatest distinctness, so that from them the listener would *divine* the entire curve. Viewed superficially, the new form seemed like several musical movements put together, each of them apparently representing a single enduring state, in reality however a moment in the dramatic course of the passion. It could happen that the listener would think he was hearing the old music of mood but failing to grasp the relationship of the several parts to one another, which could no longer be understood by reference to the old canon of antithetical parts. Even among com- posers there arose a contempt for the demand for the construction of an artistic whole, and the sequence of the parts of their works became arbitrary. The invention of the grand form for the ex- pression of passion led via a misunderstanding back to the single movement with whatever content the composer might choose, and tension between different parts of a work ceased altogether. That is why the symphony after Beethoven is such a strangely confused structure, especially when in its individual parts it still stammers the language of Beethovenian pathos. The means are not appropriate to the objective, and the objective as a whole is not at all clear to the listener because it was never clear to the composer either. But the demand that one should have something quite definite to say, and that one should say it as clearly as possible, is the more indispensable the higher, more difficult and more ambitious a species of work is.

That is why Wagner's whole struggle was to find every means of procuring *clarity*; to this end he needed above all to liberate himself from every prejudice and claim of the older music of static states and to put into the mouth of his music, which may be called the operations of feeling and passion become sound, a speech free of all ambiguity. If we look at what he achieved, it must seem to us as though he has done in the realm of music what the inventor of free-standing sculpture did in that of the plastic arts. Measured against Wagner's, all earlier music seems stiff or timid, as though it were ashamed to be seen from all sides. Wagner seizes every degree and every shade of feeling with the greatest sureness and definiteness: he takes the tenderest, most remote and wildest emotions in hand without fear of losing his grip on them and holds them as something hard and firm, even though to anyone else they may be as elusive as a butterfly. His music is never indefinite, indicating only a general mood; everything that speaks through it, man or nature, has a strictly individualized passion; storm and fire take on the compelling force of a personal will. Over all the individuals realized in sound and the struggles their passions undergo, over the whole vortex of opposing forces, there soars in the supremest self-possession an overwhelming symphonic intelligence which out of all this conflict brings forth concord: Wagner's music as a whole is an image of the world as it was understood by the great Ephesian philosopher:* a harmony produced by conflict, the unity of justice and enmity. I wonder at the fact that it is possible to calculate the grand course of a total passion out of a multiplicity of individual passions each heading in a different direction: that such a thing is possible I see demonstrated by each individual act of a Wagnerian drama, which narrates the personal history of various individuals together with a general history of

---

*Heraclitus (sixth century BC).

all of them. At the very beginning we sense that we have before us individual conflicting currents but at the same time a stream with a powerful directionality which is master of them all: this stream moves restlessly at first, over hidden jagged rocks, the flood sometimes seems to divide as though it wanted to go in different directions. Gradually we notice that the inner general movement has become more powerful, more compelling; the convulsive restlessness has passed over into a broad, fearfully strong movement towards an as yet unknown goal; and suddenly the whole breadth of the stream ends by plunging down into the depths with a demonic joy in the abyss and in its seething waves. Wagner is never more Wagner than when difficulties multiply tenfold and he can rule over great affairs with the joy of a lawgiver. To subdue contending masses to a simple rhythm, to subject a multiplicity of demands and desires to the rule of a single will – these are the tasks for which he feels he was born, in the performance of which he feels himself free. He never loses his breath in the process, he never arrives at his goal panting. He has striven as ceaselessly to impose the harshest laws upon himself as others strive to lighten their burden; he is oppressed by life and art when he cannot play with their most difficult problems. Consider, for instance, the relation between sung melody and the melody of unsung speech, and how Wagner treats the pitch, volume and tempo of passionate human speech as a natural model which it is his task to transform into art: – consider how this sung passion is then ordered within the total symphonic complex of the music and recognize a miracle of difficulties overcome: his inventiveness here, in great things and small, the omnipresence of his spirit and his diligence, is such that at the sight of a Wagnerian score one could believe that before him there was no such thing as labour and exertion. It seems that, in regard to the toil involved in art too, he could have said that the actual virtue of the dramatist consists in self-sacrifice; but he would probably retort: there is only one kind of toil, that of him who has not yet become free; virtue and goodness are easy.

Taken as a whole, Wagner as an artist has about him something of *Demosthenes*: a tremendous seriousness as to his subject combined with a strength of grip that seizes it every time without fail; he lays hold of it in a moment and his hand clings fast as though it were of brass. Like Demosthenes, he conceals his art or makes his audience forget it by compelling them to concentrate on the subject; and yet, again like Demosthenes, he is the last and highest exemplar of a whole series of artistic spirits and consequently has more to conceal than the first in the series had; his art, as nature reproduced and rediscovered, has the effect of nature. He has nothing epideictic about him, as have all earlier composers who occasionally played a game with their art and put their mastery on display. At a performance of a Wagnerian art-work one is not aware of what is interesting or enjoyable, or of Wagner himself, or of art at all: one feels only the *necessity* of it all. What severity and uniformity of purpose he imposed upon his will, what self-overcoming the artist had need of in the years of his development so as at last in his maturity to do with joyful freedom what was necessary at every moment of creation, no one will ever be able to calculate: it is enough if we sense in individual cases how, with a certain cruelty of decision, his music subordinates itself to the course of the drama, which is as inexorable as fate, while the fiery soul of this art thirsts to roam about for once unchecked in the freedom of the wilderness.

10

An artist who possesses this power over himself subjugates all other artists even without wanting to do so. To him alone, on the other hand, do those he subjects, his friends and adherents, represent no danger or limitation: whereas lesser characters who seek support from their friends generally lose their freedom through them. It is wonderful to see how his whole life long Wagner has avoided any kind of party, but how nonetheless a circle of adherents has formed itself behind every phase in the development of his art, apparently in order to keep him fixed at that phase. He was always able to frustrate this intention and to pass through to the next phase; his path has been too long, moreover, for any other individual to have found it easy to accompany him the whole way and so unusual and steep that even the most loyal would find themselves out of breath. At almost every stage of Wagner's life his friends would have liked to have laid down the law to him; and so, for different reasons, would his enemies. If the purity of his artistic character had been only a degree less firm he could have become the uncontested master of contemporary art and music a great deal sooner: – which is what he has finally become, though in the much higher sense that everything that takes place in any domain of art sees itself involuntarily set before the judgment seat of his art and his artistic character. He has subdued even the most reluctant: there is no longer any musician of

talent who does not inwardly listen to him and find him more worth
listening to than his own and all other music together. Some, determined to mean something at all cost, wrestle with this overwhelming
inner influence, exile themselves to the circle of the older masters
and prefer to found their 'independence' on Schubert or Handel
rather than on Wagner. In vain! By struggling against their better
conscience, they themselves grow meaner and pettier as artists, they
ruin their character by having to endure base friends and allies: and
after all these sacrifices they still find themselves, perhaps in a
dream, giving ear to Wagner. These opponents are pitiable: they
believe they have lost a great deal when they lose themselves, but
they are here in error.

Now, it is plain that Wagner is not very much concerned whether
composers from now on compose in a Wagnerian manner or
whether they compose at all; indeed, he does what he can to destroy
the unfortunate current belief that a school of composers must now
necessarily attach itself to him. Insofar as he exercises a direct
influence on present-day musicians he tries to instruct them in the
art of grand execution; it seems to him that the evolution of the art
has reached a point at which the will to become an efficient master of
performance and practical musicianship is far more estimable than
the thirst to be 'creative' at any cost. For, at the stage the art has now
reached, such creativity, by multiplying and then wearing out
through everyday use the techniques and inventions of genius, has
the fatal consequence of trivializing the effect of what is truly great.
In art, even the good is superfluous and harmful when it originates
in imitation of the best. Wagnerian means and ends belong together:
to feel the truth of this requires nothing more than artistic honesty,
and it is dishonesty to observe the means and then employ them for
quite different, pettier ends.

If Wagner thus declines to live among a crowd of composers all
composing away in the Wagnerian manner, he is all the more insistent
in setting every talent the new task of discovering together with him
the *stylistic laws of dramatic performance*. He feels a profound need to
found for his art a *stylistic tradition* by means of which his work could
live on unalloyed from one age to the next until it attains that *future*
for which its creator has destined it.

Wagner possesses the insatiable urge to impart everything pertaining to this foundation of a style and thereby to the continuing
existence of his art. To make his work, as a sacred deposit and true
fruit of his existence (to employ an expression of Schopenhauer's),

the property of mankind, to lay it down for a posterity better able to judge it, has become to him a goal which takes precedence over *all other goals* and for the sake of which he wears the crown of thorns which shall one day blossom into a laurel-wreath: his efforts are concentrated on the safeguarding of his work just as decidedly as are those of the insect in its final stage on safeguarding its eggs and on caring for the brood whose existence it will never know: it deposits the eggs where it knows for sure they will one day find life and nourishment, and dies contented.

This goal, which takes precedence over all other goals, inspires him to ever new inventions; the more clearly he feels himself in conflict with his most unresponsive age and its utter unwillingness to listen, the more abundantly does he draw on the well of his demonic genius for communication. Gradually, however, even this age begins to give way before his unwearying promptings and enticements and lends him its ear. Whenever an opportunity, great or small, of elucidating his thoughts by practical example appeared in the distance, Wagner was prepared for it: he applied his ideas to the circumstances obtaining and made them speak even out of the most inadequate embodiments. Whenever an even halfway receptive soul appeared he cast his seed into it. He attached his hopes to things at which the cold observer shrugged his shoulders; he was willing to deceive himself a hundred times if it meant being once in the right as against this observer. As the wise man traffics with living men only so far as he can thereby augment the treasury of his knowledge, so it almost seems as though the artist can have no traffic with the men of his age except that through which he can perpetuate his art: to love him means to love his art and its perpetuation, and he likewise understands only one kind of hatred directed at himself, that which seeks to break down the bridges between his art and its future. The pupils Wagner reared for himself, the individual musicians and performers to whom he spoke a word or illustrated a gesture, the great and modest orchestras he directed, the towns which saw him earnestly at work, the princes and women who, half timidly, half with love, participated in his plans, the various European countries of which he was temporarily the judge and bad conscience: all gradually became an echo of his idea, of his inexhaustible striving for a fruitfulness in the future; if this echo often returned to him distorted and confused, in the end it grew to the overwhelming chorus which the overwhelming intensity of the message he cried to the world was bound finally to evoke; and soon it will be impossible not to hear him or to misunderstand him. Already this chorus is making the art-centres of modern man tremble; whenever the breath of his spirit has wafted into these gardens, everything withered and ready to fall there has been shaken; and even more eloquent than this trembling is a universal uncertainty: no one knows any longer where the influence of Wagner may not suddenly break out. He is quite incapable of regarding the welfare of art as being in any way divorced from the general welfare: wherever the modern spirit represents a danger of any kind, there with the most observant mistrust he also suspects a danger to art. In his imagination he takes apart the building of our civilization and lets nothing decayed, nothing frivolously constructed, escape; if he encounters firm walls or durable foundations, he at once thinks of a way of employing them as bulwarks and protective roofs for his art. He lives like a fugitive whose aim is to preserve, not himself, but a secret; like an unfortunate woman who wants to save the life of the child she carries in her womb, not her own: he lives like Sieglinde, 'for the sake of love'.*

For it is, to be sure, a life full of torment and shame, to be a home-less wanderer in a world to which one nonetheless has to speak and of which one has to make demands, which one despises and yet is unable to do without – it is the actual predicament of the artist of the future; he cannot, like the philosopher, hunt after knowledge all by himself in a dark corner, for he needs human souls as mediators with the future, public institutions as guarantees of this future, as bridges between the now and the hereafter. His art is not to be embarked on the ship of the written word, as the philosopher's work can be: art wants *performers* as transmitters, not letters and notes. Across whole stretches of Wagner's life there resounds a fear that he will not meet these performers and that, instead of the practical example he ought to give them, he will be forced to confine himself to indications in writing, and instead of active demonstration present the merest shadow of it to those who read books, which means on the whole those who are not artists.

Wagner as a *writer* is like a brave man whose right hand has been cut off and who fights on with his left: he always suffers when he writes, because a temporarily ineluctable necessity has robbed him of the ability to communicate in the way appropriate to him, in the

---

*In *Die Walküre*, Sieglinde, the mother of Siegfried, is urged by Brünnhilde to 'live for the sake of love' by saving herself from the wrath of Wotan, not for her own sake, but for that of the child she is carrying.

form of aluminous and victorious example. His writings contain nothing canonical, nothing strict and severe: what is canonical is in his works. They are attempts to comprehend the instinct which impelled him to create his works, and as it were to set himself before his own eyes; if he can only manage to transform his instinct into knowledge, he hopes the reverse process will take place within the souls of his readers: it is with this objective that he writes. If it should in the event prove that he was here attempting the impossible, Wagner would nonetheless only be sharing the same fate as all those who have reflected on art; and over most of them he has the advantage of being the repository of the mightiest instinct for all the arts collectively. I know of no writings on aesthetics so illuminating as Wagner's; what is to be learned about the birth of a work of art is to be learned from them. It is one of the truly great artists who here appears as a witness and through a long course of years deposes his testimony ever more freely, clearly and distinctly; even when he blunders in a point of knowledge he nonetheless strikes fire. Certain of his writings, such as *Beethoven, On Conducting, On Actors and Singers* and *State and Religion*, strike dumb every urge to contradiction and compel one to regard them with the silent reverence appropriate to the opening of a precious shrine. Others, especially those of earlier years and including *Opera and Drama*, are disturbing: they evidence an irregularity of rhythm through which they are, as prose, thrown into disorder. Their argumentation is full of gaps, and their emotional leaps hinder rather than accelerate their progress; a kind of reluctance on the part of the writer lies over them like a shadow, as though the artist is ashamed of intellectual demonstration. The hardest thing of all about them for those not wholly initiated is, perhaps, an impression they give of dignified self-assertiveness; it is a tone peculiar to them and one hard to describe: to me it seems as though Wagner were often *speaking in the presence of enemies* – for all these writings are in spoken, not in written style, and one will find them much clearer if one hears them read well aloud – enemies with whom he cannot be familiar or intimate and at whom he is thus compelled to declaim from a distance. But sometimes his passionate engagement breaks through this deliberate dignity of style, and then the artificial, verbose and laboured periods vanish and there escape from him sentences and whole pages which are among the most beautiful in all German prose. Even supposing, however, that in such passages he is speaking to his friends and that the spectre of his enemies has for the moment vacated its place by his chair, all the friends and enemies

Wagner addresses as a writer nonetheless have something in common which distinguishes them fundamentally from that 'folk' for whom he creates as an artist. In the refinement and unfruitfulness of their culture they are altogether *divorced from the world of the folk*, and he who wants to make himself understood by them has to speak in a manner divorced from that of the folk: as our best prose writers have done and as Wagner also does. With what degree of self-constraint we can guess. But the force of the drive, protective and as it were motherly, which he brings to every sacrifice draws him back into the atmosphere of the scholar and the cultivated to which as a creator he has said farewell for ever. He subjects himself to the language of culture and to all its laws of communication, even though he was the first to feel the profound inadequacy of this form of communication.

For if there is anything that sets his art apart from all other art of modern times it is this: it no longer speaks the language of the culture of a caste and in general no longer recognizes any distinction between the cultivated and the uncultivated. It therewith sets itself in opposition to the entire culture of the Renaissance, which had previously enveloped us modern men in its light and shade. By transporting us for moments out of this mantle of light and shade, Wagner's art enables us for the first time to see how uniform that whole period was: Goethe and Leopardi then appear to us as the last great followers of the Italian philologist-poets, *Faust* as a representation of the riddle propounded by modern times of the theoretical man who thirsts for real life – an enigma the furthest removed from the world of the folk; even the Goethean song is an imitation of a folk-song, not an example of it, and the poet well knew why he admonished one of his followers with the words: 'My things cannot become popular; whoever thinks they can and tries to make them so is in error.'

That it was in any way possible for an art to exist which was so bright and warm that it would both enlighten the poor and lowly and melt the arrogance of the learned was something that could not be divined before it had come about. But now that it has come about, it must transform every notion of education and culture in the spirit of everyone who experiences it; it will seem to him that a curtain has been raised on a future in which there are no longer any great and good things except those which all hearts share in common. The ill odour which has hitherto clung to the word 'common' will then have been removed from it.

If we venture thus to gaze into the future, we are also aware of the uncanny social insecurity which characterizes our own times and cannot conceal from ourselves the peril facing an art which seems to have no roots at all if it does not have them in the distant future, and which reveals to us its blossoming branches rather than the foundation out of which it grows. How can we preserve this homeless art so that it shall survive into this future? How can we dam the flood of the apparently ineluctable revolution in such a way that this happy anticipation and guarantee of a better future, a freer humanity, is not also swept away with all that which is dedicated to and worthy of destruction?

Whoever feels this anxiety participates in Wagner's anxiety; with him, he will feel himself driven to seek out those existing powers which have the will to be the guardian spirits of mankind's noblest property through these coming times of earthquake and upheaval. It is only in this sense that Wagner in his writings inquires of the cultivated whether they are willing to take his legacy, the precious ring of his art, into their treasure-house; and even the sublime trust which Wagner has reposed in the German spirit even in respect of its political goals seems to me to have its origin in his crediting the nation of the Reformation with that strength, kindness and bravery needed to 'divert the sea of revolution into the quietly flowing stream of humanity': and I could almost think that this and nothing else is what he intended to express through the symbolism of his *Kaisermarsch.*[*]

In general, however, the creative artist's urge to help is too great, the horizon of his philanthropy too spacious, for his purview to be limited to the area bounded by any one nation. His conceptions are, like those of every great and good German, *supra-German*, and his art speaks, not to nations, but to individual men.

But to men of the future.

This is the faith which characterizes him, his torment and his distinction. No artist at any time in the past has received so remarkable a dowry from his genius, no one but he has had to imbibe with that draught of nectar enthusiasm has dispensed for him so sharp a drop of bitterness. It is not, as one might suppose, the misunderstood, mistreated and as it were fugitive artist who adopted this faith as a means of defence: success or failure in the eyes of his contem-

[*]The Emperor March, composed by Wagner in 1871 to celebrate the founding of the Reich.

poraries could neither raise it up nor account for it. Whether it praised or rejected him, he did not belong to this generation: – that was the judgment of his instinct; and that there will ever be a generation that belongs to him cannot be proved to him who does not already believe it. But even this unbeliever can, however, pose the question as to what a generation would have to be like if Wagner was to recognize in it his 'folk', as the epitome of all those who feel a need in common and want to be redeemed from it through an art in common. Schiller, to be sure, was more believing and more hopeful: he did not ask what an age would be like *if* the instinct of the artist who prophesies it should prove sound, he rather *demanded* of the artists:

> Erhebet euch mit kühnem Flügel
> Hoch über euren Zeitenlauf!
> Fern dämmre schon in eurem Spiegel
> Das kommende Jahrhundert auf!

– Raise yourselves on daring wing high above your own age! Let the coming century distantly dawn already in your mirror!

11

May sane reason preserve us from the belief that mankind will at any future time attain to a final ideal order of things, and that happiness will then shine down upon it with unwavering ray like the sun of the tropics: with such a belief Wagner has nothing to do, he is no utopian. If he cannot cease to believe in the future this means no more than that he perceives in the men of today qualities which do not belong to the unalterable character and bone-structure of human nature but are changeable, indeed transitory, and that it is precisely *for the sake of these qualities* that art has to be homeless among them and he himself has to be the herald of another age. No golden age, no cloudless sky is allotted to this coming generation to which his instinct directs him and whose vague lineaments can, so far as it is possible to infer the nature of the need from the nature of the gratification, be discerned in the secret writing of his art. Neither will suprahuman goodness and justice span the fields of this future like an immovable rainbow. Perhaps this generation as a whole will even seem more evil than the present generation – for, in wicked as in good things, it will be more *candid*; it is possible, indeed, that if its soul should speak out in free full tones it would shake and terrify our soul as would the voice of some hitherto concealed evil spirit of nature. Or how do

251

these propositions strike us: that passion is better than stoicism and hypocrisy; that to be honest, even in evil, is better than to lose oneself in the morality of tradition; that the free man can be good or evil but the unfree man is a disgrace to nature and is excluded from both heavenly and earthly solace; finally, that he who wants to become free has to become so through his own actions and that freedom falls into no one's lap like a miraculous gift. However shrill and uncanny all this may sound, what speaks here is the voice of that world of the future which *has a genuine need of art* and which can thus expect genuine satisfaction from it; it is the language of nature restored also in the world of man, it is precisely that which I earlier called right feeling, in contrast to the false feeling which predominates today.

But only nature can enjoy genuine satisfactions and redemptions: unnature and false feeling cannot do so. If it should become aware of itself, unnature can only long for nothingness, while nature desires transformation through love: the former wants *not* to be, the latter wants to be *different*. Let him who has grasped this pass in review, in all quietness of soul, the simple themes of Wagner's art, and ask himself whether it is nature or unnature, as they have just been described, where here pursues its goals.

A man homeless and despairing finds redemption from his torment through the compassionate love of a woman who prefers to die rather than be unfaithful to him: the theme of the *Fliegende Holländer*. – A loving woman, renouncing all happiness for herself, becomes, in a heavenly transformation of *amor* into *caritas*, a saint, and saves the soul of him she loves: the theme of *Tannhäuser*. – The highest and most glorious descends to men out of desire for them and will not be asked whence it has come; when the fatal question is asked, under a painful compulsion it returns to its higher life: the theme of *Lohengrin*. – The loving soul of woman and of the folk are happy to receive the new beneficent genius, although the preservers of tradition defame and repulse it: the theme of the *Meistersinger*. – Two lovers who are unaware they are in love, but believe on the contrary that they are deeply wounded and despised by one another, demand from one another a death-potion, apparently to expiate their offence but in reality from an unconscious impulse: they want to be freed by death from all separation and dissimulation. The supposed proximity of death unbinds their souls and conducts them to a brief, dreadful happiness, as though they really had escaped from day and delusion, indeed from life: the theme of *Tristan und Isolde*.

In the *Ring des Nibelungen* the tragic hero is a god who thirsts after power and who, through neglecting no path to its attainment, binds himself with treaties, loses his freedom, and becomes enmeshed in the curse which lies upon all power. His unfreedom is brought home to him especially by the fact that he no longer has any means of getting possession of the golden ring, the epitome of all earthly power and representing at the same time the most extreme danger to himself so long as it is in the possession of his enemies: he is overcome by fear of the ending and twilight of all the gods and by despair at being able only to watch this ending approach and do nothing to prevent it. He needs a free, fearless human being who, without his assistance or advice, indeed in conflict with the divine order, will of his own volition perform the deed denied to the god: this human being is nowhere to be seen, and it is precisely when a new hope of him dawns that the god is compelled to obey the constraint that binds him: what he loves most he has to destroy, and has to punish an act of the purest pity. At length he comes to feel a disgust for power, which bears in its womb only evil and unfreedom, his will breaks, he himself longs for the ending that threatens him from afar. And only now does there come to pass that which previously he had most desired: the free, fearless human being appears, born in conflict with all that is custom and tradition; his begetters expiate the fact that their union was counter to the order of nature and morality: they perish, but Siegfried lives. At the sight of his wonderful evolution and blossoming, disgust gives way in Wotan's soul, he follows the hero's fortunes with the eye of fatherly love and anxiety. How he forges the sword for himself, slays the dragon, gains the ring, eludes the cunningest deception, awakens Brünnhilde; how the curse that lies on the ring does not spare even him but approaches him closer and closer; how, loyal in disloyalty, wounding through love her he loves most, he is engulfed by the mists and shadows of guilt, but at last emerges as clear as the sun and goes under, igniting the whole heavens with his fiery glow and cleansing the world of the curse: all this the god – whose commanding spear has been shattered in combat with the freest of men, who has thereby deprived him of his power – beholds with joy at his own defeat, rejoicing and at one with his conqueror: his eye reposes with the light of a painful blissfulness upon the concluding events, he has become free in love, free from himself.

And now ask yourselves, you who are living today! Was this created *for you*? Have you the courage to point to the stars in this celestial vault of beauty and goodness and say: it is *our* life that Wagner has set among the stars!

Where among you are those able to interpret the divine image of

Wotan by reference to their own life and who themselves, like him, grow ever greater the further they withdraw? Which of you will renounce power, in the knowledge and experience that power is evil? Where are those who, like Brünnhilde, relinquish their wisdom out of love and yet in the end learn from their life the highest wisdom of all: 'deepest suffering of sorrowing love opened my eyes'.* And where are the free and fearless, those who in innocent selfishness grow and blossom out of themselves, the Siegfrieds among you?

He who thus asks, and asks in vain, will have to look towards the future; and if in some remote age his glance should discover precisely that 'folk' for whom Wagner's art is a record of its own history, he will also have finally come to understand *what Wagner will be to this folk*: something he cannot be to any of us, namely not the seer of a future, as he would perhaps like to appear to us, but the interpreter and transfigurer of a past.

*Words of Brünnhilde in one of the many different versions Wagner wrote of the closing scene of *Götterdämmerung*: not in the final version set to music, but included in a passage appended as a footnote to the scene in the 1872 edition of the *Ring* text.

GLOSSARY OF NAMES

AUERBACH, Berthold (1812–82): novelist and story-writer.

BURCKHARDT, Jacob (1818–97): Swiss historian, author of the *Civilization of the Renaissance in Italy*; he was an elder colleague of Nietzsche's at Basel University.

DEMOSTHENES (384 or 383–322 BC): Greek orator and statesman.

DEVRIENT, Eduard (1801–77): German actor, producer and dramatist.

DIOGENES LAERTIUS (*fl.* AD 222–35): biographer of the Greek philosophers.

DUBOIS-REYMOND, Emil (1818–96): scientist and advocate of agnosticism.

ECKERMANN, Johann Peter (1792–1854): German writer who became an associate and assistant of Goethe during the latter's last years and produced in his *Gespräche mit Goethe in den letzten Jahren seines Lebens* (1836–48) the German equivalent of Boswell's *Johnson*.

ECKHART, Meister (1260–1327): German mystic.

EMPEDOCLES (*c.* 490–430 BC): Greek philosopher and statesman.

ERWIN VON STEINBACH (d. 1318): principal architect of Strasbourg Cathedral, which is the 'monument' alluded to on p. 73. Goethe's essay 'Von deutscher Baukunst' (1772) is the source of Nietzsche's observations here.

GERVINUS, Georg Gottfried (1805–71): German literary critic and a pioneer of the study of literary history.

GOTTSCHED, Johann Christoph (1700–66): German philosopher and literary critic; the 'literary dictator' of German letters for roughly 30 years (about 1730 to 1760).

GRILLPARZER, Franz (1791–1872): Austrian dramatist and critic.

GUTZKOW, Karl Friedrich (1811–78): dramatist, novelist, journalist.

HARTMANN, Eduard von (1842–1906): German philosopher; author of the *Philosophy of the Unconscious.*

HÖLDERLIN, Friedrich (1770–1843): poet. Unappreciated in his own day, he is now regarded as one of the greatest masters of German poetry. Like Nietzsche, he died insane.

KLEIST, Heinrich von (1777–1811): dramatist and story-writer.

LEOPARDI, Giacomo, Count (1798–1837): Italian poet.

LESSING, Gotthold Ephraim (1729–81): dramatist and critic; the most admired literary figure of the age preceding that of Goethe.

LICHTENBERG, Georg Christoph (1742–99): aphorist and satirist.

LUCRETIUS (Titus Lucretius Carus: 99/94–55/51 BC): Roman philosophical poet.

MERCK, Johann Heinrich (1741–91): close friend of Goethe's during the latter's earlier years; noted in German literary history for his influence on Goethe as a knowledgable, if sometimes wounding, critic of Goethe's literary productions.

MOLTKE, Helmut Count von (1800–91): Prussian general and for 30 years (1858–88) chief of staff of the Prussian army.

MOMMSEN, Theodor (1817–1903): historian and Nobel prizewinner; author of the *History of Rome.*

255

Glossary of names

NIEBUHR, Barthold Georg (1776–1831): historian, his history of Rome being his most famous work.

POLYBIUS (c. 201–c. 120 BC): Greek historian; his *Histories* are essentially the story of the rise of the Roman Empire.

RAMLER, Karl Wilhelm (1725–98): poet and translator of classical poets.

RANKE, Leopold von (1795–1886): historian, author of the *History of the Popes*.

RIEHL, Wilhelm Heinrich (1823–97): writer, historian and composer; his *Hausmusik* – settings of 50 poems – was published in 1855; the title-page design shows a family of at least eight people and a cat gathered around a piano – a clear indication of the character of Riehl's music.

SAVONAROLA, Girolamo (1452–98): Florentine religious reformer.

SCALIGER, Julius Caesar (1484–1558): classical scholar.

SCHLEIERMACHER, Friedrich Daniel Ernst (1768–1834): theologian; the founder of modern Protestant theology.

SCHOPENHAUER, Arthur (1788–1860): philosopher, author of *The World as Will and Idea* (1819), one of the great philosophical texts of the nineteenth century. Although he had no genuine successors and founded no school, his influence was very widespread from about the middle of the century onwards, his most famous disciple being Richard Wagner, who believed that Schopenhauer had revealed to him the meaning of his own works and who then consciously pursued a Schopenhauerean line. In his youth Nietzsche counted himself a disciple of Schopenhauer, though he later repudiated all his doctrines. In the present century Schopenhauer's philosophy of will has been one of the influences behind the development of existentialism and Freudian psychology.

STAËL, Anne Louise, Baronne de (1766–1817): French writer; noteworthy in the present context for her study of German life and letters and her efforts to make the French understand them.

STRAUSS, David Friedrich (1808–74): theologian who, under the influence of the philosophy of Hegel, propounded in his *Das Leben Jesu, kritisch bearbeitet* (1835–6) the thesis that the events narrated in the Gospels are not historical but mythical – a thesis which ensured his exclusion from teaching in German universities. In his last work, *Der alte und neue Glaube* (1872), he renounced Christianity altogether in favour of a form of scientific materialism. Though he is now a familiar name only to students of nineteenth-century theology, Strauss enjoyed considerable fame and notoriety in his own time.

VISCHER, Friedrich Theodor (1807–87): theologian, aesthetician and man of letters.

WAGNER, Richard (1813–83): composer, dramatist and man of letters. His career in the theatre over the half-century 1832–82, as opera composer and librettist, conductor, reformer and finally as the creator of the Bayreuth Festival, and his influence on the course not only of opera composition and production but of music in general, are unexampled in the history of music and possibly in that of any other art. A wholly exceptional personality, he polarized all who knew him into devoted friends and admirers or unconditional enemies; Nietzsche, who met him in 1868 and became an intimate acquaintance, was at first the former, subsequently the latter.

WACKERNAGEL, Wilhelm (1806–69): Germanist and poet.

WINCKELMANN, Johann Joachim (1717–68): archaeologist and historian of art; his view of the world of ancient Greece became canonical for eighteenth century Germany.

WOLF, Friedrich August (1759–1824): German scholar and the founder of modern classical philology.